# Dimensions of Learning
## Education for Life

Bernice Duffy Johnson • Debra Owens Parker •
Magnoria Watson Lunsford • Lenneal J. Henderson, Jr.

Copyright © 2009 by Bent Tree Press.

All rights reserved. No part of this book may be reproduced in any form whatsoever, by photograph or xerography or by any other means, by broadcast or transmission, by translation into any kind of language, nor by recording electronically or otherwise, without permission in writing from the publisher, except by a reviewer, who may quote brief passages in critical articles and reviews.

Printed in the United States of America.

ISBN: 978-1-60250-114-0
       1-60250-114-9

# TABLE OF *contents*

**CHAPTER 1** Becoming a Master Student .................................................................................... 1

**CHAPTER 2** Dimensions of Critical Thinking ............................................................................ 23

**CHAPTER 3** Dimensions of Testing & Study Skills .................................................................... 49

**CHAPTER 4** Dimensions of Resource Management .................................................................. 83

**CHAPTER 5** Dimensions of Communication ............................................................................ 111

**CHAPTER 6** Dimensions of Computer Technology .................................................................. 133

**CHAPTER 7** Dimensions of Research ........................................................................................ 155

**CHAPTER 8** Dimensions of Diversity ........................................................................................ 183

**CHAPTER 9** Etiquette, Professional Protocol, and Ethics ...................................................... 201

**CHAPTER 10** Dimensions of Leadership .................................................................................. 225

**CHAPTER 11** Dimensions of Service Learning ........................................................................ 253

**CHAPTER 12** Dimensions of Career Development .................................................................. 267

**CHAPTER 13** Dimensions of Global Learning .......................................................................... 299

**INDEX** .......................................................................................................................................... 315

# ACKNOWLEDGMENTS

The authors are grateful to many individuals who contributed in a variety of ways to make this project a reality and to bring to the students a textbook that will assist them in being successful throughout college and beyond. We owe much to students in previous classes who have shown us the need for this text. Their styles of learning and their pace of obtaining knowledge made us keenly aware that the current texts used were not serving either our purpose as a faculty or the students' purpose as learners.

Comments and suggestions made by the instructors who used this text, were appreciated. Special recognition is given to Mr. Turner R. Coggins a former colleague in the Department of Human Sciences and Dr. Sherry Cole-Eaton, a colleague in the Department of Psychology, as contributing authors of Chapter Three - Testing and Study Skills.

The authors, Dr. Bernice Duffy Johnson, Dr. Debra Owens Parker, Dr. Magnoria Watson Lunsford, and Dr. Lenneal J. Henderson, extend special thanks to our reviewers, Mindi Thompson and Chandra J. Glover, from Alabama A &M University and to Shawn Allen, Bent Tree Press publisher, for encouraging us, and providing invaluable assistance throughout the entire process of revising the text for publishing.

And finally, to our families who provided the daily encouragement needed to reach our goal. We love you and could not have completed this project without your patience, love, and continuous support. Thank you!

# ABOUT THE AUTHORS

Bernice D. Johnson, Debra O. Parker, Magnoria W. Lunsford, and Lenneal J. Henderson, Jr., have captured their experiences in working with youth, teaching, administration, professional development, community, and civic service in Dimensions of Learning: Education for Life. The authors received their Ph.D. degrees from the University of North Carolina-Greensboro (Johnson, Parker, and Lunsford) and the University of California at Berkeley (Henderson) and are colleagues at North Carolina Central University, Durham, North Carolina. Johnson, Parker, and Lunsford are all recipients of the Award for Teaching Excellence, presented by the University. As certified Family and Consumer Scientists and distinguished professor of Political Science, the authors' research and experience in teaching total 25 years in secondary schools and 80 years in higher education in the states of Arkansas, California, North Carolina, Indiana, Maryland, Tennessee, and the District of Columbia.

Bernice Duffy Johnson is an Associate Professor of Family and Consumer Sciences and Assistant Vice Chancellor for Academic Services at North Carolina Central University in Durham, North Carolina. Dr. Johnson is a leading scholar in professional development. She has published and conducted numerous workshops in the areas of social and professional ethics, communication, conflict resolution, time and stress management, managing finances, and professional leadership. In addition, she has been awarded more than four million dollars in research and training grants by the U. S. Department of Education (DOE), National Science Foundation (NSF) and the National Aeronautics and Space Administration (NASA). Dr. Johnson has taught courses in Leadership Development, Family Resource Management, Research and Evaluation, Meal Management, Management Theories and Principles, Housing and Home Furnishings, and Family and Consumer Sciences' Freshmen and Senior Seminars.

Serving as the point person for retention and student success at NCCU, Dr. Johnson and her staff organized in the 2007-2008 academic year, a University College designed to ensure academic success of first time freshmen, sophomores and new transfer students.

Debra Owens Parker is Professor of Family and Consumer Sciences and presently Chair of the Department of Human Sciences at North Carolina Central University. Her areas of specialization are Curriculum Development; Child Development, Family and Community Studies; and Individuals with Exceptionalities. Dr. Parker has taught courses in Research, Program Planning and Evaluation, Child Development, Group Work Techniques, and Curriculum Development, and has authored several publications that focus on youth and curriculum development. In addition, she has received instructional and professional development grants totaling more than four million dollars. In 2002, Dr. Parker received the esteemed Board of Governors Award for Teaching Excellence. She now gains national recognition for her work with learning communities and academic success.

Magnoria Watson Lunsford is an Associate Professor of Family and Consumer Sciences and CEO of L &U Contractors. She has been teaching, consulting, and publishing in education for more than thirty years. In addition, she has conducted numerous workshops on critical thinking, inquiry based learning, teaching strategies, team-building, curriculum development, professional development, and career development.

Dr. Lunsford is a former chair of the Textiles and Apparel Division of the American Association of Family and Consumer Science, and Coordinator of Family and Consumer Sciences Education and Textiles and Apparel Programs in the Department of Human Sciences. She is also a former k-12 director of School Improvement, Curriculum, and Technology. Under her leadership, the schools in the district received Comprehensive School Reform grants and technology grants totaling millions of dollars. Currently, she is the Historical Minority Colleges and Universities curriculum specialist for the Supplemental Educational Services K-8 programs in North Carolina.

Lenneal J. Henderson is a Distinguished Professor of Government and Public Administration at the University of Baltimore, the Daniel T. Blue Endowed Professor of Political Science at North Carolina Central University, and part-time faculty of the School of Educational Leadership and Change at the Fielding Graduate Institute. He has served on the faculties of Howard University, the University of Tennessee, Knoxville, the University of San Francisco, and St. Mary's College of California, and taught Statistics and Research in Singapore, Hong Kong, and Malaysia. He has consulted or lectured in Europe, Africa, Asia, and Latin America. He was the recipient of the Distinguished Teaching Award at Howard University and the Distinguished Teaching Award at the University of Baltimore. He obtained his A.B., M.A., and Ph.D. degrees from the University of California, Berkeley, and conducted postdoctoral research at the Paul Nitze School of Advanced International Studies at Johns Hopkins University.

# PREFACE

The twenty-first century has ushered in a new wave of knowledge sound bytes, making it imperative that all students receive a comprehensive education during the first year – first semester, even – in order to experience college and career success. Course content in the first year, first semester curriculum, must focus on real-life practical issues, skills, and competencies for preparing students for multifaceted areas, such as the new home and family life, graduate and professional schools, and careers of the future. The need for knowledge of group dynamics and skills in being part of a team is more important now than ever. Students who take the plunge into a serious discipline of learning, studying, and networking during the first year will reap the benefits of a well-rounded college education during the fourth year.

This second edition of Dimension of Learning: Education for Life is designed to prepare students early on in their college career to master basic concepts needed for academic success for life and work in a global society. These concepts include communication, leadership, protocol, social and professional ethics, resource management, research, information technology, critical thinking, testing and study skills, multiculturalism, career planning, global learning, and service learning. The Dimensions of Learning: Education for Life text provides the basics needed for a first year college course, designed to prepare students for life and work in a global society.

Objectives and key concepts are presented at the beginning of each of the chapters. At the end of each of these chapters are a summary, a glossary, references, and activities. Activities for each chapter are integrated into an experiential approach to learning. Students are required to think critically and provide periodic assessment of themselves in regard to competencies addressed.

The first four chapters of the text – Becoming a Master Student, Critical Thinking, Test Taking Skills, and Resource Management –provide freshmen, students new to the university, and students in transition, a solid foundation for succeeding in the remaining eight chapters of the text, in other courses taken simultaneously at the university, and in future courses. These chapters pose provocative questions and paint visual scenarios of the results of effective attention to concepts and strategies for college and career success.

The second set of chapters – Dimensions of Communication, Information Technology, Introduction to Research, and Diversity – will require the students to test skills gained in previous chapters as they plunge deeper into the world of information and computer technology to analyze research utilizing diverse media. A higher level of communication will be required as students work to become sensitive to all peoples' languages and cultural needs.

The third and final set of five chapters – Etiquette, Social Protocol, and Professional Ethics; Dimensions of Leadership; Academic and Community Service Learning; Career Planning; and Global Learning – will enable students to effectively use communication skills, research techniques, information technology, testing & studying skills, resource management skills, critical thinking skills, and other foundational skills as they experience using proper etiquette and social protocol, taking on leadership roles, performing academic community service, mapping career paths for the future, and living and working in a global society.

Students are reminded throughout the book of the broader communication tasks faced by professionals: building cooperation, leading and participating in meetings, using today's technology, and working with a wide diversity of people, personalities, and lifestyles. Throughout one's life, challenges, choices, opportunities, and successes are created by knowledge, which is power. Mastery of the skills required to apply that knowledge in practical situations is paramount for today's college students.

The courses in which this text may be used include core curricula first-year courses, and introductory courses in specialized departments, schools, and colleges. Many core curricula focus on common themes of effective writing, integration of content across disciplines, global/international perspectives, critical thinking applications, interdisciplinary development and implementation, and active student involvement and participation in university programs and events. If the text is studied carefully and practices followed, students will finish the course as self-directed, disciplined learners, destined to achieve successful college adjustment and high academic goals.

# CHAPTER *one*

## Becoming a Master Student

### INTRODUCTION –"TAKING THE FIRST STEP"

Success in college and beyond is determined as much by attitude as by aptitude! First of all, you are here by design. It is no accident that you have researched various universities, thoroughly examined the options for advancing your search for knowledge, and decided to come here! Congratulations on making the decision to further your studies. By enrolling in this university, you have **"taken the first step."**

Before actually arriving on campus, you probably wondered whether you would make friends easily, whether the people would be different from you, whether you would ever learn your way around, and, probably, whether you could handle the level of work expected of you by your professors. These are questions that most, if not all, students ponder at the start of their college experience or in coming back to school to retool. In addition, students who are returning to school after an extended period of time or who are transferring from another university may be even more anxious and wonder how things will be different from another university or whether things have significantly changed since the last time they were enrolled.

*Most students arrive on campus with questions, but there are a variety of resources available to help you through the transition period.*

Whether you are here as an undergraduate, transitional, or a returning student, you must first develop the mind set that you are responsible for you. You must learn how the university operates and how you can best achieve your goals within this environment. Such strategies may include exploring various fields of study. Although you may have come to school with an intended major, you should keep an open mind about fields of study that are new, changing, or developing. One of your first steps should be to visit the university's website to review the various programs offered by the different schools and colleges. Secondly, you may want to visit some of the program directors or department chairs and ask questions about what the major entails, the experiences one may encounter, professional organizations, achievements of program graduates, enrollment size, and other concerns that may come to mind. Perhaps you have already declared a major and need additional information on the requirements for your degree program.

You should be certain to acquire copies of the Student Handbook and the university catalog. These two documents should contain all of the policies and guidelines you need to know to be successful. Students who have

been the most successful tend to be familiar with the policies and procedures. Specific information that you should know includes the following:
1. The attendance policy and penalties.
2. Academic regulations and procedures related to minimum course load requirements, how to drop a class, the last day to register, the lowest grades that can be earned to receive course credits, and the academic honor code.
3. Who your academic advisor is, where your advisor is located, and how you were assigned to that advisor. How do you best monitor your progress as you matriculate through the program?
4. What academic support services are there on campus, and what are their hours of operation?
5. What are the hours of operation for the main library and for departmental libraries, and what services do those libraries provide?
6. Where is the career placement center located? What are the hours of operation, and what services does the center provide?
7. Where is the health care unit located, and what services are provided? Where are the counselors located, and how do you access their services?
8. Who are the faculty and staff in your intended major? How soon can you meet them to review requirements? Can you select a double major or minor? Which ones complement your current program of study?
9. What resources are available to support your spiritual growth and development?
10. What is the mission and vision of this institution, past and present.

## OBJECTIVES

The objectives of this chapter are to help you
1. evaluate strategies for adjusting socially and academically to the university environment,
2. become familiar with the rules and regulations of the university,
3. discover self-knowledge, and
4. examine college as a total system.

### KEY CONCEPTS

- University System
- Style Manual
- Accreditation
- Academic Advisor
- Degree Program
- Resource Management
- Degree Audit
- Master Student

## ADJUSTING SOCIALLY

*"But I don't know anyone!"* When I first attended college, I was no different from many of you–in a new place, at a new time in my life, and did not know many people. In fact, I only knew one other person on the entire campus. I, like you, was anxious and apprehensive about meeting other people and wondered if we would "get along." You will be surprised just how many people who appear very confident outwardly have the same concern. Some of the best and lifelong friendships that you will establish will start right here on campus. There area few things that you can do to help foster such relationships:

1. Be confident in who you are.
2. Speak to people as you pass.
3. Be open to assisting others with assignments in your classes.
4. Feel free to ask others for help as needed.
5. Organize study groups for various classes.
6. Do not become so socially oriented that you lose sight of why you are attending school. Stay focused on your goals.

There are various sororities, fraternities, and social groups that will appear inviting. There is nothing wrong with belonging to clubs and organizations. However keep in mind that many such activities will vie for your attention and may very well be more of a distraction and hindrance to your education than a support.

## *Living Arrangements*

Let's examine some probable responses to many of these questions. What is college living like? Some of you will choose to live in a residence hall on campus and will have the option of selecting a roommate prior to arriving on campus or even the residence hall in which you will live. However, some universities have a carefully designed system for assigning roommates. And often, some residence halls have been specified for students with a specific focus, such as learning communities, honor students, athletic scholarships, and special programs of study. Whichever process is in effect at this institution, remember that there is an expected adjustment period in which you will need to take time to learn about your new living environment, your roommate, and the guidelines for that particular residence hall. You will need to refer to many of the concepts presented in this book to help with a smooth transition.

Such concepts include communication strategies, conflict management, appreciating diversity, learning styles, leadership, resource management, and collaboration. In fact, it appears that this entire book will be very helpful to you as you plunge into new

*There is an expected adjustment period for learning about your new living environment, your roommate, and the guidelines of your particular residence hall. Give yourself time to get used to your new home.*

**Becoming a Master Student**

experiences. It may even be helpful for you initially to scan the book to get an overview of its content so that you will know where to turn for assistance.

Others of you will not choose to live on campus for a number of reasons; possibly there may not be enough housing, off-campus living may better suit your lifestyle, or you may have relatives in the same town. Some students are married, may have children or established careers, and operate their own household. These students are referred to as non-traditional students. You will also find this book to be very helpful as you learn to effectively manage school, work, and household responsibilities. Some general guidelines to follow in learning to live with others, particularly when you may have had the benefit of your own private room and personal items, include the following:

1. Learn to listen to the other person before responding: listening does not simply mean waiting for your turn to speak.
2. Try to identify and appreciate the differences that may exist in the way you do things.
3. Give your roommate the benefit of doubt.
4. Sit down over lunch maybe and discuss the way you like to do things.
5. Brainstorm ways to approach differences in how you operate.
6. Develop an agreement on how you can have both of your needs met without compromising the values, attitudes, and privileges of the other person.

Do not forget that it will take a positive attitude to make the social adjustments that are expected. It is far less important who your roommate is than how you interact with him or her.

*Attending college requires students to take on new levels of personal responsibility: you are responsible for you.*

## UNIVERSITY ENVIRONMENT

Colleges and universities differ from high schools. The entire mode of operation is different. High school settings have lots of policies in place to govern behaviors, are much smaller, and the level of work is not as demanding. These types of changes are to be expected. How well you adjust to these changes depends on what you did prior to coming to college. Students just out of high school generally have the most difficulty with the new level of personal responsibility expected of them. For example, there may not be policies for mandatory class attendance, or visitation in the residence hall, or set times for meals, or travel to and from campus at will.

Non-traditional students, on the other hand, have had more experience in managing unstructured settings, defining their own boundaries, and becoming self-disciplined. The challenges for the non-traditional student, however, focus more on managing multiple responsibilities and demands, remaining self-disciplined even when torn between two desires, and often choosing reduced course loads, which results in a longer time frame to complete the course of study. As time progresses, students become more skilled at managing their time, money, and human resources. Refer to Chapter Four—Resource Management—for additional content on time and stress management, in particular.

## COLLEGE AS A SYSTEM

Colleges and universities are not, for the most part (except for private colleges) separate units that operate independently of any other colleges or universities. In most cases, colleges and universities (and I will use the terms interchangeably in this discussion) are part of a constituency of schools with a governing body. Each college or university in a constituency, however, has its own mission that distinguishes it from each of the other institutions in the system. The head administrator at a university is the chancellor or president. The chancellor has the responsibility for ensuring sound, well-developed programs and services for students, staff, and faculty. These offerings are strongly related to the mission of the university (See Activity 1).

The chancellor reports to a governing board, often referred to as the board of trustees. The members of the board are appointed in various ways. It is common for the governor of the state to appoint some members of the board in state institutions. There is an even larger board to which the university must report, frequently called the board of governors or board of regents, which oversees the operations of all of the universities in the constituency. It would be interesting for you to explore the organizational structure at your university. Who are the trustees? Who are the members of the board of governors? What are some of the decisions made by each level of the organizational structure?

### *Organizational Structure within the University*

As you can imagine, managing a university is a major responsibility and requires the assistance of various individuals, divisions, and departments. Following is a list of common appointments in the chancellor's or president's cabinet. As an out-of-class activity, you may want to obtain a copy of the catalog and identify the individuals in those positions at your institutions. Take a moment and, as the opportunity arises, and introduce yourself to these individuals. The various individuals will be very happy that you took the time to do so.

- Chancellor
- Legal Assistant to the Chancellor
- Special Assistants to the Chancellor
- Executive Assistants to the Chancellor
- Provost (Second Person in Command)
- Vice Chancellor for Academic Affairs
- Vice Chancellor of Financial Affairs
- Vice Chancellor for Student Affairs
- Vice Chancellor for Development
- Vice Chancellor for Graduate Education and Research
- Associate Vice Chancellors
- Directors of Services and Special Programs

Deans of Schools and Colleges
Department Chairs and Program Directors

This list is not complete by any means, as each organizational structure may differ from school to school. As you can imagine, it takes many layers of individuals to effectively manage a school of this size.

The university is divided into undergraduate and graduate programs of study. The undergraduate programs normally house the vast majority of the students and are headed by deans of the various schools and colleges. The graduate programs are also headed by deans. The schools and colleges are then broken down by units, which may be departments or programs. Departments or programs, which are headed by chairs and directors, offer degrees (majors), concentrations, or areas of specializations. Some universities also have professional schools, such as law or medicine.

## *Accreditation–Department/University*

The university is often accredited by an organization that reviews its programs and operations. You should investigate the accrediting bodies throughout the United States and compare their standards. It would also be wise to learn about the accrediting bodies for your professional fields of study. What is the name of the accrediting body that accredits your institution? When is the next site visit?

The accreditation takes place every five to ten years. The accreditation process requires a lot of work on the part of students, faculty, and staff. During the accreditation site visit, do not be surprised if you are stopped by a person or group of persons who inquire about how services are provided to you. This could be a representative of the accreditation team. The review and accreditation process indicates a high level of quality in the academic and service operations of the university, which keeps a school competitive with similarly ranked schools.

## **Degrees**

Each college or school offers various degrees and/or certifications. The degree options at most universities are as follows:

Bachelor of Science
Bachelor of Arts
Bachelor of Business Administration
Bachelor of Sciences in Family and Consumer Sciences
Bachelor of Music
Bachelor of Social Work
Master of Arts
Master of Science
Master of Business Administration
Master of Education
Master of Information Science
Master of Public Administration
Juris Doctor
Doctor of Philosophy
Doctor of Public Health
Doctor of Education

What is your intended major? What degree are you pursuing? It is never too soon to start researching the requirements for the proposed degree or minor fields of study. Yes, you should consider a minor field of study, if not a double major. A minor field of knowledge under you belt will broaden you career choices and increase your marketability. It is often best to select related fields. For example, if you are majoring in Political Science because you want to become a family law attorney, consider a minor in Family Science, Family Studies, or Human Development and Family Studies. Another example would be a major in Public Health with a minor in Nutrition or vice versa. Many degree programs have student organizations or specific student engagement activities with which you may become involved to learn more about the field prior to making a selection.

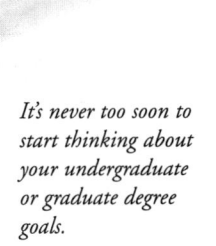

*It's never too soon to start thinking about your undergraduate or graduate degree goals.*

What is the color of the academic regalia for your discipline? How might majors and minors be combined? What degree programs are housed together? Why? How do they relate? Perhaps you can determine potential majors for new and developing careers. Professional degrees often require a major research study frequently referred to as a dissertation for a doctorate degree and a thesis or project for a master degree. The requirement for each study varies from school to school and department to department. This may appear to be a distant goal–pursuing a doctorate degree. However, the time to plan for that is now–the first day that you enter undergraduate school.

## *Admissions*

Universities are typically committed to equality of educational opportunity and do not discriminate against applicants, students, or employees based on race, color, national origin, religion, sex, age, or disability. As with any university, I am sure that this one has application deadlines and procedures for freshmen, transfer students, and special students.

Once you have been admitted to the university, it is important that you remain in good academic standing. Keep your student accounts current and monitor the attempted course credits and the earned course credits. Some universities will assess your account a surcharge for exceeding a set number of credit hours before graduating. This is typically done to ensure that you stay focused and not waste time and resources. If you exceed the number of hours and are charged a surcharge, you will need to be readmitted to the university. How can you make sure you do not exceed maximum credit hours?

## *Resources*

There are various resources available to assist students in successfully matriculating through the various degree programs. Such resources include the library, computer labs throughout the campus, services for students with special needs, support servic-

Becoming a Master Student

es, academic advising services, scholarships, work-aid, and other forms of financial assistance. Each student is also assigned an academic advisor to help in the identification of classes and activities that lead to degrees.

You have probably never had to manage so many demands at one time nor had the responsibility of managing monetary and human resources over a period of time. It is easy to be tempted to "want" and "need" a lot of the things that others may have. You may even want to move off campus and get an apartment. This could lead to needing your own or more reliable transportation or to working or working more hours. Before you know it, you could be spending more time on work than studying and school combined. From time to time ask yourself, "Why am I here? Am I here to work or to get an education?" Remember that the sacrifices that you make today will advance you that much further into the future. Be sure to pay special attention to the Resource Management chapter (4) in this textbook.

## *Learning Communities*

Many universities have reinvigorated learning communities. Learning communities are an **intentional** restructuring of the environment so that students have opportunities for deeper understanding and integration of the material they are learning, and more interaction with one another and their teachers. They occur in a variety of settings and make be adapted to the organization and to the student and faculty culture of a campus. Often there are communities established for freshmen or students in transition, non-traditional students, specific disciplines such as liberal arts, behavioral and social sciences, or the natural sciences.

Joining a learning community has many benefits. You have an opportunity to meet and interact with a smaller group of individual with whom you share common interests and goals. There are many other benefits such as to:

Organize students and faculty into smaller groups thus bringing them together in more meaningful ways,

- Encourage the integration of the curriculum,
- Help students establish academic and social support networks,
- Provide a setting for students to be socialized to the expectations of college,
- Keep students focused on learning outcomes,
- Offer critical lens for examining first year experiences and selecting majors and minors, and
- To gain hands on experience through student engagement activities that enhance academic programs of study.

In essence, learning communities can broaden your experiences and help you to stay focused by understanding the academic and social cultures early in your college experience. To gain more information about such organizations you should consult the university's First Year Experience Office, your advisor or academic department, or freshman seminar instructor.

## *Academic Success*

Your academic success is measured not only by your ability to comprehend the information, but also by your ability to relate the information to others, in and out of academic settings. Thus, a large part of academic success is attitude. Therefore, it is critical, to your success, that you personally meet each of your instructors at the start of class. Simply introduce yourself and discuss your expectations for the class. It is equally important for you to visit your instructors periodically for clarification of concepts and guidance in preparing assignments. Many students find it easier to stay focused when they know the individuals to whom they are held accountable – your instructors.

Technical papers and research papers are often assigned by professors in classes to provide students with the opportunity for in-depth study of a topic. There exist manuals to assist you in writing a professional formal paper. However, style manuals vary from discipline to discipline. Some disciplines use style manuals of the American Psychological Association (APA), the Chicago Style, Kate Turabian, or Modern Language Association (MLA). See the chapter on Dimensions of Research (7) for references to style manuals for each discipline or field of study.

You university may provide you with a student planner to assist in staying organized and which also states school policies and procedures. An excellent strategy for 'framing your attitude' about academic success is to first collect copies of all of your course syllabi, Secondly, read through each very carefully and note the due date of the assignment in the planner. Highlight this date with any color except green. Next, after carefully examining the work load, select a start date for each assignment and highlight it in green. Some assignments – papers, reading, research, midterm, finals, projects – may be due near the same time. It is critical that you space out the start dates and even complete assignments ahead of time so that you do not become too overwhelmed. And yes, you can even factor in that Step Show or concert that you do not want to miss. It is simply a matter of prior planning and follow-through.

## *Academic Evaluation System*

Each school has its own point system for determining grades of A, B, C, D, and F. In addition to these grades, some universities assign plusses and minuses for each of the grades above. What does your university do in this regard? Research the grading scale at your university and respond to Activity 3.

The university expects students to be personally responsible for themselves, to maintain a solid grade point average, and to use sound decision-making skills. Students are also expected to have prompt and regular class attendance, and to display respect for themselves and the professor. There are guidelines and policies that govern student conduct. The Student Handbook is normally the document that houses such policies.

*The university operates on an honor system for exams and assignments. These policies can be found in the Student Handbook.*

Students also have expectations of the faculty and the university that involve being offered a competitive, structured, and current program of study within the major. Advisement of which courses to take or not to take is often expected. Do not hesitate

**Becoming a Master Student**

to let your needs be known to your instructors as you matriculate through your program of study.

A major part of the expectations of students is for students to be responsible in completing assignments and performing other activities in a timely manner.

The university operates on an honor system and cheating on exams or assignments, such as not giving credit to authors whose ideas you use, is dishonest and could result in expulsion from the university. Please refer to the Student Handbook for the related policies of this university. Personal responsibility also includes a sense of responsibility for the community and the university at large. Please read carefully the chapter (11) on Dimensions of Academic and Community Service-Learning.

## *Tips for Academic Success*

1. Know what is expected of you in each class. Once you receive the course syllabus for each course, create a schedule of when assignments are due, allowing enough time for mishaps. It would also be good for you to build in a regular study schedule.
2. Discuss assignments with fellow students before or after class or at other times. Assist other students and ask for assistance as needed from other students, the teacher, and from the academic enrichment program.
3. Visit your instructors to discuss major concepts on a regular basis. The instructor will appreciate your interest and you will undoubtedly benefit from the one-on-one discussions.
4. Set up a regular study schedule. Review your notes from each class at least once after class. Prepare a list of questions that you have regarding the previous or current lesson. Asking questions is the key to learning. Do not study information in isolation. This means that you should attempt to draw relationships

*Discuss assignments with fellow students before or after class. If you need additional assistance, join a study group, or form one of your own. There is always someone in your class who would like a study partner.*

between and among concepts. Ask questions such as, "How does this relate to what was discussed yesterday–or even last week–in class ?" You should also compare and contrast the various perspectives on a given topic.
5. Seek a tutor if you need additional assistance. Take the initiative to seek help–before you perform below par–when you see that help is needed.
6. Join a study group or form your own. There is always someone in your class who is conscientious and who would like a study partner.

## *Safety and Security*

There is much that individuals can do to ensure some measure of safety for themselves: do not walk in dark secluded places; learn self-defense tactics; do not move around the campus late at night, particularly alone; know where the safety lights are on campus that will alert security should you feel threatened; and trust your instincts.

A major factor in remaining safe and secure is not having too many people in your room. The vast majority of rapes, thefts, and other serious crimes are perpetrated by individuals who were acquaintances of the victim. Be very guarded in whom you trust with your valuables. It is not a good idea to leave valuables out in your room when your roommate may have visitors also. Visit the campus police for the property tools to have valuable items engraved with your identifying marks. The campus police also tend to offer various sessions on effective safety practices.

*Take measures to ensure your personal safety: avoid walking around campus late at night, know where the safety lights are, and learn self-defense tactics.*

# SELF-ACTUALIZATION/SELF DISCOVERY

## *Self-Direction*

As you continue to develop at this stage of your life, you will learn more about who you are and what you want to achieve. It is critical to your success that you set realistic goals for yourself and that you plan concrete steps for achieving these goals. This will require a skill known as self-direction.

A self-directed learner is the best type of learner to be. This means not needing to rely on others to set the boundaries or to remind you of limitations, rules, and dates when assignments are due. A good way to become a self-directed learner is to search constantly to understand what you want and how you best learn. Knowing both pieces of information will help to build your self-esteem (how you feel about yourself) and your self-concept (how you view yourself).

It is also common to become confused as you are faced with so many options, experiences, and challenges. Rely on you basic teachings and what feels right to you. Do not allow yourself to be guided by others at random. It is far better to seek the advice of a wise counselor, mentor, instructor, or someone more experienced in life issues than you might be.

## *Values Clarification*

Exercises in clarifying your values will help you to keep focused and maintain a positive attitude. Attitude is strongly influenced by one's set of values. Some people are unclear about their values and ways to identify or even change their value system. Use Activity 4 to evaluate your value system. If your priorities are not in order, you will find it difficult to be successful at reaching your goals. One such goal area could be maintaining a good grade point average.

Once you have clarified your value system, you should map out a Four-Year Plan for Success. Always look four years ahead, anticipating where you will be, how you plan to get there, and what you will be doing. The plan should be visible. Post it on your mirror or closet door. Share it with friends, family, and mentors. Revise as needed. Do not be discouraged if your plan changes. That change may very well be the result of growth and development. You see, your views, needs and expectations will not be the same at the end of four years as they were when you first arrived on campus. Expect and embrace the changes that will occur, but be tempered in all things.

## *Learning Styles*

Many people differ in the way they interact with and gain knowledge from the environment. For example, some people prefer to have information presented visually, while others prefer activities that require them to listen (auditory). The unique way that a person perceives and processes information is that person's learning style. It is one's preferred method of learning. Knowing your own learning style can help you to learn more efficiently. You will be able to adapt each learning situation to fit your own preferences. This means that as you continue with classes, you will have a variety of instructors with varied teaching styles. Knowing how you learn best will help you to adapt to the different teaching styles. You should also visit your instructors and discuss how you learn best with each of them. Knowing your style of learning will also prepare you to seek out those experiences especially suited to your way of learning.

When trying to design a learning environment that maximizes your potential, it may be helpful to determine if you are an auditory, visual, or tactile kinesthetic learner. Included in this chapter is a brief learning style assessment that will help you to start identifying the approach to learning that works best for you. Your instructor may have more extensive forms of assessment that will examine other factors that contribute to learning, such as the time of day or the number of students working together.

Activity 7 will help you to discover your preferred style of learning quickly and easily. If you checked items 1, 3, 8, 9, and 13, you may be a visual learner. You learn most effectively when you are able to visualize objects and create mental images. You should make sure that you are able to "see" the information that you are attempting to learn. Use charts, notes, diagrams, and books when studying. Try to picture words or concepts in your head to help you to remember. Writing out lecture notes will also aid in learning. Make sure that you write down assignments and other important information.

If you checked items 2, 5, 10, 11, and 15, you are most likely an auditory learner. You learn most effectively when materials are presented orally. It may be beneficial to tape lectures to listen to later. Make sure you sit close enough to clearly hear the instructor. It may also be helpful to read written materials aloud. Allow yourself extra time when completing written assignments.

If you checked items 4, 6, 7, 12, and 14, you may be a tactile or kinesthetic learner. You learn most effectively through touch and physical movement. When studying, give yourself frequent breaks so you can get up and move around. It may be necessary for you to rewrite several times the material that you need to learn. Study groups may also be helpful since you enjoy physical contact and interaction with others.

Don't be concerned if you don't seem to have a "preferred" learning style. It is possible to use all three types of learning styles in different settings depending on the nature of the materials being taught. The key is knowing which style will allow you to get the most out of each learning situation that you encounter. If you need additional assistance in identifying or understanding your learning style, you should contact the academic enrichment center, the university testing center, or the counseling center–all located on campus.

## SUMMARY

The first year experience is an exciting new beginning. It is one that will present you with a lot of choices and new experiences. You will undoubtedly be concerned about making the right choices. Remember that you are not alone. Your family, advisor, faculty, and staff in your major department, and various other individuals throughout the campus are here to support and assist you as needed. You must, however, stay ever vigilant about your reason for being here. Know the rules. Follow the rules. Stick to your four-year plan.

## GLOSSARY

**Academic Advisors:** people employed by the university to help; they can clarify the university's degree requirements, help you identify potential majors and special academic programs, and address other academic concerns.

**Accreditation:** an assessment of the university's programs and operations to determine the quality of academic, financial, and student services. The review usually occurs every 5 to 10 years.

***Audit Class:** to enroll in a class for no credit. Enrollment is usually contingent upon availability and requires permission from the instructor.

**Bachelor of Science Degree:** an academic degree conferred after successfully completing undergraduate studies with the majority of courses in the sciences, such as human sciences, physical, science, mathematics, chemistry, and biology.

**Bachelor of Arts Degree:** an academic degree conferred after successfully completing undergraduate studies with the majority of courses in the arts, such as social studies, humanities, music, and fine arts.

**Board of Governors/Board of Regents/Board of Trustees:** "elected or appointed officials responsible for making major policy decisions. The university chancellor or president usually reports to the board. And the board is accountable to whoever appointed them, i.e. the state governor or the electorate" (Holkeboer, p. 2, 2004).

**Chancellor/President:** the title given to the top administrator of the university or college.

**College System:** a framework or structure that comes together to provide the necessary support that's needed in order to achieve a rewarding and successful academic experience. A group of colleges operated under a single governing body (UNC-System).

**Dean:** the top administrator of academic and non-academic disciplines, for example, Dean of the College of Arts and Sciences and Dean of Student Services.

**Degree Program:** a course of study leading to an academic degree.

**Department Chair or Head:** the title given to the person in charge of an academic department or unit, such as Human Sciences or Mathematics, who reports to an academic dean.

**Honor System:** a philosophical way of running a variety of endeavors based on trust and honor. Something that operates under the rule of the "honor system" usually does not have strictly enforced rules behind its functioning.

**Learning Styles:** an individual's preferred mode of learning to think, process information, and demonstrate learning.

**Major:** the primary course of study requiring 30-45 semester hours concentrated in a single discipline.

**Major Advisor:** a faculty member in your declared major assigned to assist you in planning your major, identifying research opportunities in the major, and discussing fellowship and post-graduate opportunities in your academic field.

**Non-traditional Student:** attributes include delayed enrollment, attending part time, and family responsibilities such as being financially independent, having dependents to support, or working full time while enrolled.

**Provost:** the title given to the administrator who is second in command at the university and is in charge in the chancellor's absence.

**Self-directed Learner:** taking charge of yourself; you do not need others to set limits, remind you of deadlines, or rules.

**Style Manual:** a guide or reference book for writing professional and scholarly papers.

**Traditional Student:** students who enroll in college immediately after high school and attend full time until graduation.

## REFERENCES

Ellis, D. & Toft, D. (2009). *Becoming a master student* (12th ed.). Boston, MA: Houghton Mifflin.

Cuseo, J.(2007). Thriving in college and beyond: Research- based strategies for academic success and personal development. New York: Kendall Hunt.

## WEBSITES

http://dictionary.reference.com
http://encyclopedia.thefreedictionary.com

# ACTIVITY 1

**Directions:** Record below the mission and vision of this university. Then respond to the remaining items.

_____

_____

_____

_____

What major points of focus do you see in the mission statement? The vision statement?

_____

_____

_____

_____

How does this mission statement impact upon your academic, social, and professional development at this institution?

_____

_____

_____

_____

Describe how the mission and vision of the university directly relates to the history of the university.

_____

_____

_____

_____

_____

_____

Becoming a Master Student

# ACTIVITY 2

**Directions:** Identify the chancellor/president of this university. Research his or her background and write a brief biography of major achievements.

_____
_____
_____
_____
_____
_____
_____
_____
_____
_____

Now, make a list of the major university administrators. Refer to the listing of positions commonly found at most universities given earlier in this chapter. Where are their offices located, and what are their major responsibilities?

_____
_____
_____
_____
_____
_____
_____

# ACTIVITY 3

Name _____

**Directions:** Respond to each of the items below.

1. The grading scale at my university is _____.

2. The minimum acceptable grade point average (GPA) to avoid probation by the university is _____.

3. The minimum acceptable GPA in my major is _____.

4. The GPA requirements for admission into graduate school are

   Overall _____.

   Major _____.

5. What is the last day that you can add a class?

6. What is the last day that a course can be dropped?

7. What is the school's procedure on dropping classes? What is the refund policy after dropping a class? How might your financial aid be affected?

8. What is the school's policy on receiving an incomplete as a grade?

9. What is the policy regarding challenging courses at your school?

10. With which office would you consult if you were interesting in transferring to another university?

11. What is the appeal policy for challenging a grade?

12. What is plagiarism, and how do you avoid it? What is the penalty for acts of academic dishonesty?

13. Describe the breakdown of credit hours needed for the core curriculum, for your major field of study, for electives, and for a minor field of study.

14. Where is the financial aid office located on your campus? What are work-aid and work study?

15. What services are available for students with special academic needs? What is the name of the office providing these services, and where is it located?

16. What distance education programs are available at your university?

17. How do you register for a distance education course?

18. List some of the student organizations on your campus.

19. Who is the President of the Student Government Association?

20. What is the transportation system for the university and the surrounding community?

# ACTIVITY 4

Name _____

**Directions:** Complete the following exercise to gain more insight into what is important to you. Make a random list of ten things most important to you. Now prioritize the list of important things. Was this a difficult task? Now work with a colleague to compare your lists. Together, develop one list of the ten most important things to both of you. You must agree on the items and the rankings. What did you learn about values? What did you need to consider as you prioritized your individual and combined lists?

# ACTIVITY 5 - CHALLENGES

**Directions:** What are your biggest personal challenges while attending college (i.e., finances, child care, ill family member, health care, etc.)? What is your plan to manage these issues?

# ACTIVITY 6 - VALUES

**Directions:** Describe the value of your college experience to you now and in the future.

## ACTIVITY 7 - LEARNING STYLE INVENTORY

**Directions:** Place a check beside the items that apply to you most of the time.

_____ 1.  I prefer information in written form (i.e., books or on the chalkboard).

_____ 2.  I have difficulty with charts and graphs.

_____ 3.  I often ask for verbal directions to be repeated.

_____ 4.  Writing things down helps me to remember.

_____ 5.  I have the radio or television on even when I am alone.

_____ 6.  I enjoy working with my hands.

_____ 7.  I enjoy physical contact with others (i.e., hugging and handshaking).

_____ 8.  I enjoy designing charts and diagrams.

_____ 9.  I lose concentration during long lectures.

_____ 10. I learn how to spell new words by sounding out the words phonetically.

_____ 11. I prefer listening to the news rather than reading the newspaper.

_____ 12. I enjoy "doing" versus seeing or hearing.

_____ 13. I enjoy jigsaw and crossword puzzles.

_____ 14. I "fiddle" with objects (pencil, paper clips, etc.) when in class and when studying.

_____ 15. I follow oral directions better than written ones.

# Forum (Laboratory)

Date _____ Name _____

## TOPIC:

Description of the activity:

_____

_____

_____

_____

List three things that you learned in this activity.

_____

_____

_____

_____

List three things about which you still have questions.

_____

_____

_____

_____

What suggestions do you have for enhancing this forum?

_____

_____

_____

_____

_____

# CHAPTER *two*

## Dimensions of Critical Thinking

### INTRODUCTION

One dimension of a liberal arts education is learning how to think. Your activities, including the interaction patterns in your classes, will contribute to growth in your ability to think. Learning how to think critically is a necessary condition for being educated. Learning how to think is important for several reasons. One reason is that learning how to think will develop cognitive skills that will last a lifetime. While bodies of knowledge are important, they become outdated; thinking skills do not. Thinking skills enable us to acquire knowledge and reason with it.

*Learning how to think critically is a skill that will last you a lifetime. Good thinking skills enable you to acquire knowledge and reason with it.*

A second important reason for learning how to think is the rapid growth of information that is available to us. Today, information is at our fingertips, just a click away. The twenty-first century ushered in the "Age of Information," which has changed the way we learn, work, and interact with others at home and abroad. For example, many Americans are living in one part of the country, while simultaneously going to school in another part of the county (e-learning) and working outside of the United States (e-commerce).

Most of the jobs, responsibilities, and activities encountered outside of the classroom require responses at higher levels of behavioral complexity, which is the third reason for learning how to think. Higher-level responses often involve analysis, synthesis, and decision-making behaviors in the cognitive domain, organization and characterization behaviors in the affective domain, and articulation behaviors in the psychomotor domain.

If you are to develop into an adult who is comfortable with and skilled in thinking critically, you must learn to do the following:
- value the authority of your own reasoning capacities,
- comprehend principles of rational thought,
- compare and contrast,
- consider it natural that people differ in their beliefs and points of view, and learn from others, even from their objections, contrary perceptions, and differing ways of thinking.

To think dimensionally means to think critically. Critical thinking is an active, purposeful, integrated, and systematic approach used to examine thought processes and content to develop creative solutions to problems. Identifying the dimensions of your thinking will require you to reason (Paul & Elder, 2004).

## OBJECTIVES:

This chapter is designed to help you
1. understand the processes involved in thinking;
2. examine relationships among values, moral reasoning, problem-solving, and decision making;
3. become aware of how you think by exploring the dimensions of thinking through various activities;
4. become aware of strategies that will help you to arrange information, and data, into meaningful patterns; and
5. Assess your own thoughts and actions through reflecting.

> **KEY CONCEPTS**
>
> Your reasoning skills will be revealed as you explore the concepts in this chapter. Understanding the concepts presented will help you to comprehend and retain information and give you a rationale for doing so.

### *Hierarchies in Building Thinking Skills*

Your ability to solve problems rests on the premise of hierarchies in skill building. Teachers often sequence instruction from simple to complex, a process that encourages thinking. Bloom's taxonomy of education (1956) presents a hierarchy of cognitive skills. The cognitive skills in Bloom's taxonomy include knowledge, comprehension, application, analysis, synthesis, and evaluation. The taxonomy defines the skills according to the various levels of applications. This classification of objectives relates one level of cognitive operations to another, with each level including at least some of those beneath it. For example, to evaluate data you must also recall, understand, apply, analyze, and synthesize the data. Utilizing the skill of evaluation will require you to engage in the other cognitive levels or skills.

### *Thinking Deductively*

Deductive thinking is a methodical, logical way to draw conclusions. Deductive thinking proceeds from a broad or general statement (premise) to a more-specific premise. If you accept one premise or reason to be true, then you must accept the conclusion to be true. For example:

    Premise: All manufactured fibers are made from chemicals.
    Premise: Nylon is a manufactured fiber.
    Conclusion: Therefore, nylon is made from a chemical.

Another example:
    Premise: Students are poor readers because they watch too much television.
    Premise: Sara is a poor reader.
    Conclusion: Therefore, Sara watches too much television.

Deductive reasoning is constructed as a syllogism. A syllogism is a deductive reasoning format consisting of two supporting premises and a conclusion. An example of the syllogistic reasoning format follows.

Premise: All A (manufactured fibers) are made from B (chemicals).
Premise: S is an A (Nylon is a manufactured fiber).
Conclusion: Therefore, S is B (Nylon is made from a chemical).

Classification A (manufactured fibers) falls within classification B (chemicals). S (nylon) is a member of classification A (manufactured fibers). Logically, S (nylon) must fall within classification B (chemicals).

Let's practice what we have learned. Using the other example, construct a syllogism. When you begin to study materials from a particular discipline and you look for definitions and examples to help you understand the concept, you are applying deductive skills. You know this method well. Throughout your career as a student, teachers have told you what to think, what to do, and how to do it. In college, many of your professors will continue to use this method (lecture) to introduce concepts, provide salient attributes, give examples, and then have you to practice. You are learning the how-to, gathering information that you will rely on to make decisions.

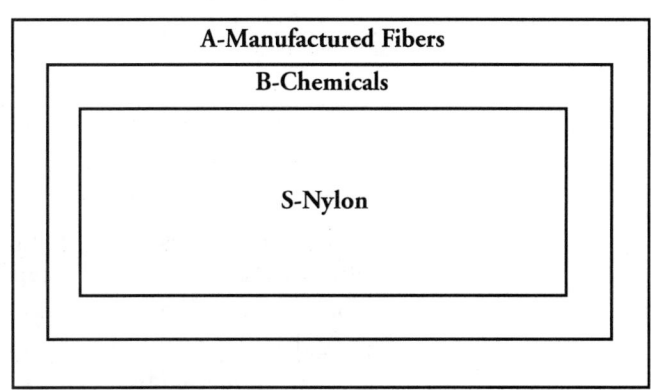

Inductive thinking goes from specific facts toward general premises. If the facts support the premise, then the conclusion is true. Inductive thinking is the reverse of deductive thinking; a conclusion is reached from the premise (fact). For example:
    Premise (fact): Every nylon fiber ever examined contained chemicals.
    Conclusion: Therefore, all nylon fibers comes from a chemical.

In the classroom, the inductive approach will require you to classify, group, and label data. Then, based upon those observed facts, you make generalizations and form conclusions. Your instructor will provide examples and then you will begin to explore possibilities. Your instructor will give you examples of inductive thinking (concepts). Next, the instructor will ask you to generate or infer a definition. When you apply inductive thinking, you understand the concept (premise) by applying your own experiences.

An example of how a textiles class uses inductive thinking is illustrated below. The teacher tells the class that nylon is a manufactured fiber, used in many domestic and industrial applications from making tooth bristles and stockings to making car tires. What characteristics and properties must nylon have to be used in so many different applications? Students in a textiles class observed that the same chemicals used to make nylon carpets were also used to make nylon stockings. The students observed that the liquid chemical was being extruded through different spinnerets (A spinneret is similar to a showerhead). Some spinnerets had more holes than the others. The holes also varied in width and shape, producing thin, strong, lightweight filaments as well as thicker, stronger filaments. The observations provided evidence that led the students to conclude that even though nylon was lightweight, it was strong. The size of the polymer and the amount of draw determined its strength and properties.

This form of inductive reasoning is known as empirical generalization. Empirical generalization occurs when a general statement is made about a particular population based on observing a sample of that population. A population is all members of a group, whereas a sample makes up some members of the group. Can you explain why the above example is an empirical generalization?

_____

_____

_____

_____

Another form of inductive reasoning that we use in thinking is causal reasoning. Causal reasoning is based on the premise that an event occurred because of the results of another event. Most of us use causal reasoning every day and perhaps many times during the day. If we oversleep, we wonder why the alarm didn't go off. The causal reasoning to this question may be, "The clock probably did not alarm today because the current went off sometime during the night." Or you may ask, "Why didn't I make an A in this course?" The causal reasoning may be, "The grade I received in this class is probably caused by turning in assignments late." It is natural for us to look for reasons or factors associated with occurrences. Understanding empirical generalization and causal reasoning will require practice. This discussion is overly simplified because it is an introduction to what is to come later in Chapter 7. Complete Activity 2 before continuing.

## *Mind Mapping and Graphic Organizers*

Mind maps are visual representations that provide an effective dimension for recall and a visual adjunct to brainstorming. Mind mapping is a concept developed by Tony Buzan that can help you create patterns in logical, orderly, and sequential thought processes. Creating mind maps will help you to see visually the relationship between ideas quickly and accurately. Mind mapping will help you to think deductively, from general to specific.

Draw a detailed map of how to get to where you live from where you are now.
1. Describe your thought process.
2. What did you have to do before you could create your map?

Maps, like the one you just drew, are really groups of symbols organized to depict certain relationships. In creating your visual map, perhaps you tried to organize various aspects of your experiences into patterns and symbols that made sense to you and to others. As you constructed your map, you probably traveled the route home "in your mind," trying to recall the correct turns, street names, buildings, and so on. You then symbolized these experiences and organized the symbols into a meaningful pattern, your map.

Creating mind maps is a strategy we can apply to many different areas that express the patterns of our thinking processes. Let's test this theory. Do Activity 3: Mind Mapping, page 42.

Graphic organizers are similar to mind maps; they too use a visual framework to represent and organize data. Graphic organizers are visual communication tools that will help you to understand and manage your own thinking and learning. Graphic organizers are used to
- develop, organize, and communicate ideas.
- visually represent connections, patterns, and relationships.
- depict understanding and comprehension of events and ideas.
- clarify and categorize ideas.
- integrate new concepts with prior knowledge.
- aid in retention of factual information.
- evaluate and predict.

Another great reason to use a graphic organizer would be to help organize information that you receive from oral communication. For example, how do you take notes? Do you try to write sentences and quotes that the teacher has said? Do you try to paraphrase what the instructor has said? Do you listen to what the instructor has said and then write it down? If your response to any of the questions was yes, then more than likely when you begin to study your notes, you may find key words or ideas missing. The notes are not adequate because they do not include the various relationships among the ideas expressed. A spider map is one graphic organizer used to describe a central idea, thing, process, concept, or proposition with support. This organizer will help you to answer three key questions: What is the central idea? What are its attributes? What are its functions? An example of a Spider Map is shown below:

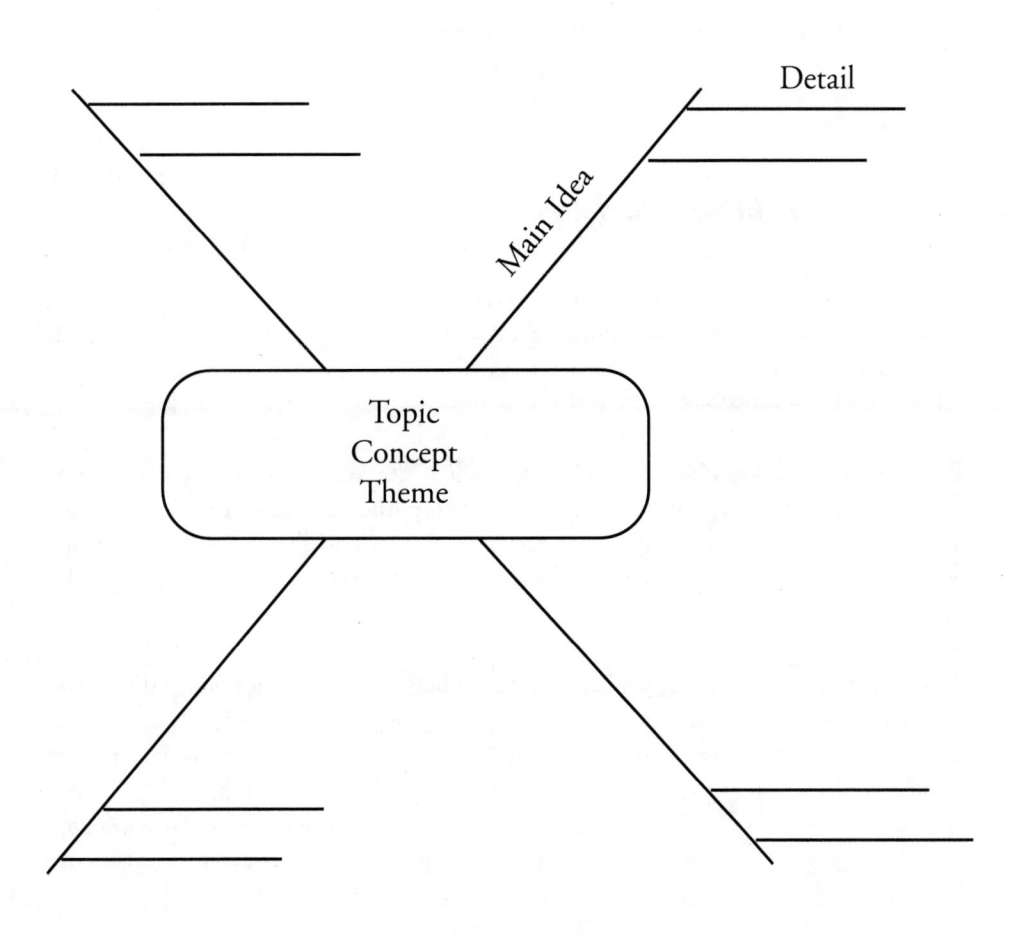

Graphic organizers can be very effective for making oral and written presentations. You can see at a glance all of your key ideas and their relationships. By having a clear map of the main ideas and their relationships either in your mind or in your notes, the chances of you "freezing-up" are greatly reduced. A concept map, a flow chart (linear) or a Venn diagram are a few examples of graphic organizers that can be used to show relationships.

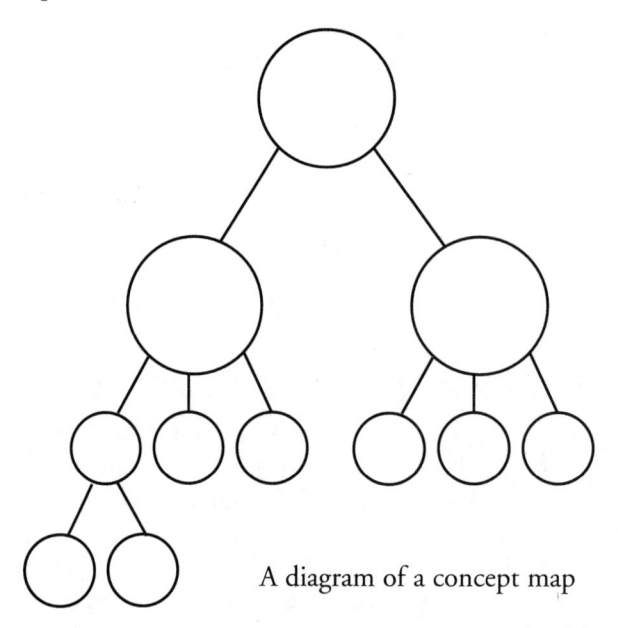

A diagram of a concept map

Once you have constructed a graphic organizer or a mind map, you can place the ideas in whatever order you may need by numbering or circling them in different colors. Thus, graphic organizers and mind maps are effective tools for creating outlines or speaking notes.

### *Processing Cognitive Operations*

Understanding cognitive operations will help you to monitor and extend your learning and make connections with the material being studied. Cognitive processes are mental activities that include acquiring information, making choices, thinking, and valuing, which are interrelated rather than discrete. Cognitive processes are actions taken with or upon subject matter.

Processes or thinking skills are applied to the facts that include mathematical computations, blending sounds in decoding, map reading, the mechanics of writing personal and business letters, English grammar, applying scientific laws, solving algebraic equations, or tuning an automobile engine. You learn a general rule that is then applied to new situations.

There are ten basic thinking processes that can help you build a foundation for learning any content, applying knowledge, or producing new knowledge. The thinking processes for learning any concept are concept formation, principle formation, comprehension, knowledge acquisition, oral discourse, problem-solving, and knowledge application. Decision-making, research, and composition are ways in which we apply new knowledge. The thinking skills embedded in these processes that could be used

in the integration of learning thinking skills with subject matter are as follows:
- Focusing: defining problems and setting goals
- Information-gathering: observing and formulating questions
- Remembering: encoding and recalling
- Organizing: comparing, classifying, ordering, and representing
- Analyzing: identifying attributes and components, relationships and patterns, main ideas and errors
- Generating: referring, predicting, and elaborating
- Integrating: summarizing and restructuring
- Evaluating: establishing criteria, verifying

You are not required to master one skill before moving on to the next. These skills can be used at any point in the thinking process, and the same thinking skill may be repeated.

Thinking processes often begin with an unresolved problem. The first step is to define the problem and set goals. Next, information is gathered by observing and formulating questions or activating prior knowledge by remembering. At certain points in this process, information is organized by comparing, classifying, or ordering. Data are organized and checked for accuracy, identification of main ideas, attributes and components, relationships and patterns. Additionally, ideas may also be generated by inferring, predicting, and elaborating. Occasionally information is combined, summarized, and reconstructed. Eventually, you arrive at a solution, construct new meaning, or create a product. Established criteria are used to evaluate and verify aspects of the proposed solution or product.

One integrated thinking process is the scientific method of inquiry. The six phases of scientific inquiry are: 1) identify the problem, 2) define the puzzling event, 3) gather data, 4) develop a conclusion, 5) apply the conclusion, and 6) summarize the experience.

During phases one and two, the puzzling event is presented. The puzzling event is either a problem dealing with a real-life situation, an experiment, or a question. You will then hypothesize (make a guess) about the solution to the problem.

The third phase, data-gathering, allow you to test the hypotheses. Data needed and the procedures for testing the hypotheses are identified.

In phase four, you reach conclusions from the organized data, formulate explanations, and evaluate the reasonableness and quality of ideas.

Patterns of inquiry are analyzed in phase five by applying the conclusion. What you have learned becomes apparent in phase six. In this phase, you will summarize the content, which is what you have learned (Lunsford, 1991).

## *Cooperative Learning*

It was not until the last twenty years in the twentieth century that educators began to value cooperative learning. Up until then, we were taught to be competitive. Phases such as, "There are winners and there are losers; you must win by any means necessary" were taught early and became a part of who we are. It is not easy to let go and embrace this relatively new phenomenon, the new meaning, of cooperation.

Cooperative learning is a team-building strategy, designed to increase communication skills and the opportunity to experience various roles. The authors of this text define cooperative learning as the formation or grouping of individuals who share expertise, interest, resources, and responsibilities to get the job done. Cooperative learning is the pooling of student resources to complete an assignment or project, study or review for a test, or accomplish what an individual cannot, under given time restraints. By working cooperatively, you will have the opportunity to experience various roles –leader, facilitator, follower, timekeeper– and develop the skills necessary to build collaborations (Lasley, Matczynski, & Rowley, 2002). According to Johnson and Johnson (1989-1990), there are five basic elements of cooperative learning:

- positive interdependence
- face-to-face interaction
- individual accountability
- collaborative skills
- group processing

Inherent in these elements are the advantages of cooperative learning. These advantages are higher academic achievement, better interpersonal relationships, increased productivity, and a more positive attitude toward the subject and the classroom.

Okay, I know some of you are saying, "I thought I was leaving group work behind me when I graduated from high school. "Oh, no! I hate group projects." It is true that your success is contingent upon the success of the other members in the group. And, yes, there are times when some members of the group may not carry their load. But, isn't this the case in your family or with your roommate? No one is reliable, 100% of the time. It is to everyone's advantage to help other group members. Cooperative learning forces us to help each other, to motivate each other, and to build self-esteem. Learning this skill requires practice. Chances are you will be assigned a group project in all of your classes. Developing team skills is an important part of your education. Very few jobs–as a matter of fact, I do not know of any that will advertise for a recluse, a person who communicates only with self and lacks people skills.

## *Multiple Intelligence*

The purpose of this chapter is to help you to assess ways in which you learn by focusing on cognitive processes. In Chapter 1 you were introduced to learning styles and engaged in activities that helped you to determine how you learned best. Not once did you discuss your IQ, take an IQ test, or even wonder about your IQ. Do you know your intelligence quotient (IQ)? Is it important to know your IQ? The authors of this text (and many cognitive psychologist) believe that it is more important for you to know "how" you are "smart": multiple intelligences (MI). The multiple intelligence theory emerged from the works of Dr. Howard Gardner. According to Dr. Gardner (2006), there are eight different ways we learn:

- linguistically (words, language, sounds, meanings)
- mathematically (numbers or logic)
- spatially (pictures, capacity to perceive the visual-spatial world accurately)
- musically (ability to produce and appreciate rhythm, pitch)
- intrapersonally (self-reflection, access to one's own feelings)
- kinesthetically (a physical experience, body movement)
- interpersonally (a social experience, relate to people)
- naturally (an experience in the natural world)

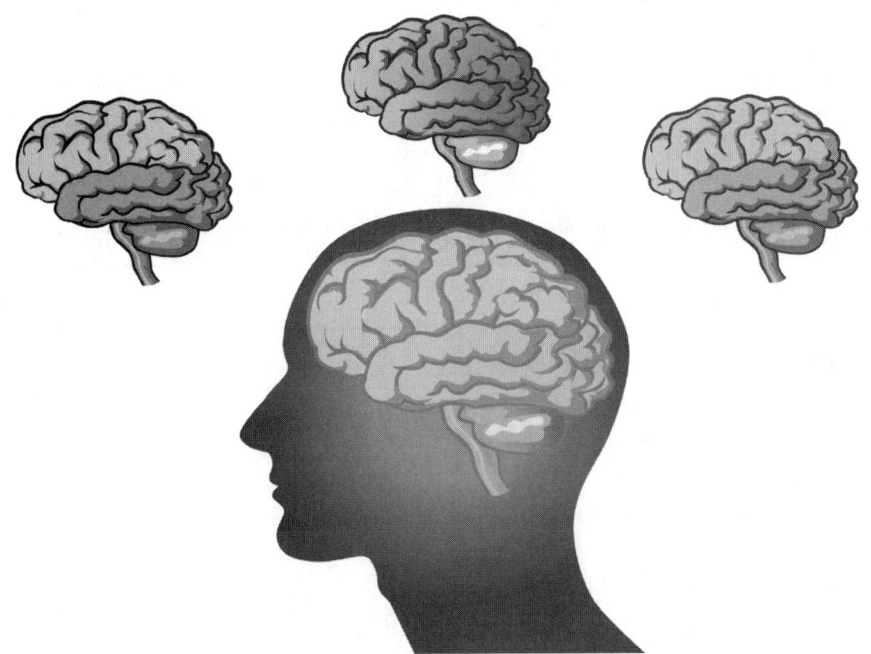

*Multiple intelligences provide eight potential pathways to learning. Understanding how you learn best can help you interact with new information in a way that promotes more effective learning for you.*

Throughout your educational pursuits, learning has probably occurred in two domains: logical-mathematically and linguistically. And what happens when this is not the best way you learn? More than likely, you will say, "I can't remember that stuff." Or, you may say, "I read that material twice, and I still do not understand." The adults in your life, your cheerleaders, probably advised–encouraged–you to read it again; read it aloud. After several years of learning in the more traditional linguistic way, you have probably concluded that you have a learning disability, when in actuality; you need to find a different way to interact with the information. One thing is sure, more of the same is not the strategy for you. If we employ the multiple intelligence theory, there are several other ways to interact with the material to facilitate effective learning. You could visualize the material (pictures, symbols, graphic organizers), personalize it, set it to music, or relate it to the natural world.

Multiple intelligences provide eight different potential pathways to learning. If you are having a problem with learning the data using the traditional ways, there are other ways to do so. For example, if you're learning about the law of supply and demand in economics, you might read about it (linguistic), study mathematical formulas that express it (logical-mathematical), examine a graphic chart that illustrates the principle (spatial), observe the law in the natural world (naturalist) or in the human world of commerce (interpersonal); examine the law in terms of your own body [e.g., when you supply your body with lots of food, the hunger demand goes down; when there's very little supply, your stomach's demand for food goes way up and you get hungry] (bodily-kinesthetic and intrapersonal); and/or write a song (or find an existing song) that demonstrates the law (perhaps Dylan's "Too Much of Nothing"?), Armstrong, 2000.

We are not suggesting that you use all eight ways to learn something. What we are suggesting is that you explore the possibilities, examine the pathways that interest you the most, and then apply it in your studies.

# DIMENSION OF PROBLEM-SOLVING

Solutions to realistic and practical problems often require a problem-solving framework. Practical, real-life problems are complex. There are no quick solutions to many of them. And sometimes there will be a best answer rather than a right or correct answer. Your ability to solve complex problems successfully will be contingent upon how effective you are at problem-solving. Problem-solving skills employ a general framework that will help you systematically process the questions to which you will seek answers. The questions asked are

1. What is the problem?
2. What are the alternatives?
3. What are the advantages of each alternative?
4. What are the disadvantages of each alternative?
5. What is the solution?
6. How well is the solution working?

## *Problem-Solving Framework*

Components of the problem-solving framework will include goal-setting, values, and moral reasoning. Everything you do in life, from setting goals to making complex decisions, becomes easier when you have an established personal value system.

Being able to articulate your own personal values will help you to see the differences between your current beliefs and those of your parents, peers, the church, and the media. Additionally, you will discover and appreciate value differences of people from various cultures.

Values represent basic convictions that a specific mode of conduct or end-state of existence is personally or socially preferable to an opposite or converse mode of conduct or end-state of existence (Rokeach, 1973, p. 5, in Robbins, 2002, p. 174). Since values are "your beliefs," they are what you believe to be right, good, or desirable. Values have both cognitive content and emotional attributes. The cognitive content attribute uses facts to state that it is important. The emotional attribute specifies the importance of the value. For example, if being educated is more important than preparing for a specific job, you will choose a liberal arts education and attend a liberal arts university. On the other hand, a community college education will more than likely lead to a specific job. Ranking your values in terms of how important they are to you determines your value system. Thus, a hierarchy of values forms your value system.

## *Dimensions of Decision-Making*

Decision-making is a comprehensive process that helps you to control destiny. According to Ellis, Mancina, McMurray, & Toft, (2007), "Our lives are largely a result of the decisions we've made and the actions that followed from those decisions" (p. 220). The decisions we make are based on our values: what we believe to be important. Knowing what we believe will help us to set realistic, meaningful goals, and make sound, positive decisions.

To make a realistic, sound decision, you must know your goal or problem. Then you can determine the best way to reach the goal or solve the problem. The process begins with problem identification, which includes defining the problem, finding the cause,

and considering the effects of the problem on the people involved. The next step is to define solution objectives. The questions to be answered are:
1. What do you want to happen?
2. What are you going to do?
3. What do you expect the outcome to be?

The third step in decision-making is to generate. All possible solutions should be evaluated based upon the solution objective. Generating viable alternatives to a decision includes addressing the following questions:
1. What resources do you need?
2. What will happen as a result of each solution?
3. Will the outcome give lasting satisfaction?
4. Will everyone involved be satisfied?
5. What assumptions are you making?

Clarification of personal values is critical in step three. How you answer the aforementioned questions will depend on your value system. Clarification of personal values can be frustrating, especially for young adults. Decisions you make will be based on what is important to you. Seeking an answer to the question, "Whose values should you emulate – your parents, your peers, those of your professor, your religious leader?" creates the dilemma.

Since all possible alternatives are not equally feasible, the next step is to evaluate alternative solutions. Which solution is best? Is the solution based on solid information?

The fifth step is choosing one of the alternatives. After implementing step four by evaluating several alternatives, one is selected based upon the solution objective.

Step six is implementing the chosen alternative. During this step, you will take action to carry out your solution.

The seventh and final step is the follow up. You must monitor the effectiveness of the solution to the problem. Hopefully, you have chosen the best alternative, but you will not know unless you follow up. There will be times when you may need to choose another alternative or may not have identified the real problem. Ask yourself:
1. Does the problem still exist?
2. Am I satisfied with the decision I've made?
3. Has implementation of the solution caused new problems?

Self-evaluating the solution and seeking feedback from others will let you know if the problem has been solved.

# DIMENSIONS OF MORAL REASONING

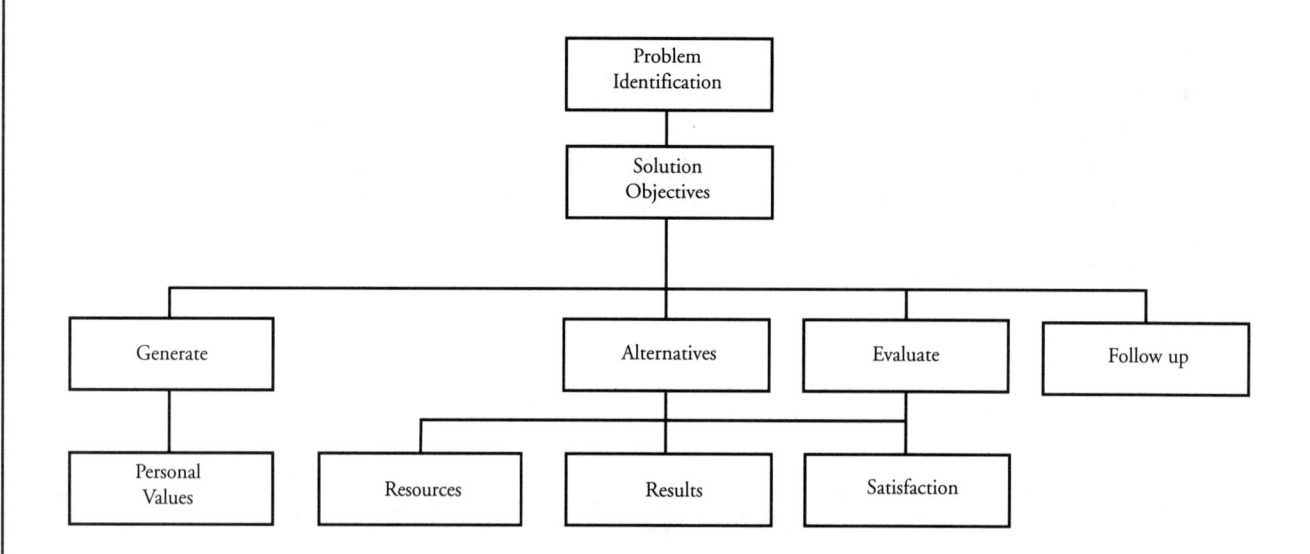

```
                    Problem
                  Identification
                        |
                    Solution
                    Objectives
        _____|_____
        |           |          |         |
     Generate   Alternatives  Evaluate  Follow up
        |        ___|___      ___|___
        |        |     |      |     |
     Personal  Resources Results  Satisfaction
      Values
```

Many of the decisions made are judgmental and involve morals or ethics. Ethical or unethical actions, for the most part, are based on individual characteristics and the environment. Scores of decisions are mentally processed, determined in a millisecond of time, and may have dire consequences. How well you are able to judge what is morally right will be dependent upon where you are in the stages of moral development. Lawrence Kolberg, a leading proponent of the cognitive developmental approach to moral education, has defined a hierarchy of three levels of moral thinking with six stages. Let's apply Kolberg's theory (stages) by analyzing a story that was reported in the Raleigh News and Observer in 2004.

**Stages of Moral Reasoning and The Sentence**
In 1970, a man stole a black-and-white television set valued at $140 from an elderly lady in a southern town in rural North Carolina. A few days later this man was captured, charged with second-degree burglary, tried by a jury, and found guilty of the crime. This man has already spent 34 years in the NC jail, and parole is still uncertain.

I. Preconventional Moral Reasoning
  1. Goodness defined in terms of the physical consequences: reward or punishment. The concern is about self.
  2. Instrumental cooperation: I'll scratch your back, if you'll scratch mine. How it benefits me is the basic motivation.

The Sentence: In this story, the desire to have the television outweighed the fact that stealing from another person to satisfy own desires is illegal and unethical. Moral immaturity causes persons to function at the level of "I desire," regardless of the consequences. During this stage, the primary concern is to obtain what is desired.

**II. Conventional Moral Reasoning**
  3. "Good Boy" orientations: goodness is defined by the approval of others. Conforming to group norms and being concerned about groups of people are the foci.

4. "Law and Order" orientation: goodness is maintaining the social order.

The Sentence: A jury convicted the man, and the judge sent the man to prison with a life sentence based on a second-degree burglary conviction.

### III. Postconventional Moral Reasoning
5. Morality based on "social contract": agreement among individuals, which may be changed for reasons of social utility. The entire society decides what is right.
6. Morality based on "principles of justice": equality and cooperation are dependent on respect for the dignity of human beings and freedom of conscience.

The Sentence: Lastly, we examine the crime and the punishment imposed for the crime. In society, we have laws that endeavor to protect the society. Authority must be respected and order maintained.

The Sentence: A prosecutor became the man's most unlikely ally in 2001, when he worked for the county that put this man behind bars. He was quoted as saying, "I've never heard anything like this. In my personal opinion, it's time to let him go, turn the key." This prosecutor wrote a letter to the North Carolina Parole Commission and helped the convicted man find a lawyer. The Parole Commission responded with the following statement, "Your release at this time would unduly depreciate the seriousness of the crime." This statement mirrored 25 others. For 25 straight years, this man has been denied parole. His lawyer commented of his imprisoned client, "It's a lost life." This man spent 34 years in the NC jail.

After examining where you are in the stages of moral development, do you think justice has been served?

## DIMENSIONS OF QUESTIONING

Asking questions that are relevant to the situation is a requisite to critical thinking and practical problem-solving. One of the most powerful thinking skills you can have is the ability to ask appropriate and probing questions.

A high correlation exists between asking good questions and thinking. Throughout your adult life, you will make decisions based upon the answers to the questions you ask. Thinking requires us to think about something. And when we think, we think for a purpose. It is the purpose that will generate our questions and the process we use to generate, gather information, draw conclusions, and make inferences. Questions come in many different forms and are used for various purposes. The types of questions discussed in this section are based on the eight basic thinking processes that were identified earlier in this chapter. Five of the eight basic thinking processes were remembering, information-gathering, analyzing, integrating, and evaluating. The question types corresponding to the thinking processes are fact, analysis, interpretation, synthesis, evaluation, and application. These question types are taken from Chaffee, 2007. Let's analyze the question types by looking at the rules and regulations that govern academic success.

Some of the questions asked will be to seek information. Factual question types are relatively straightforward and objective. They seek information about who, what, when, where, and how. Your thought pattern is to recall the information. Questions to ask concerning academia are, "How does the university define academic success?" "Where is the administration building?"

Interpretation questions seek to discover relationships between facts and ideas. Examples of such relationships include
- Chronological relationships: relating things in time sequence
- Process relationships: relating aspects of growth, development, or change
- Comparison relationships: relating things in terms of their similar features
- Contrast relationships: relating things in terms of their different features
- Causal relationships: relating events in terms of the way some events are responsible for bringing about other events.

"What is the relationship between my GPA and my academic standings?"
"How does my course of study compare to the course of study at another university?"

Analysis question types examine the entire process or situation by breaking its component parts into manageable and understandable pieces. The relationship of these parts to a whole is realized. These questions attempt to classify various elements, outline component structures, articulate various possibilities, and clarify the reasoning being presented. Thinking analytically infers that you understand the interrelated functions that all thinking includes. What are the organizational structures in your department? In general administration? In paying your bills? Answers to these questions will require classification and a comparison of the various types of structures.

Synthesis combines ideas to form a new whole or come to a conclusion. Making inferences about future events, creating solutions, and designing plans of action are goals of this question type.

"What goals will you set in order to graduate in four years?" is a question of synthesis.

Students make judgments or express value when evaluation questions are asked. Evaluation questions help us to make informed judgments and decisions by determining the relative value, truth, or reliability of things. Evaluation involves identifying the criteria or standards we are using (being used) and then determining to what extent the things in common meet those standards. Informed critical thinkers use this approach when they are deciding what courses to take, which alternatives to pursue in solving a problem, or what to believe about a serious issue. Questions may be, "What are the criteria for determining my classification?" "Where am I going to live during my last semester of college?"

## *Reflecting*

The purposes of reflections are to facilitate learning (e.g., academic, professional, and personal growth) and the sharing of ideas with one's peers and, later, colleagues. Students, teachers, and other professionals need to understand that one's own perspective is only one of a number of potentially valid views and knowledge is often not absolute (e.g., neither definite nor certain). This gives the individual a broader and more-flexible perspective that is better suited to the changing demands of our personal and professional lives.

Having an opportunity to reflect on our experiences can promote
- Analytical and critical thinking
- Creative (novice) thinking
- Consideration of alternative points of view
- Fact-based learning
- Insight into various issues and problems
- Practical thinking (i.e., application to one's own personal and professional life)

If you are serious about "lifelong learning" you need to find time to reflect on your experiences in order to grow, change, understand, and increase your professional knowledge and skill foundations. Self-reflection must be both a conscious and intentional (purposeful) process. Intentional self-reflection can provide clarity and understanding to your experiences, making them more accessible for effective use in your personal and professional life.

Reflective practice requires all of us to provide reasons for our pedagogical goals and decisions and to explore them from multiple perspectives. Through reflection, you will learn to critique: assess, analyze, and evaluate what you do as you do it, or later when we have more time to critically reflect without pressure for some performance or decision. You can then use that information to make corrections, improvements, enhance your understanding, or add something successful to your repertoire of knowledge and skills. Thus, reflecting can help us make new sense out of our experiences. Reflecting over past experiences allows us to see the themes and patterns of our thinking, feelings, and behaviors.

## SUMMARY

Learning to think critically is exercising the mind to analyze, synthesize, and evaluate. Critical thinkers engage in deductive and inductive thoughts to identify the issue or problem to be solved. It addition, critical thinkers ask tough questions, collect data, make inferences, organize information, and make decisions, taking into account fair-mindedness and morality. Once the decision is made, critical thinkers will reflect upon the process and the conclusions drawn.

## GLOSSARY

**Causal Reasoning:** based on the premise that an event occurred because of the results of another event.

**Cognitive Processes:** mental activities that include acquiring information, making choices, thinking, and valuing, which are interrelated rather than discrete.

**Concept Map:** a web diagram used to explore knowledge and gather and share information. A concept map consists of nodes or cells that contain a concept, item, or question, and links. The links are labeled and denote direction with an arrow symbol. The labeled links explain the relationship between the nodes or cells. The arrow describes the direction of the relationship and reads like a sentence.

**Critical Thinking:** an active, purposeful, integrated and systematic approach used to examine thought processes and content to develop creative solutions to problems.

**Decision-making:** a comprehensive process that helps you to control destiny.

**Deductive Reasoning:** proceeds from a broad or general statement (premise) to a more-specific premise.

**Empirical Generalization:** occurs when a general statement is made about a particular population based on observing a sample of that population.

**Inductive Reasoning:** goes from specific facts toward general premises.

**Mind Maps:** visual representations that provide an effective dimension for recall and a visual adjunct to brainstorming.

**Syllogism:** a deductive reasoning format consisting of two supporting premises and a conclusion.

**Values:** what we believe to be important.

## REFERENCES

Armstrong, T. (2000). Multiple intelligence in the classroom (2$^{nd}$ ed.). Alexandria, VA: Association for Supervision and Curriculum Development.

Bloom, B. S. (1956). Taxonomy of educational objectives: The classification of educational goals, handbook I: Cognitive domain. New York: McKay.

Chaffee, J. (2007). Thinking critically (9th ed.). Boston, MA: Houghton Mifflin.

Ellis, D., Mancina, D., McMurray, E.L., and Toft, D. (2007). Becoming a master student (12$^{th}$ ed.). Boston, MA: Houghton Mifflin.

Gardner, H. (2006). Multiple intelligence: New horizons in theory and practice. New York, NY: Basic Books.

Johnson, B. (1992). Values classification survey.

Johnson, D. W., & Johnson, R. T. (1989/1990). Social skills for successful group work. *Educational Leadership* 47 (4): 29-33.

Lasley, T., Matczynski, T. J., and Rowley, J. B. (2002). Instructional models strategies for teaching in a diverse society (2nd ed.). Belmont, CA: Wadsworth/Thomson Learning.

Lunsford, M. W. (1991). Effectiveness of the inquiry method of instruction in teaching a secondary home economics textiles unit. Unpublished doctoral dissertation, University of North Carolina-Greensboro.

Norris, S. P. (1992). Synthesis of research on critical thinking. *Educational Leadership*, 40-45.

Paul, R., & Elder, L. (2004). The elements of critical thinking helping students assess their thinking skills. FT Press.

Robbins, S. P. (2002). Organizational behavior: concepts, controversies, and applications (10th ed.). Englewood Cliffs, N J: Person Prentice Hall.

Sternberg, R. J. (1987). Teaching critical thinking: Eight easy ways to fail before you begin. *Phi Delta Kappa*, 456-459.

Schon, D. (1984). The Reflective Practitioner: How Professionals Think in Action. San Francisco, CA: Jossey-Bass.

Toseland, R. W. & Rivas, R. F. (2008). An introduction to group practice (6th ed.). Boston, MA: Allyn & Bacon.

## WEBSITES

### *Critical Thinking*

http://www2.sjsu.edu/depts/itl/graphics/main.html
www.criticalthinking.org
www.nwrel.org/scpd/sirs/6/cu11.html.

### *Multiple Intelligence*

http://www.newhorizons.org/strategies/mi/front_mi.htm
http://www.ericfacility.net/ericdigests/ed410226.html
http://www.thirteen.org/edonline/concept2class/month1/

### *Values*

http://www.worldvaluessurvey.com/news/index.html
http://3sc.environics.net/surveys/3sc/main/3sc.asp
http://www.pbs.org/endgame/home.php

### *Moral Reasoning*

http://www.stedwards.edu/regist/stuinfo.htm
http://plato.stanford.edu/entries/reasoning-moral/
http://www.csuchico.edu/    ****Nice PowerPoint presentation****

### *Decision Making*

http://faculty.fuqua.duke.edu/daweb/lexicon.htm
http://wvvw.mapnp.org/library/prsn_prd/decision.ht

## ACTIVITY 1: DEDUCTIVE AND INDUCTIVE THINKING

Directions: Go back to the definitions given for deductive and inductive thinking. Consider the following discussion between two friends.

"Adham: I've noticed previously that every time I kick a ball up, it comes back down. So I guess this next time when I kick it up, it will come back down, too. Rizik: That's Newton's Law. Everything that goes up must come down. And so, if you kick the ball up, it must come down" (Mission, 2004, p.1).

Answer the following questions:

1. Which friend is thinking deductively? _____

2. What processes (thinking) did you use to answer question #1?

3. Which one of the guys is thinking inductively?

4. What processes did you use to answer question #3?

5. Can an inductive premise be stated deductively? YES ? NO ?

Explain

_____

_____

6. Can a deductive premise be stated inductively? YES ? NO ?

Explain

_____

_____

## ACTIVITY 2: CAUSAL REASONING

Problems that we encounter in life are usually complex and multifaceted. For example, Tony and Susan have been dating for six months. Both of them are ready to take it to the next level and have gone to a nice restaurant to celebrate. A former boyfriend spots Susan and comes over to the table. He insists on joining Susan and Tony, even though they have made it clear that they want to be alone. Susan's old flame starts down memory lane, telling one story after another, each one getting more personal. In the middle of the main course, Tony leaves. Write the outcome of this dilemma by using inductive/causal reasoning. An excellent reference to use with this exercise is Causal Arguments and Exercises for Causal Arguments found on the website below.

http://www2.sjsu.edu/depts/itl/graphics/main.html

# ACTIVITY 3: MIND MAPPING

Read the following paragraph.

Thinking processes often begin with an unresolved problem. The first step is to define the problem and set goals. Next, information is gathered by observing and formulating questions or activating prior knowledge by remembering. At certain points in this process, information is organized by comparing, classifying, or ordering. Data are organized and checked for accuracy, identification of main ideas, attributes and components, relationships and patterns. Additionally, ideas may also be generated by inferring, predicting, and elaborating. Occasionally information is combined, summarized, and reconstructed. Eventually, you arrive at a solution, construct new meaning, or create a product. Established criteria are used to evaluate and verify aspects of the proposed solution or product.

Directions: Answer the following questions.

1. How would you represent the ideas and other relationships presented in the paragraph?

2. Create a mind map for the above paragraph. Your ideas should be either written on lines connected to other lines, or within shapes connected by lines to express clearly the relationships between the various ideas. Print the ideas in all capital letters so that they can be easily read and identified. Order your ideas by numbering or circling them with different colored markers.

3. Exchange your graphic organizer with a classmate.

4. Compare and contrast your graphic organizer with the one created by your classmate.

## *Mind Mapping Group Assignment:*

Working in a group of three to four members, brainstorm as many examples of cultural diversity activities as you can think of in five minutes. Create a mind map that organizes the ideas you have generated. Use the following format to structure this assignment.

What is your point? (Explain the concept of characteristics of culture.)

How will I prove my point? (Give examples of various activities that will increase acceptance of different cultures. Explain why you think these examples would be useful.)

## ACTIVITY 4: COGNITIVE OPERATIONS

On a textiles exam, students were given multiple-choice items that consisted of two parts. Students were instructed to choose the best answer to both parts. Two of the questions are below. Apply the cognitive processing skills to both questions. Two of the cognitive operations may not be used.

16A    A garment made from which fabric would be most comfortable on a hot humid day?
1. cotton
2. rayon
3. acetate
4. polyester

16B.    The reason for your choice in 16A is that a garment made from this fabric will
1. absorb moisture.
2. wick moisture away from the body.
3. trap moisture between the fibers of this fabric.

### *Cognitive operations and the thinking skills:*

1. Focus _____

2. Information-gathering _____

3. Remembering _____

4. Organize data _____

5. Analyze _____

6. Generate _____

7. Integrate _____

8. Evaluate _____

# ACTIVITY 5: MULTIPLE INTELLIGENCES SURVEY

**Part I**
Let's review what the researchers say about multiple intelligences.
- All humans have at least eight different types of intelligence.
- Some intelligence is more developed than others.
- We all have an aptitude for all intelligences.
- Each of us learns through specific intelligences/learning styles

Directions: Take the Multiple Intelligence Survey that is located on the website http://surfaquarium.com/MI/inventory.htm. This exercise will help you identify your strengths. By knowing your preferred learning style, you can work to strengthen the other intelligences. It will also help you identify the strengths of your classmates. This information can be very helpful when working on group projects. Analyze your results. Plot your scores on a bar graph. Your instructor will plot the class scores. Your instructor will use this information when planning lessons and activities and when making group assignments.

# ACTIVITY 6: PROBLEM SOLVING

Describe in detail a problem you have encountered within the last year. Apply the six steps to reach a solution.

Situation (problem): _____

1. What is the problem? _____

2. What are the alternatives? _____

3. What are the advantages of each alternative? _____

4. What are the disadvantages of each alternative? _____

5. What is the solution? _____

6. How well is the solution working? _____

*Dimensions of Critical Thinking*

## ACTIVITY 7: WHAT DO YOU VALUE?

Rate the items below on how important each is to you on a scale of 0 (not important) to 100 (very important). Record your rating on the line to the left of each item. (Adapted from Robbins, 2002 and Johnson's survey, 1992).

```
              Not            Somewhat             Very
         10  20  30  40  50  60  70  80  90  100
```

_____ 1. Job satisfaction.
_____ 2. Money.
_____ 3. Love and commitment to family.
_____ 4. Eating together, social events.
_____ 5. Environmental and global issues.
_____ 6. My religious convictions.
_____ 7. Recreation, playing sports.
_____ 8. Education.
_____ 9. A challenging career with advancement opportunities.
_____ 10. Material success–expensive cars, designer clothes, home, etc.
_____ 11. Spending quality time with my entire family.
_____ 12. Spending time with close friends.
_____ 13. Volunteering, working in the community.
_____ 14. Honesty, morality, quiet time to think, pray, etc.
_____ 15. Recreation, relaxing, healthy eating habits.
_____ 16. Relaxation, reading, TV, self-improvement programs.

**Directions:** Add the item pairs to determine your value set.

| Professional | Money | Family | Friends |
|---|---|---|---|
| 1. _____ | 2. _____ | 3. _____ | 4. _____ |
| 9. _____ | 10. _____ | 11. _____ | 12. _____ |

Totals _____   _____   _____   _____

| Community | Spirituality | Health | Intellectual |
|---|---|---|---|
| 5. _____ | 6. _____ | 7. _____ | 8. _____ |
| 13. _____ | 14. _____ | 15. _____ | 16. _____ |

Totals _____   _____   _____   _____

The higher the total in any value group, the higher the importance you place on that value set. Your highest-ranking value should be the one that helps define your morality or form the foundation of your moral judgment. The closer the numbers are in all eight pairs, the better rounded you are, which may indicate difficulty in finding a guiding principal in making a major decision (Adapted from Robbins, 2002, A-27).

## ACTIVITY 8: VALUES CLARIFICATION

### *Values*

Make a list of examples of values changing in our society, as well as in your own group of friends. Share your list with at least 4 other classmates. Compile to make one list.

### *Personal Values*

Make a list of the personal values you hold now. Do your personal values mimic those of society? (the compiled list) Explain.

## ACTIVITY 9: YOUR DECISION-MAKING STYLE

1. Assess your decision-making skills by completing a decision-making style questionnaire identified by your instructor or career counselor.

2. Working in groups, analyze the case study provided by your instructor. If you do not remember the steps, refer to "Dimensions of Decision-Making" discussed earlier in this chapter. Answer the questions following the model in the text.
    a. Apply the steps of decision-making to the case study.
    b. How can the steps of decision-making be used to explain the decision?
    c. What is the relationship between personal values and the decision that you recommend?
    d. What is the relationship between personal values, specific goals, and the decision made?

## ACTIVITY 10: MORAL REASONING

Examine the honor code at your university. How do you, your classmates, professors, and administrators feel about the code of honor? Give examples to illustrate your points.

## ACTIVITY 11: POSING QUESTIONS

Read about an issue such as affirmative action, human cloning, or same-sex marriage. Critically examine it, posing questions from each of the six question types previously discussed: fact, analysis, interpretation, synthesis, evaluation, and application.

Questions of

1. Fact _____
2. Analysis _____
3. Interpretation _____
4. Synthesis _____
5. Evaluation _____
6. Application _____

What conclusion do you make based upon questions asked and answers derived from the article?

## ACTIVITY 12: REFLECTION

**Directions:** Reflect on your experiences as a student at your university. Discuss the following in your reflection:

1. Identify and briefly describe one or both of the following:
   - ❑ An experience in your class or on campus that involves students, colleagues, and/or an instructor.
   - ❑ Two or three main ideas or issues from a reading assignment.

2. How can you apply (or what are the implications for) what you learned from the lesson and/or your experience to your current responsibilities, your role as a student, your role as a colleague, or to this course?

3. In writing about a personal experience, include the following to help with the reflection process:
   - ❑ A brief outline or description of the experience (e.g., a student situation, a presentation you made).
   - ❑ A description of how it went (e.g., what worked, what didn't work, what you would change).
   - ❑ One or two questions about the experience that you would like to reflect on and discuss with your classmates in this course.

# CHAPTER *three*

## Dimensions of Testing & Study Skills

### INTRODUCTION

As a student, I longed for the day when the thought of yet another examination would be the least of my concerns. However, now, as an instructor, I have come to the realization that such a day does not exist. Examinations, tests, quizzes...a challenge by any other name are still a challenge. In the academic arena, examinations play an instrumental role in assisting both the student and instructor in assessing the level of comprehension (for the student) and the effectiveness of subject matter presentation (for the instructor). Therefore, the exam is mutually beneficial to both parties involved. A student, in part, should be able to determine his or her progress in a course, based on examination results. Additionally, the exam is your opportunity to let the instructor know that you have mastered the material and you can successfully demonstrate it if asked to do so. Examinations do not always, however, reflect one's full competence (or the lack thereof) of a given subject on a given day. Not all exam days are good student days, and some might say that no exam day is a good day. Hopefully, this chapter will furnish you with some of the strategies that will make you look with great anticipation for the next opportunity to go to battle with an exam.

*A test lets you show the instructor you have mastered the material and helps you determine your progress in a course.*

### OBJECTIVES

1. Discuss the different types of tests.
2. Analyze the relationship between the test-maker and the test-taker.
3. Become aware of research-based, test-taking strategies.
4. Apply skills of studying, managing time, listening, memorizing, and note-taking to become a successful learner.

### KEY CONCEPTS

- Profile of the test-maker and the test-taker
- Analyzing exam questions
- Stress
- Computerized testing
- Listening
- Preparing for the test
- Time management
- Memorization
- Note-taking

## *Anatomy of the Test-Maker*

Ms. Anne N. Structor is in the process of preparing a test for her 10:00 a.m. Foods and Nutrition class. The exam will cover the first three chapters of the unabridged, dictionary-sized, used textbook ($45.12) that you have yet to open. Chapter One is an introductory kind of chapter, really general and easy-going. Chapter Two contains a bit more detail on the various classes of nutrients. Chapter Three is dedicated to carbohydrates, everything that you ever wanted to know, and then some. If we take a moment to observe Ms. Structor, we will find the following: 1) class begins at 10:00 sharp and the lecture ends at 10:50; 2) she is a stickler for details and is well organized; 3) one of her favorite topics is carbohydrate metabolism (she spent a significant amount of time discussing the metabolic pathways); 4) she has taken the time to develop an in-depth course outline from which she hardly ever strays; and 5) when Ms. Structor writes on the board, she circles and underlines the terms that she wants to emphasize. The stage is set, and if we take into consideration the aforementioned qualities and characteristics of our test-maker, we can perhaps hypothesize (make an educated guess, Chapter 2) as to the type of questions that Ms. Structor might ask on an exam. I'm no psychic, nor do I have a 1-800-FOR-TEST hotline, but together we can probably picture Anne N. Structor's exam. In the following space, list some of the things (in general) that you might expect or would not expect on the exam (i.e., "I foresee calculations and at least two questions that compare the nutrients to one another").

_____

_____

_____

_____

What makes the instructor ask what he or she asks on an examination is the $64,000 question. The answer, however, is my two cents worth of take-it-or-leave-it advice. As a

*Prepare for an exam by reviewing information every day–immediately after class, if possible. Studying with a classmate will help you reinforce concepts.*

student, I would ask the same question, especially after receiving an exam that posed questions that had very little in common with the material that I had reviewed. "Am I in the right class?" "Did he give us someone else's exam?" "I knew I should have dropped this class." These are a few of the comments that I have heard in response to some exams. These were the exceptions.

The majority of exams has rhyme and reason and questions that address and are consistent with the course competencies. One can expect that the test-maker's questions will reflect 1) the relative degree of importance of a topic as it relates to the subject, (each subject has its own "you've got to know this topic": i.e., in nutrition, you need to know the six classes of nutrients), 2) the instructor's personal areas of interest, ("I'll ask you a few questions about carbohydrate metabolism..."), and 3) specific requirements for competence (in order to say that you have successfully completed an introductory course in nutrition, you must be able to demonstrate that you can calculate the basal metabolic rate for an individual, based on given information).

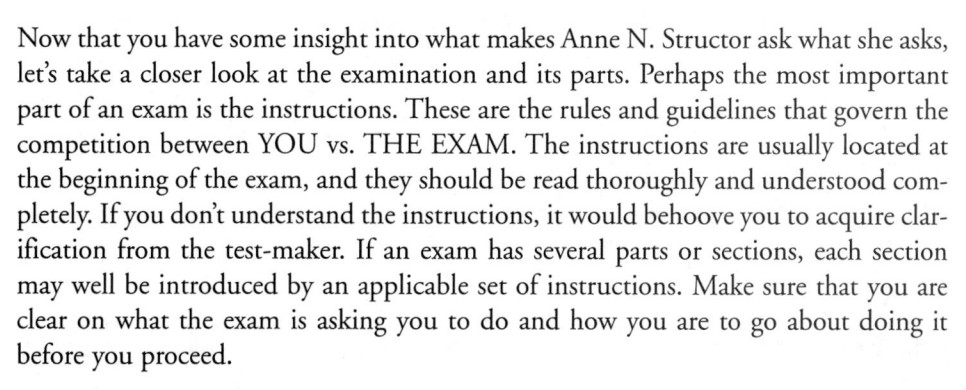

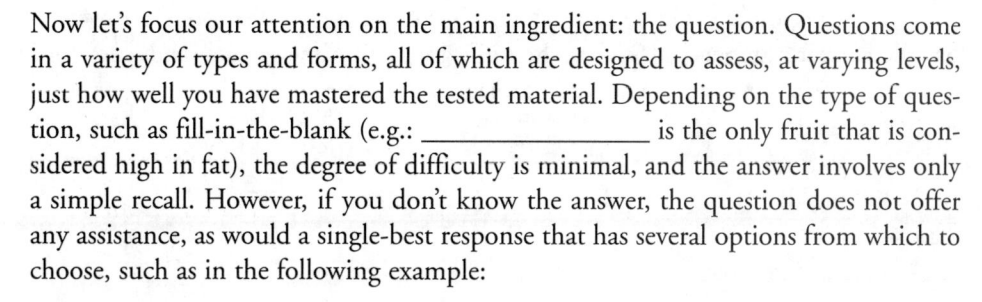

*You can usually deduce what types of questions an instructor will ask on an exam, based on the importance of a topic in relation to the subject, the instructor's personal area of interest, and the subject's specific requirements for competence.*

Now that you have some insight into what makes Anne N. Structor ask what she asks, let's take a closer look at the examination and its parts. Perhaps the most important part of an exam is the instructions. These are the rules and guidelines that govern the competition between YOU vs. THE EXAM. The instructions are usually located at the beginning of the exam, and they should be read thoroughly and understood completely. If you don't understand the instructions, it would behoove you to acquire clarification from the test-maker. If an exam has several parts or sections, each section may well be introduced by an applicable set of instructions. Make sure that you are clear on what the exam is asking you to do and how you are to go about doing it before you proceed.

Now let's focus our attention on the main ingredient: the question. Questions come in a variety of types and forms, all of which are designed to assess, at varying levels, just how well you have mastered the tested material. Depending on the type of question, such as fill-in-the-blank (e.g.: _____ is the only fruit that is considered high in fat), the degree of difficulty is minimal, and the answer involves only a simple recall. However, if you don't know the answer, the question does not offer any assistance, as would a single-best response that has several options from which to choose, such as in the following example:

Which of the following fruits is considered high in fat?
  a.) apples
  b.) avocados
  c.) bananas
  d.) tomatoes

Other questions may require a more in-depth thought process. Thought-provoking questions often require an assimilation of separate bits of information in order to satisfy the final solution. Word problems that incorporate calculations are able to achieve a heightened degree of difficulty by requiring the synthesis of answers for which a subsequent answer is the same, or even another, question is dependent. For example,

**Dimensions of Testing & Study Skills**

Jack weighs 220 lbs. and is 5'4". At age 33, he is considered moderately active, but he has recently been diagnosed with Type II, (non-insulin dependent) diabetes mellitus. Based on the information provided, how many Kcal should Jack's diet include? How many grams of CHO, protein, and fat should Jack consume daily? Make recommendations that will perhaps help Jack improve his overall status of health.

The following question might be posed: "Based on your response to the previous question, outline a one-day meal plan for Jack." As you can see, this can become rather involved, especially if you don't know "jack" about Jack's problem. One question builds upon the other, and a substantial familiarity with several formulas and the ability to then apply this information is requested. Don't you just love questions like this? Well, you should, because Anne N. Structor will undoubtedly have at least one such question on the exam.

Let's draw our attention to a differently structured type of question. The types of questions that provide answers are single-best response questions, key-type questions, and questions with distracters. Distracters, as the name implies, offer an added challenge. The distracters are usually choices that are close, but not correct. In your reviewing, you have probably seen the distracter terms used, perhaps even in the same paragraph or section of your class notes, as the correct answer. Distracters may also contain partially correct information; but, as is the case with true-or-false questions, if part of the response is incorrect, then it is no longer the best option.

Example: The normal fasting blood glucose level is _____.
   a.) 115 mg/dl
   b.) 300 ppm
   c.) 115 g/dl
   d.) 240 mg/dl

The correct response would be "a," 115 mg/dl. The others are distracters. Answer "c" has the correct number—115—but the units are 1,000 times greater and, therefore, "c" would be incorrect. If the question remained the same and the following responses were offered
   a.) 115 g/dl
   b.) 300 mg/dl
   c.) 72 ppm
   d.) none of the above
the correct response, of course, would now be "d".

## ANATOMY OF AN EXAM QUESTION

Just as a cell is made up of several different organelles, each having a specific function in the maintaining of the cell and the organism, an exam may have different types of questions. The question type may vary, but the function is to assess the test-taker's familiarity with and understanding of the information given. Let's look at a few of the ways in which the test-maker can "pick your brain."

## True or False

The true-or-false question is an oldie but goodie. It is an objective-type question that has a relatively high chance (50%) of being answered correctly. True-or-false questions are not extremely difficult to construct, but depending on their length (and they can be lengthy), and the subtleness with which one or two facts are deleted, reversals, or erroneous insertions can be made, they can become somewhat challenging to follow and, as a result, a bit difficult to answer. But you can do them. When you approach a true-or-false question, there are a few tips that might be helpful. Read the question thoroughly, and make sure that you understand the statement that is being made. Look for words like not, always, only that are pivot words in the statement. If a statement has the word not, which may not be highlighted, then the statement can be approached like a mathematical equation where two negatives make a positive, and any other combination of a positive and a negative is a negative. Examine, for instance, this statement: "Raleigh is the state capitol for North Carolina." If the question is stated as thus, the response is true, since Raleigh is North Carolina's capitol. However, the question is false if stated like this: "Raleigh is not the capitol of North Carolina." The response is also false if the statement is this: "Charlotte is the capitol of North Carolina." But if the word not is inserted into this equation, the double negative mathematical precept now comes into play. Therefore, "Charlotte is not the capitol of North Carolina" is a true statement. The words only, always, never, and other such terms that denote absolute, without-exception descriptions should be approached with caution, especially for subject matters that are not empirical, governed by laws, or that leave room for individual interpretations of their concepts, as evidenced in this question: "Diabetes is always the result of a prolonged diet that is extremely high in sugar." Even though we associate diabetes with elevated blood glucose (sugar) levels, this statement may sound good, but it is misleading. The variables in this question are too relative (How long is "prolonged?" And how high is "extremely high?"). The statement is not 100% foolproof. In fact, the cause of diabetes is physiologically linked and, in some cases, genetically inherited. The word always is too strong an adjective in this statement. Remember, if any part of a true-or-false statement is false, the entire question is considered false.

## Single-Best Response

The single-best response introduces another variable: the distracter. Distracters are bad-news bait. They lure you in and make you select the wrong answer. They are designed to lead you astray. The distracters are sometimes close, and may not contain the single-best response. Examine the following question:

*Questions can be tricky in their wording. Read each question carefully before selecting an asnwer. Look for distractors and qualifying words like "not," "always," "only," and "never."*

The capitol of Maryland is
 a.) Columbia
 b.) Annapolis
 c.) Baltimore
 d.) Largo
 e.) none of the above

Dimensions of Testing & Study Skills

Option "a" is a state capitol, but not of Maryland. Baltimore is perhaps the best-known city in Maryland, and it has the largest population, but it isn't the capitol. Largo is the home of the Capitol Center, and choice "e" none of the above is a personal favorite, but the correct answer is "b," Annapolis. The probability of guessing the correct answer for a single-best response question of this sort is 1 in 5. You have a 20% chance of getting it right if you guess. Of course, if you know the correct answer because you learned the information, your chances are dramatically increased. The following question has the probability of having more than one correct answer based on the available options:

A cup _____.
   a.) is equal to 1/2 pint
   b.) is equal to 240 ml
   c.) is equal to 240 cc
   d.) all of the above are correct
   e.) none of the above

The question can likewise have either one or no correct response. The addition of "all of the above" as an option gives the test-taker yet something else to consider. When a question is structured in this manner, the test-taker can turn it into a series of true-or-false statements. For example, a cup is equal to 1/2 pint (true or false). Repeat this for "b" and "c." If your conclusion is that each of the three is applicable, then the correct answer is "d" (which it is). This same method can be used in answering the infamous multiple/multiple or key-type response questions.

### *Key-Type Response*

Key-type response questions not only require the knowledge of selected facts, but they also have a key (as the name implies) that corresponds with the answer selection process. The alphabet (A, B, C, D, or E) is selected if you feel that the number or combination of numbers that correspond with the letter is correct. The standard key is usually arranged as follows:

A = 1,2,3  B = 1,3  C = 2,4  D=4 only
E = 1,2,3,4 (all choices are correct)

Although key-type questions appear somewhat involved, they are not overwhelmingly difficult. In fact, the pattern of the key assists the test-taker to some degree. If you examine the answer key pattern, you will note that in each case, when the number one (1) is observed, the number three (3) is likewise present. By default of the pattern, if "1" is correct, then "3" is also correct. Your choices are narrowed down to either, "A," "B," or "E." If "1" and "4" are correct, then your correct response must be "E." If "1" is incorrect, then, by design, your answer is either "C" or "D."

Once you have mastered the key pattern, these questions become less difficult. Guard against selecting an incorrect response because you think you must have missed something somewhere in your notes. Examine this question:

Which of the following foods is a good source of Vitamin A?
1. Carrots
2. Pumpkins
3. Sweet Potatoes
4. Citrus Fruits (i.e., oranges)

As you read and understand the question and then select your response, systematically start with the first response, "carrots", and ask yourself if this response is true to the question asked (employ your true-or-false strategy, based on the wording of the question). Carrots are a good source of vitamins, so since that is true, sweet potatoes must be also, whether you knew it or not. The next step is to put the test to response "4." Are citrus fruits a good source of vitamin A? If you answered no, (which is correct, since they are not), then your corresponding choice would be either "A" (1,2,3) or "B" (1,3). Since "2" and "4" don't correlate like "1" and "3," you must determine if "2" is correct or not in order to make your final selection. Pumpkins are a good source of vitamin A, so the correct answer is "A" (1,2,3). If you are not sure about a choice (unless it has a "must be right" correlation, like 1 and 3, then it might not be to your advantage to figure it into your solution. Don't say to yourself, "Oranges and citrus fruits might have been somewhere in my notes, and I must have inadvertently skipped over it; so just in case I didn't see it, I'll answer 'E' to be on the safe side." This will in many instances place you on the wrong side. Your first impression is usually the correct one.

## *Matching*

Questions that ask you to match a term with a statement or a numerical response with an equation are somewhat like fill-in-the-blank questions with a pool of potential answers. In some instances, a single response can be used more than once, so make sure that you read the instructions or ask the test-maker or test administrator if this is the case. When completing matching questions, be sure to select the very best response, since answers may tend to be somewhat close, but one is more exact or descriptive than another. Take, for example, this matching exercise:

1. \_\_\_\_\_ Site of protein synthesis

2. \_\_\_\_\_ Number of ATPs generated by one glucose (aerobic)

3. \_\_\_\_\_ Author of this textbook

4. \_\_\_\_\_ Watson and Crick

a. 36 to 38
b. Johnson, Parker, Lunsford, and Henderson
c. devised model of DNA
d. ribosomes

It is obvious from some of the questions that a certain type of answer is requested. The word site in a question may suggest a place; number is self-explanatory; author is looking for a proper name, or perhaps research organization (i.e., American Red Cross); the names Watson and Crick don't give you much to go on. With each question, go down the list of probable responses, and make a notation by any that are applicable. If there are two that are very close, select the one that you feel better answers the question. If there are the same number of answers as questions, and no duplicate responses, then this may help you isolate the best choice for each question. The answers to the above questions are

1. d; 2. a; 3. b; 4. c

### Fill-in-the-_____.

Fill-in-the-blanks are usually straightforward. You know it, or you don't. They are rote memory types of questions: "The speed of sound is _____." "The capitol of Ohio is _____."

These questions are too easy. When you see a fill-in-the-blank section on an exam, it's time to exhibit an ear-to-ear smile and get ready to score points. A slight variation of the fill-in-the-blank is the labeling or identification question. Expect labeling or identification questions in classes where equipment, visual applications, or audio applications are utilized. A biology instructor may design an exam that asks you to label the parts of a microscope. An art appreciation instructor may ask you to identify a particular painting or architectural style. A music appreciation instructor may require that you train your ear to differentiate between periods of musical influence or identify a composition by name and give its composers. These are the types of answers that you either know, or you don't, and since it is up to you to supply a response, the thoroughness of your preparation is your primary insurance.

### Calculations

Calculations separate the grown folks from the growing folks, and they are not just reserved for courses that are taught by the math department. Chemistry, biology, nutrition, and music are just some of the disciplines that can incorporate numerical computations. If formulas for the calculations are needed, but are not provided, write them down (while the exam is in session, not prior to its start) on the exam copy, or on a scrap sheet of figuring paper (while the formulas are fresh in your mind). You can then refer to the formulas as called upon by the exam. It is usually a good idea to show all of your work in a step-by-step sequence. This will suggest to the instructor that you understand how your answer was derived, and in the event you make an arithmetic error, you may be eligible for partial credit, since the mechanics are there on paper. Be sure, if time permits, to check and re-check the steps leading to your answer. The answer should be a logical one. If decimal points are involved, make sure that the decimal is placed correctly. If units are a part of the answer (i.e., grams, mg/dl, etc.), be sure to attach them to your answer. Since you may have several notations on your paper, it is probably a good idea to either circle or highlight your final answer so it stands out from the rest of the numbers.

*If formulas for calculations are needed, but not provided, write them down on your test at the start of the exam. You can then refer to the formulas, as needed.*

## Word Problems

One of my favorite types of exam questions is the word problem. Word problems can really force you to analyze a given situation and render a plan of resolution that may require several formulas, definitions, and then logical explanations. Here's one of my classic word problems from yesteryear:

Bill weights 220 lbs. and his wife, Ruth, weights 132 lbs. Assuming that Bill and Ruth are in good physical condition and do not have a history of any serious ailments, what is the difference between the weight of the bone protein that is contributing to Bill's total body weight and the muscle protein that is contributing to Ruth's total body weight? Express your answer in Kgs.

Now, from an instructor's perspective, it doesn't get much better than this. Let's examine the question so that we can reveal why this question type is an instructor's favorite. For what are we looking? When you read the question, you will note that we are comparing Bill to Ruth, and we need to derive some kind of difference, which suggests subtraction. "Oh, my goodness! What have I gotten myself into?" one might ask. "Nothing that you can't handle," is your response. Always have an "I can do this" attitude, especially when you have prepared. To answer this problem, go through the following steps:

1. Since the answer is to be expressed in Kgs, we must convert our lbs. to Kgs. Let's do that now, and get it out of the way, lest we forget.
2. Approximately 20% of a person's total body weight is protein. Use this information in the next calculation.
3. The weight of the protein that is contributing to one's total body weight can be distributed into the following areas:

    50% Muscle
    20% Bone
    20% Other
    10% Skin

    Take the answer you obtained in Step 2 and figure out the weight percentages, as indicated above.

4. The difference between the protein weight of Bill's bone and the protein weight of Ruth's muscle can now be calculated.

Ask yourself the following: "Does this answer look reasonable?" (Do you have an answer that is greater than what you started with, when you know that it should be less?) "Have I given the instructor what he or she has asked?" (Or, does this answer reflect what he should have been asking?) Make sure that you have not left out any step(s), and always show your work. Read the question carefully, and before proceeding, make sure that you understand exactly what is being asked. If you are altogether clueless, and the question's point value is not comparatively high, wait until you have completed some of the less time-consuming sections of the exam before you tackle the word problems.

## Essays

The essay puts you in the driver's seat. You are responsible for expounding on the question, and writing at your discretion what you want to say. There are no "distracters," and you are, for the most part, in complete control. As always, read the question carefully and understand what the instructor is asking. If time is on your side, a brief outline of your thoughts might be in order. Include key points and terms that will jog your memory. In some instances, the question might ask that you compare, contrast, and/or show relationships between two or more variables. If the question asks that you do so, writing out in your response "the relationship between" or "to compare X to Y" will alert the instructor that you are addressing the particulars of the question. Be aware of spelling, grammar, and subject-verb agreement, just as if you were constructing an English course composition.

Like word problems, essays tend to be time-consuming. Depending on the time available, and the relative point value of the essay(s), monitor your time such that each question can be adequately addressed. Remember, be careful not to spend twenty minutes on a 7-point essay and leave 93 points (assuming the exam is based on 100 points) unattended. That's only common sense. Neatness is always a plus. If your handwriting is not that legible, printing is an option. When constructing an essay, use the "SCAB" approach: Simplicity, Clarity, Accuracy, and Brevity, but don't forget to be as thorough as necessary.

## Take-Home Exams

Take-home exams give you the luxury of having resources at your access and time at your disposal; but for a take-home exam to be truly beneficial, the test-taker must take advantage of both. All too often, test-takers wait until the last hour to take an exam that they have had several days to complete. By pacing yourself and sticking to an established completion schedule, you can make take-home exams an uncomplicated, enriching learning experience.

## Open-Book Exams

Open-book exams are definitely not the better of two worlds (the access of notes and textbooks, without the extended time allotment of the take-home). Instead, an open-book exam can be a potential time trap, if the test-taker is not extremely well organized. The false security of knowing that you can just look up the answer in the book does not always work out as planned. Open-book exams can be administered in most disciplines, but they are more common in courses that require tables, lots of formulas, and information such as listings of sine, co-sine, specific heats, and variables that are required for calculations. When an instructor announces that an upcoming exam will be open book, take the time to organize your notes and text such that everything that you will need is readily available and easy to find. Use stick-em notes to identify sections of your book and highlight formulas, definitions, and other pertinent information (in different colors, if you like) so that your time is not spent searching during the exam.

*Take time to organize your notes and text before an open-book exam, using stick-em notes to highlight important information.*

## COMPUTERIZED TEST

Using the computer to administer a test is becoming the preferred mode in the halls of higher education. Most of the standardized tests have a computer-based version, which has been an alternative to the pen-and-paper version since 1993 (Miller, Linn, & Gronlund, 2008). There are several advantages of using the computer to take a test.

1. You can schedule to take the test at your convenience, rather than having to take it on the national testing date.
2. You can have your test results almost immediately.
3. You can separate speed and accuracy of responses. Thus, the computer allows you to do things that would be almost impossible to do with a more traditional test version.
4. The computer administers adaptive test; the subsequent question is based upon the previous answer. The questions posed are modified to the taker's performance level and provide precise information about your abilities using fewer test questions than traditional paper-based tests. At the start of each section, you are presented with test questions of middle difficulty. As you answer each question, the computer scores that question and uses that information, as well as your responses to any preceding questions and information about the test design, to determine which question is presented next. As long as you respond correctly to each question, questions of increased difficulty typically will be presented. When you respond incorrectly, the computer typically will present you with questions of lesser difficulty. Your next question will be the one that best reflects both your previous performance and the requirements of the test design. This means that different test takers will be given different questions (ETS, 2004, p. 5).

*To take an online test, you will need a computer, access to test software, and a connection to the Internet.*

## ONLINE, COMPUTER-BASED TESTING/TUTORIALS

In order to take an online, computer-based test, you will need test-preparation software and a service provider for Internet access that will link you to online programs and specialized "mini-courses" designed to help with math, vocabulary, or other skill sets. The advantage is that you will have access to the test, just for the asking. The test will be available, accessible whenever you are ready for it. The disadvantage is obvious: Internet access. You can take a test any place, any time, as long as you have Internet access to a computer. Many of the computer-based programs offer a "live, online" chatroom, which offers students that personal, face-to-face contact.

## ANATOMY OF A TEST-TAKER

As a student at Morehouse College, I recall walking into a classroom with my head cocked to one side and lying somewhat on my shoulder. I would walk to my seat and, within seconds, one of my classmates and study buddies would enter with his head displayed in similar fashion. What started as a humorous gesture later became a some-

**Dimensions of Testing & Study Skills**

what common occurrence. The action was suggestive of our having studied so much that our heads were heavy with history or English or whatever the class might have been. The symbolism of our side-cocked heads was a message to our friends that we were prepared to "ace" the exam.

How do you prepare for an exam? The answer is "every day." Don't wait until the night prior to an exam to begin studying (How many times have you heard this advice?). Review each subject as though you were trying to learn it and not just pass an exam. Develop a routine study schedule that exposes you to each subject for an adequate amount of time each day. What is adequate? You judge your feeling of competence in each area. Some courses require more time than others, as I'm sure you are aware. If your schedule allows for it, immediately following a class session is perhaps one of the best times to review new information. The more you see it and review it, the more saturated your memory becomes with the information. It is even a good idea to look over the new information that is scheduled to be taught the night before the class, so at least the terms will be familiar when you hear them during the lecture.

*A study group can help you prepare for exams. Selecting a group leader can help the group stay focused and productive.*

Avoid cramming for exams! However, sometimes you have to "do what you have to do," and in the event you find yourself between this proverbial rock and hard place, cram like your grade depended upon it. Cramming involves getting the big picture and as many of its major components as possible. If you have ever painted by numbers, you will recall that the image of the picture comes into focus prior to all of the fine details being in place. You can make out what it is, even though it's not finished. That's cramming at its best. With cramming, you select the major concepts, focal points, and seven to ten of the terms (vocabulary words) that are related to these main points. You learn (not really learn, but more like apply to your short-term memory) these points and supporting information and try to reiterate them in the morning or whenever the exam takes place. Cramming is stressful for some folks, and since it is a relatively short-term application, you will still need to learn the information to truly benefit from its worth.

College is full of distractions. Some are worthwhile, and others are undoubtedly not as valuable. Becoming a disciplined student is perhaps as challenging as organic chemistry. It's close, but organic may have a slight edge. Being disciplined does not necessarily mean staying in your room or in the library behind a book all the time. However, when there is a step-show at the gym, it's Homecoming week, and your friends are on their way to the gym and then to the after-the-gym jam, you have to make a serious decision, because your criminal justice instructor has no mercy and has scheduled an exam for Monday at 8:00 in the morning. You feel ready, but you could stand to give the material the once-over, and so you tell your friends to go on without you. By all means, if you have the time and the money, go to the show, if that's your cup of tea. It's a part of college life. But always keep school in the proper perspective and prioritize your time wisely. If you miss some of these events during your freshman year, you'll want to be in a position where you can, hopefully, see them as a sophomore (if you know what I mean).

### *Before the Exam*

Now you can take this for what it's worth, but the period before the exam (from the night before until you walk through the classroom door) is crucial time. You have probably heard folks say to the last-minute reviewer who is standing outside of the door with notes in hand, "If you don't know it by now...," but for some, it is a common practice. Who knows what little tidbit of information you may stumble across? If you are well prepared, you really should not have to take anything to an exam but your pen and your pencil. Everything else is stored upstairs. It might be a good idea to get there a little early to find a seat (one with minimal distraction).

Sometimes you have to feel the pre-exam crowd out. You need to be on time, but in some instances, the too-early crowd can give you the blues. Something that can get on your last nerve (well, at least my last nerve) is when you haven't studied for a test and there are students who are asking some of everything about everything before the test, right outside of the room. If you like it, be my guest; engage in dialogues if you care to. But I'm looking for peace and quiet before the storm, instead of confusion.

### *After the Exam*

Experienced test-takers will go back and analyze their mistakes on an exam. Doing so improves upon their test-taking skills, as they are searching for the careless mistakes that can cost points and make the difference between an "A" and a "B+," or as the registrar sees it, "a letter grade." If your instructor passes back exams for you to review and keep, it is always a good idea to review the types of questions asked, as well as the content within the questions, to get a better feel for the approach that the instructor uses. Review your exam with the instructor if there are questions that you still find puzzling, and make sure that you understand why you missed each question and how the correct response was derived.

## HIGH-STAKES TESTING

Testing is a big deal. Before college, you took achievement tests–the PSAT, the SAT, or the ACT. Universities use the results to predict how well you will do in college and if you are the "kind of student" they are looking for. If you pursue graduate studies, you will take the GRE or the GMAT, or LSAT to enter various professional schools. Your teachers, and later your employer, will evaluate your performance using some type of test. Yes, it is important that you do well on tests, but keep testing in its proper perspective. That is, don't get caught up in the moment–compromising all that you have worked for just to do well on a test. What am I getting around to? The answer is an easy one, honesty. Every college and university expects you to honest. Being honest in your academic pursuits is important and appears as a pledge on the enrollment application, in the course catalog, on the professor's syllabus, etc. The consequences of dishonesty are severe: receiving an "F," academic and disciplinary action, and expulsion. As a matter of fact, many universities hold all students responsible and accountable for each other's actions when it comes to ethical behavior. Knowledge is not advanced when students corrupt the essential process by engaging in falsification and cheating. The misconduct includes, but is not limited to, plagiarism, bribery, cheating, lack of net-etiquette, abuse of computer use policy, misrepresentation (passing off someone else's work as your own), and giving someone your access code to do your work. What can you do to avoid being charged with academic dishonesty?

Dimensions of Testing & Study Skills

It begins by preparing thoroughly for tests and assignments. Take the initiative to prevent others from copying tests by shielding your answer sheet during a test and looking in the direction of other students' papers during tests. Also, avoid talking to other students during tests.

Check the course syllabus for additional guidelines regarding academic honesty in a particular course. Discuss course expectations with the instructor and do not lend assignments to other students.

Remember to give credit to the author. Use a recognized handbook, visit the library, or visit this campus's website: http://www.spcollege.edu/central/libonline for instruction on citing source materials in papers. Consult with the instructor or program director when in doubt.

Encourage honesty among other students. Refuse to help students who cheat and when you need assistance, use the tutoring services that are available on your campus.

## TESTING ANXIETY

You have probably heard that a little anxiety is good for you. And most experts would agree it is. Experiencing nervousness and apprehension prior to, during, or after an exam are signs of "good" anxiety. This kind of anxiety is common among college students and can motivate you to do well on exams. From time to time, most college students will feel some level of anxiety or stress regarding upcoming exams, papers, or presentations.

While most students can reduce anxiety levels through preparation, some may need additional strategies. For example, if you know the material, but worry too much and become emotionally and physically ill prior to, during, or after an exam, your emotions are running amuck. This kind of anxiety may cause you to perform poorly and decrease your ability to do well.

### *Sources of Testing Anxiety*

Various situations trigger anxiety. Anxiety is an emotional response to a frightening situation alerting the mind that something is wrong "prepare to take action," "fight or take flight." Testing is one of those trigger situations.

The term "test anxiety" refers to the emotional reactions that some students have to exams (www.utdallas.edu). The fear of taking exams is a reasonable response. After all, how you perform on college exams can shape the course of your academic career. But, excessive fear of exams will keep you from doing your best in college.

There are three components of test anxiety: physical, emotional, and cognitive. If you are physically worried (acute anxiety), you may experience nausea, upset stomach, sweaty palms and shaky hands, dry mouth and/or a pounding heart. Emotional test anxiety involves fear or panic. As one student put it, "I become completely unglued!" (www.utdallas.edu). Problems with attention and memory (freezing-up, forgetfulness) are symptoms of cognitive test anxiety. "My mind jumps from one thing to another"; "I worry that I'm certain to fail", are statements that students make when they fear they have not performed well.

There are two rather simple techniques that reduce and eventually eliminate test anxiety. One technique is to become aware of your thoughts. More than likely, they are negative. You will need to practice thinking positively, thus, replacing negative worrisome thoughts that cause the anxiety. For example, instead of saying, "I don't do well on tests; I know I am going to fail." Say, "I am going to do my best, and if I get a low grade, I will increase my score by 30 points the next time."

The other technique used to reduce test anxiety is to learn how to relax. Learning how to relax can help control anxiety during the exam. Practice the following techniques beforehand so you are comfortable with them:
- Get comfortable in your chair–slouch down if that helps.
- Tighten, then, relax different muscle groups of your body, one group at a time. Start with your feet, moving up your body to your neck and face.
- Begin breathing slowly and deeply. Focus your attention on your breath going in and out. Each time you breathe out, say, "relax" to yourself (www.utdallas.edu). Other relaxation techniques and ways to deal with stress are discussed later in this chapter and in Chapter 4.

## STUDY SKILLS

I am sure that you have been exposed to "study skills" in one way, shape or form ever since you started your formal education. And I am sure that you have used one or more of these "skills" at some point in your schooling with some degree of success. But, if you are like most students, you have yet to develop a systematic way of approaching a learning situation that will allow you to retrieve and use all the knowledge crammed into your head. There is nothing more frustrating than feeling that you truly "worked" or "studied" and still ended up with grades that did not reflect all the time and effort you put forth. This may cause you to give up, believing that you are not smart or capable enough to be successful in school.

*Being a successful learner has its rewards both in and out of college in the form of good grades, advanced degrees, high-paying jobs, and promotions.*

This section will present several types of study skills or "specific methods, behaviors, and attitudes students engage in while learning" (Chin, 2004). Research has indicated that students who are more diligent in their use of study skills tend to have higher grade-point averages. There are no magic formulas that can guarantee your place on the Dean's List. However, there are methods and techniques that can enhance your ability to master the college curriculum and become a successful learner. I emphasize "learner" because your goal should be learning, not memorizing and reciting facts and information by rote. Learning involves discovering and creating new strategies to meet the challenges of everyday living. Successful learners are those who know when to use the tried-and-true methods and when to use new or different strategies to solve problems (Chapter 2). Being a successful learner has its rewards both in and out of college in the form of good grades, advanced degrees, high-paying jobs, and promotions.

Before we begin, you should understand that it might not be easy to relearn certain habits, skills, or strategies. But if you are sincerely motivated and desire to become more efficient at acquiring, organizing, synthesizing, and remembering information, the effort will be well worth it. The specific skills that can aid you in your journey to becoming a successful learner include studying with peers, managing your time, listening, note-taking, memorizing, and reading (Cole, 1987).

## *Study Groups*

You've heard the old proverb, "Two heads are better than one." And it is certainly true when it comes to college and studying. Too often, we overlook this strategy (college can seem very competitive), which the business world uses all the time. In the "real world" you will not work in isolation. College is an ideal place and being a student is the ideal time to learn group dynamics and the power of groups. When forming a group consider the following guidelines:

- Select group members based upon purpose–in this case, students who have similar academic aspirations. Seek group members who a) stay alert in class, b) ask questions, c) take notes, and d) answer the instructor's questions.
- Choose partners with varied learning styles, "different ways of knowing" the information. More than likely, there will be different preferred learning styles among group members.
- Keep the group manageable (4 to 6 students).
- Get to know your group members prior to getting down to business. Evaluate compatibility; you will be spending a great deal of time with these peers. You want quality time and sharing from all members of the group. This may be a good time to ask the group to complete a self-assessment exercise on test-taking. A Test-Taking Checklist is one instrument that can be printed from the website and used to assess your level of satisfaction of your test-taking skills. The website is: http://www.d.umn.edu/student/loon/acad/strat/testcheck.html.
- Reflect, noting the characteristics of the group. Select a group leader, a student that can keep the group focused and productive.

When the group meets, adhere to a few guiding principles:

- Read the text and complete all assignments prior to the study session.
- Compare notes.
- Question each other on the material.
- Teach each other the concepts; you will reinforce what you know, and you will help your peers learn the material. Research studies document the power of peer teaching and learning. Oftentimes, peers can help you make connections.
- Predict what the test questions may be (refer back to the session on the "Anatomy of the Test-Maker").
- Evaluate each session. Ask, "Did everyone fully participate? Did we achieve what we set out to do? What improvements should we make?" These are just some guidelines that you can use to get started. You will add your own ideas as you engage in group activities.

## Applying Time Management

To begin our discussion, answer each of the following questions as either true or false:
1. There isn't enough time in the day to do all I need to do.
2. I procrastinate or put off things that I know I should be doing.
3. I find that I spend a lot of time doing things that aren't important.
4. Scheduling daily or weekly chores is boring and a waste of time.
5. I never learned how to budget time.

If you answered true to one or more of these questions, you need to learn how to budget time. Many people view time as their enemy, or think that there will always be enough time to do what needs to be done (i.e., I can get to that later). Both of these assumptions are false. Time, when used properly, can be your best friend. However, there are only twenty-four hours in each day, and time can easily slip by, leaving you feeling panicked if you haven't done an essential task. The key is to make the most of the time allotted through effective time management.

The first step in managing time effectively involves determining how you are currently spending your time. To do this, make a schedule and track your activities for at least one week. Be honest! Include time spent talking on the phone and hanging out on campus. At the end of the week, calculate the amount of time spent in class, studying, working, socializing, eating, sleeping, and taking care of personal business. Now, see if you can discover where you are spending large amounts of time in activities that are non-productive. Can you see times that could have been better spent studying? Can you find ways to rearrange your schedule so that you have enough time to do what is necessary and still have a personal life? Do you see times or days that are more productive than others? With this information, you are now ready to design a schedule that will allow you to do required activities, while leaving time for fun and relaxation.

## Time-Management Activity

An empty schedule is provided. To make one that is workable, do the following:
1. Write in fixed time periods, such as class time and work.
2. Schedule regular study sessions. You should study a minimum of two hours for every one hour spent in class. For example, if you are taking twelve credit hours, you should study twenty-four hours per week.
3. Schedule one-to-three-hour study sessions. If you spend less than one hour, much of the time is spent finding and organizing the study material. More than three hours at a time is ineffective for retention, as you may become fatigued and lose your concentration.
4. Schedule some study time before class for preparation and after class for review.
5. Don't plan marathon study sessions. Five two-hour sessions are better than one ten-hour session.
6. Consider your peak times, and study more difficult subjects when you are at your best.
7. Plan time for relaxation. Use this as a reward for studying.
8. Leave some unscheduled time for personal errands and unexpected emergencies.
9. Set definite start and stop times.
10. Be flexible! Rigid scheduling is doomed to fail.

Try your schedule for one week to determine if adjustments need to be made.

The TO DO list is another effective time-management tool. These lists can be done on a weekly or daily basis. The list should include projects that must be done, as well as those items that you would like to do. Weekly lists should be done on Sunday evening and daily lists the night before. For TO DO lists to work, follow these strategies:
1. Prioritize items on the list in terms of urgency.
2. Carry the list with you at all times.
3. Cross off items as they are completed. This will let you see what has been done, which gives you a sense of accomplishment.

Even the most time-conscious person may procrastinate from time to time. It is not a deadly sin unless it becomes a way of life and you find that you are always doing something at the last minute. If you are a person who seems to continually "put off until tomorrow what can be done today," you may benefit from these strategies:
1. Decide the value of the task. If it is of little value, don't spend time worrying about it. If it is important, proceed to Step 2.
2. Break the task into smaller, less-overwhelming parts.
3. Visualize yourself completing the task.
4. Set beginning and ending times or dates for completion of the task.
5. Enlist others, such as your friends, roommate, and parents, to help you achieve your goals.
6. Plan to award yourself when done. A Schedule Planner is located on pages 83 and 84.

## *Listening*

Most people assume that because they are hearing, they are listening. However, there is a major difference between the two. Hearing is a physiological process that involves the detection of sound waves by the ear. In contrast, listening is "the process by which spoken language is converted into meaning in the mind" (Steil & Bommelje, 2004). The majority of school instruction is presented orally because almost half of all verbal communication is devoted to listening, as opposed to reading or speaking.

## *Listening Skills*

The first step in becoming a better listener is to realize that listening is an active versus a passive activity. This means that you must be attentive and ready to receive the information being imparted. Being an active listener means that you have a purpose for listening. The purpose may be to learn something new or to reaffirm previously acquired information. Next, try to anticipate what the speaker is going to say next. Most speakers talk about a specific topic or concept. Your task is to identify that main idea and the supporting details. Anticipating the course of the talk will help keep you involved. Then, keep an open mind and try not to judge or criticize the message or the speaker. Criticizing or judging may cause you to miss key facts and information. Attempt to summarize the main points and pay attention to the speaker's body language.

During a lecture, listen for signal words that indicate a major point in the lecture. Examples of signal words include "first," "for example," "in conclusion," or "the basic idea," "however," "therefore," etc. Try to relate the lecture to something you already know or have experienced; this will help keep you interested. If you don't understand, ask questions. Sometimes, even when you plan to listen actively, you may lose your concentration and your mind may wander. If you find this happening, you can come back to the present by doing the following:

1. Write down the thought that has caused you to be distracted so that you can come back to it too many spaces later.
2. Change your body position. Sit up straight, cross or uncross your legs, move your head from side to side, or clench and unclench your hands.
3. Take a deep breath, hold it for five to ten seconds, and then exhale slowly. Do this three times.

## NOTE-TAKING

Now that you have seen what it takes to listen properly, you need to be able to record accurately what you have heard. The ability to take good notes is without a doubt one of the most important skills college students need and the one that most students have yet to master. You do not need to be a stenographer to be able to take notes that can aid learning and studying. However, you must have an organized system so that you can take down the essential points of an oral presentation.

### *How to Take Notes*

1. Read texts and other materials before class. This initial reading will give you an idea of the subject of the lecture, and you won't feel pressured to write each word the instructor is saying.
2. Have a notebook for each subject or a divided three-ring binder so that you will be able to find the notes for each subject quickly when studying and preparing for class.
3. As you write, leave a three-inch margin on the left side of the paper. This margin can be used to fill in additional information or to write questions that you want to ask or look up after class.

*Hearing is not the same as listening. Listening is an active process that allows you to process information and give it meaning.*

Dimensions of Testing & Study Skills

4. Use only one side of a page to allow you to spread out your notes when you study.
5. Be sure to write down key points as they occur in the lecture (see "Listening Skills").
6. Be sure to copy material written on the board.
7. Number and date your notes. Also, use a new page for each new lecture.
8. Organize your notes in a logical outline. Organized notes are much easier to use when studying.
9. A note about tape recorders: tape recorders should be used only as a backup. They should not be used in place of good note-taking. If used properly, recorders can help fill in the gaps in your notes. However, making notes from tapes can be very time consuming.
10. It may be helpful to use different colored markers to emphasize key or important points that you want to be sure to remember.
11. Develop and use your own system of shorthand and abbreviations. Some commonly used symbols are shown below:

| | | |
|---|---|---|
| * = key point | ? = unclear point | w/o = without |
| w/ = with | & = and | s/b = should be |
| + = positive or good | _ = negative or bad | ~ = approximately |
| re: = regarding | > = greater than | < = less than |
| vs = against or opposite | dx = does not | cx = can't |
| i.e, = in other words | [ ] = information that belongs together | |
| !!!! = very important | ÷ = individual | |

Note-taking does not end after the lecture. Using the study session you scheduled after each class period (see "Time Management"), you should review your notes for the following:
- check for accuracy
- edit and revise
- add information from the text
- compare with other students.

## MEMORIZATION

Of course, being able to remember is vital if you want to do well on exams. People who seem to be able to remember key facts don't necessarily have a "photographic memory." They do, most likely, have specific techniques at their disposal. Memorization is not difficult, but, as with any other skill, it requires effort and practice.

### *Aids to Memorization*

1. Have a good understanding of the material. Nothing is harder to remember than information that does not make sense.
2. Intend to remember. If you make a conscious effort, you will be more likely to remember.
3. Over learn the subject. If you spend more time than is needed for perfect memorization, you will retain the information longer.
4. Make associations between the material and previously learned information or experiences.

5. Write down the material to significantly increase retention.
6. Space your "memorization" work over several sessions. As with all studying, you will retain more with several short sessions versus one long session (see "Time Management Activity").
7. Try to review within the first twenty-four hours after class. Most forgetting occurs within the first twenty-four hours.
8. Plan to spend time memorizing right before going to bed. Then go directly to sleep without watching television, listening to music, or reading. These activities can interfere with the memorization process. Get up a little earlier in the morning to review last night's material.
9. Use key words as memory cues. Think of these words as "hooks" upon which you hang information. A key word stands for a central idea. If you can remember the key word, you can remember the central topic.
10. Use the first letters to remember the list of key words. If you can't remember the key words themselves, you might be able to remember the first letters of the key words.
11. Organize the material. Organization of the material makes it infinitely easier to remember.
12. Relax! Nothing interferes with memorization more than being tense or uptight. Take a deep breath and visualize the material to be learned.

## READING

Your ability to read may be the one single factor that influences your success in college and beyond. Even if you do not read as well as you would like, you can still develop the ability to read and comprehend the large amount of material that is required to complete a college degree. The key to reading, as with all the techniques mentioned thus far, is to be active rather than passive. This process entails becoming involved with the material by having a purpose and a plan for reading. Once this is done, you will find that you not only read more in less time, but also that you have actually learned something in the process.

One of the most referenced and well-known methods of reading are the SQ3R approach. This method was created by a psychologist named Francis Robinson as a training technique for Army recruits during World War II. Each letter stands for a particular step to be used when reading:

S= Survey

When you open the book, begin scanning the table of contents, the preface, chapter headings, and other aids such as tables, charts, chapter reviews or summaries, and the glossary. Scanning will help you become familiar with the material and general purpose of the book.

Q = Question

After you have scanned the entire text, you should develop a list of questions that you want answered. A way to do this is to turn each chapter heading into a question. Although many students think this part is not necessary, questioning keeps you focused and actively engaged with the text.

Dimensions of Testing & Study Skills

R1 = Read

Now you are ready to read. Remember, the key is to be an active reader. To do this, it is often helpful to decide beforehand how much you are going to read and to estimate the amount of time it will take you. If a particular chapter seems especially difficult, you might break it up into smaller parts. Jot down notes as you read, and underline key points (try not to underline the entire text, since this defeats your purpose). See if you can answer the questions developed in the previous stage. Remember, smaller time periods are more beneficial than longer ones.

R2 = Recite

Recite aloud the answers to your list of questions. You can do this alone or with a friend. This stage helps to solidify what you have read and aids in memorization. Try to recite the information in your own words, with the book closed.

R3 = Review

To be effective, your review should take place within the first twenty-four hours of reading (see "Memorization"). Review the introduction, summaries, headings, and main points. Review noted and underlined material. Also review your questions and answers to make sure you thoroughly understand what you have read.

## SUMMARY

You now have at your disposal all you need to become a successful learner. Reading this is just a start. Now the hard work begins. The athletes and musicians you admire did not become great through talent alone. They worked hard and practiced. You must do the same. As I said earlier, there is no magic formula. If you are committed and use the skills and methods presented, you will find that you will not only succeed in college but also in your chosen life's work.

## REFERENCES

Chin, B. (2004). *How to ace any test.* New York: John Wiley and Sons.

Chin, B. (2004). *How to study for success.* New York: John Wiley and Sons.

Cole, Sherry M. A validity study of the use of the Learning and Study Strategies Inventory with college freshmen. (1987) Unpublished Doctoral Dissertation: University of North Carolina at Chapel Hill.

Educational Testing Service (2004). What's the dif? Helping to ensure test question fairness. Retrieved May 15, 2004, from www.ets.org/research/dif.html.

Miller, D., Linn, R. L., & Gronlund, N. E. (2008). Measurement and assessment in teaching (10th ed.). Eaglewood Cliffs, NJ: Merrill Prentice-Hall.

McWhorter, K.T. (2006). *College reading and study skills* (10th ed.). Englewood Cliffs, NJ: Pearson Longman Prentice Hall.

Wong, L. (2005). Essential study skills (5th ed.). Boston, MA: Houghton Mifflin.

# WEBSITES

www.collegeboard.com
htpp://www.freevocabulary.com
www.gomath.com
http://mathforum.org
www.number2.com
www.testtakers.com
www.tc.cornell.edu/Edu/MathSciGateway
http://school.discoveryeducation.com/schrockguide/
*http://www.spjc.edu/webcentral/admit/honesty.htm*

Supportive Services Program, UMD (1995). Test taking checklist. from http://www.d.umn.edu/kmc/student/loon/acad/strat/testcheck.html

http://www.utdallas.edu/counseling/index.html
http://www.utdallas.edu/enroll/visit/slife.php

University Writing Center at the University of Central Florida: http://www.uwc.ucf.edu

*Online Writing Lab at Purdue University:*
http://owl.english.purdue.edu/handouts/index.html

# PRACTICE TEST

True-False: Answer the following questions as either true or false.

_____ 1. College instructors base grades only on tests and other assignments. Attendance in class has no effect on your final grade.

_____ 2. If a true-false question contains the word "always," it is more than likely false.

_____ 3. Meeting new people is not a reason students choose to attend college.

_____ 4. People who graduate from college are always more successful than people who don't.

_____ 5. College students tend to be happier and healthier than their peers who do not attend college.

_____ 6. You should never cram before an exam.

_____ 7. Short study sessions are more effective for retention than long ones.

_____ 8. You should stick with your first answer on a multiple choice test.

_____ 9. Over 40% of students in college are over twenty-five years of age.

_____ 10. The best students spend their time studying and are not involved in extracurricular activities.

## MULTIPLE CHOICE:

Choose the best answer for each question.

1. College can be very stressful. You can reduce your level of stress by
    a) exercising.
    b) eating properly.
    c) taking time to relax.
    d) all of the above.

2. All the following are signs of depression except
    a) excessive sleeping.
    b) increased activity.
    c) loss of appetite.
    d) low self-esteem.

3. The most commonly used drug among college students is
    a) heroin.
    b) marijuana.
    c) cocaine.
    d) none of the above.

4. Which one of the following statements is true?
   a) Most African American students attend predominantly black universities.
   b) Most African American students attend predominantly white universities.
   c) Most black college graduates go on to graduate school.
   d) More black males than females attend college.

5. The main reason students do not complete their college education is due to
   a) "flunking out."
   b) personal problems.
   c) financial problems.
   d) lack of family support.

6. When choosing a college major, the most important consideration should be that
   a) it is the most popular major on campus.
   b) it is what your parents want you to do.
   c) it matches your interests.
   d) it is where the jobs are.

7. You will get more out of the class if you
   a) read the text before class.
   b) read the text after class.
   c) read the text during class.
   d) read the text right before the exam.

8. The least effective method for taking lecture notes is to
   a) write down main points and supporting details.
   b) write down everything the instructor says.
   c) write your notes in outline form.
   d) devise and use your own system of shorthand and abbreviation.

9. Which of the following events would college students rate as being the most stressful?
   a) a serious argument with a close friend.
   b) a serious argument with an instructor.
   c) lower grades than expected.
   d) increased course load.

10. The fact that many college students take more than four years to graduate may be due to all of the following except
    a) students have jobs while in school.
    b) students have family responsibilities.
    c) students often change majors.
    d) college programs are designed for five years.

## MATCHING:

Match the word in the first column with the correct definition in the second column.

1. compare          a) to explain how something happened in detail

2. contrast         b) to show similarities between two things

3. explain          c) to show the difference between two things

4. describe         d) to tell the meaning of something

5. summarize        e) to provide a brief account

# ANSWER KEY

True-False          Multiple Choice          Matching

1)                  1)                       1)

2)                  2)                       2)

3)                  3)                       3)

4)                  4)                       4)

5)                  5)                       5)

6)                  6)

7)                  7)

8)                  8)

9)                  9)

10)                 10)

**Dimensions of Testing & Study Skills**

# ACTIVITY 1

## *Listening*

This activity will help you gain practice in effective listening. Have someone read the section on the following page entitled "Developmental Tasks" to you. Based on what was read, see if you can:

1. Identify the topic or main idea. _____
   _____
   _____

2. List at least three signal words. _____
   _____
   _____

3. State three key facts or concepts. _____
   _____
   _____

4. Summarize what was said. _____
   _____
   _____

5. Formulate two questions about what you heard. _____
   _____
   _____

## Developmental Tasks

The concept of developmental tasks is of relevance to the study of adolescent behavior and psychological maturity. By understanding developmental tasks relative to this stage, one can view the adolescent as distinct from other age groups within the family, peer group, and school situation. There are four basic adolescent tasks that represent developmental milestones the adolescent must successfully master if he or she is to become a psychologically healthy adult. The first task is to become emancipated from parents and adults. The second developmental task is the acquisition of skills for future economic independence. This task has to do with career plans and encompasses the vocational interests of the adolescent. The third is psychosexual differentiation, and learning to function in an adult role. The fourth, and perhaps the most basic and important of the tasks, is the establishment of a realistic, stable, positive, adult self-identity.

In working through these tasks, the adolescent is typically torn between dependence and independence. In striving for independence, most adolescents will engage in behaviors that will challenge their parents' expectations and values. During this time, the peer group becomes an important reference group for social norms. However, for the black, high achieving adolescent, peer pressure and its impact on academic achievement has some unique features. Authors such as Kunjufu refer to this aspect of peer pressure as the "silent killer." If the adolescent acts in ways which are not sanctioned by the peer group, for example achieving academically, the willingness to do well in school is challenged. Many adolescents may choose to go "underground," to become visible, yet invisible, by not drawing attention to their academic progress, thereby minimizing stress. Therefore, as the adolescent experiences conflicts between identity and achievement, he or she is confronted with experiencing an internal turmoil brought on by feelings of ambivalence. The impact on achievement seems even more intense since academic excellence is not viewed with respect by many adolescents.

# ACTIVITY 2

## *Note-taking*

This can be done in conjunction with the Listening Activity. As you are actively listening, try to take notes. When you are finished, take a few minutes to review your notes. Check for accuracy by reading the material yourself.

Compare what you have written to the following notes taken in outline form:

A) Developmental tasks
   1. emancipation
   2. skill acquisition
   3. psychosexual differentiation
   4. establishment of identity

B) Conflict
   1. dependence vs. independence
   2. peer group pressure
      a) "silent killer"
      b) going "underground"

# ACTIVITY 3

## *Memorization*

A psychology text lists the following as key factors that increase the likelihood that the behavior of a person will be imitated.

1. The model's behavior has <u>value</u>.
2. There are <u>similarities</u> between the model and the observer.
3. The model and the observer are engaged in <u>like</u> activities.
4. The <u>consequences</u> of the model's behavior are satisfying.
5. The model's behavior is not beyond the <u>skill</u> of the observer.

The key words have been underlined (value, similarities, like, consequences, and skill). Take a few minutes to memorize just the keywords. Then test yourself to see if you can recall the material.

The five factors that influence modeling are

1) _____

2) _____

3) _____

4) _____

5) _____

# ACTIVITY 4

## *Reading*

Set aside 1 to 1½ hours. Select a text or other college book that you have not read. The following activity will help you practice the SQ3R method:

1. Survey
   List the chapter headings and subheadings.
   _____
   _____

2. Question
   List questions you want answered.
   _____
   _____

3. Read
   Thoroughly read the material. Answer the questions previously developed.
   _____
   _____

4. Recite
   Recite the answers to your questions to yourself or to a friend.

5. Review
   Review the reading material and your written work.

## SCHEDULE PLANNER

A schedule planner is useful for getting an overview of your week as well as guarding against attempting to schedule more than one class into the same time slot. Below is a completed example planner for you to review.

| Monday | Tuesday | Wednesday | Thursday | Friday | Saturday |
|---|---|---|---|---|---|
| 8:00-8:50 | 8:00-9:15 *Class* | 8:00-8:50 | 8:00-9:15 *Class* | 8:00-8:50 | 8:00-8:50 |
| 9:00-9:50 *Class* | 9:25-10:40 *Study* | 9:00-9:50 *Class* | 9:25-10:40 *Study* | 9:00-9:50 *Class* | 9:00-9:50 *Study* |
| 10:00-10:50 *Class* | 10:50-12:05 *Study* | 10:00-10:50 *Class* | 10:40-11:30 *Study* | 10:00-10:50 *Class* | 10:00-10:50 *Study* |
| 11:00-11:50 *Class* | 12:05-12:45 *Errands* | 11:00-11:50 *Class* | 12:05-12:45 *Errands* | 11:00-11:50 *Class* | 11:00-11:50 *Study* |
| 12:00-12:50 *Lunch* | | 12:00-12:50 *Lunch* | | 12:00-12:50 *Lunch* | 12:00-12:50 |
| 1:00-1:50 | 1:00-2:15 *Lunch* | 1:00-1:50 | 1:00-2:15 *Lunch* | 1:00-1:50 | 1:00-1:50 |
| 2:00-2:50 | 2:25-3:40 *Class* | 2:00-2:50 *Study* | 2:25-3:40 *Class* | 2:00-2:50 *Study* | 2:00-2:50 |
| 3:00-3:50 *Free Time* | *Free Time* | 3:00-3:50 *Study* | | 3:00-3:50 *Study* | 3:00-3:50 |
| 4:00-4:50 *Free Time* | 3:50-5:05 *Free Time* | 4:00-4:50 *Free Time* | 3:50-5:05 *Class Lab* | 4:00-4:50 *Free Time* | 4:00-4:50 |
| 5:30-6:45 *Dinner* | 5:30-6:45 *Dinner* | 5:30-6:45 *Dinner* | 5:30-6:45 *Dinner* | 5:30-6:45 | |
| 7:00-9:30 *Study* | 7:00-9:30 *Study* | 7:00-9:30 *Study* | 7:00-9:30 *Study* | 7:00-9:30 | |

# SCHEDULE PLANNER

Use the planner below to enter your classes, study periods, work times, and lunch and dinner breaks for the week. You may obtain a printout of your classes from the registrar's office, electronically through the online register, or from your advisor.

| Monday | Tuesday | Wednesday | Thursday | Friday | Saturday |
|---|---|---|---|---|---|
| 8:00-8:50 | 8:00-9:15 | 8:00-8:50 | 8:00-9:15 | 8:00-8:50 | 8:00-8:50 |
| 9:00-9:50 | 9:25-10:40 | 9:00-9:50 | 9:25-10:40 | 9:00-9:50 | 9:00-9:50 |
| 10:00-10:50 | 10:50-12:05 | 10:00-10:50 | 10:40-11:30 | 10:00-10:50 | 10:00-10:50 |
| 11:00-11:50 | 12:05-12:45 | 11:00-11:50 | 12:05-12:45 | 11:00-11:50 | 11:00-11:50 |
| 12:00-12:50 |  | 12:00-12:50 |  | 12:00-12:50 | 12:00-12:50 |
| 1:00-1:50 | 1:00-2:15 | 1:00-1:50 | 1:00-2:15 | 1:00-1:50 | 1:00-1:50 |
| 2:00-2:50 | 2:25-3:40 | 2:00-2:50 | 2:25-3:40 | 2:00-2:50 | 2:00-2:50 |
| 3:00-3:50 |  | 3:00-3:50 |  | 3:00-3:50 | 3:00-3:50 |
| 4:00-4:50 | 3:50-5:05 | 4:00-4:50 | 3:50-5:05 | 4:00-4:50 | 4:00-4:50 |
| 5:30-6:45 | 5:30-6:45 | 5:30-6:45 | 5:30-6:45 | 5:30-6:45 |  |
| 7:00-9:30 | 7:00-9:30 | 7:00-9:30 | 7:00-9:30 | 7:00-9:30 |  |

**Dimensions of Testing & Study Skills**

# CHAPTER *four*

## Dimensions of Resource Management
*(Managing Resources Effectively)*

### INTRODUCTION

Life's challenges require that we take time to engage in those activities and responsibilities that are important to us. These challenges also require that we use the appropriate tools and skills to perform to our best potential. It is important that individuals relate life's work and challenges with resources available and accessible to them. Resource management calls into focus our responsibility to ourselves and to others in the cycle of moving from one stage in life to another.

*The effective management of time, finances, and energy can lead to hope and aspiration, self-confidence, goal accomplishment, and the motivation to accompliish more.*

**Resource management,** or the management of resources, calls for a self-evaluation of one's values, goals, and philosophies in relation to responsibilities to the micro-macro environments. The effective management of time, finances, and energy can lead to hope and aspiration, self-confidence, goal accomplishment, and the motivation to reach higher goals and accomplish more. The effective management of **stress** enables individuals to enjoy healthier emotional states and positive attitudes that are instrumental in keeping them focused on those activities and responsibilities that are important.

The use of **human** and **non-human resources** to accomplish goals requires 1) an identification and definition of resources, and 2) the relationship of the resources to individual roles and responsibilities at a particular stage in life.

### OBJECTIVES

The objectives of this chapter are to
1. identify basic resources necessary for college and lifelong success,
2. describe resources in relation to goal accomplishment,
3. determine how the effective management of resources contributes to successful academic achievement,
4. determine how the effective management of resources contributes to the successful accomplishment of family and career-related duties and responsibilities, and
5. understand the relationships among values, goals, standards, and philosophy.

> **KEY CONCEPTS**
>
> - Systems Approach-Family Ecosystem
> - Managing Time/Managing Tasks and Responsibilities
> - Managing Stress/Eustress and Distress
> - Managing Resources and Goal Accomplishment
> - Managing Resources and Performing Duties and Responsibilities
> - Managing Resources and Motivation for Success
> - Community Service and Time Management
> - Administrative Styles and Stress
> - Availability of Community Resources
> - Values/Goals/Accountability

## MANAGING RESOURCES

The **management** of **resources** calls for change. It is not possible to alter the past, but the future is ever before you to alter, to mold, and to build into what you desire to make of it. **Management** is a tool for creating purposeful change. Jean-Henry Fabre, a French naturalist, studied the unusual habits of the **processionary caterpillars**. In an experiment, Fabre enticed the insects to the rim of a large flowerpot where he connected the first one with the last one. The **insects** formed a **complete circle** that started moving around in a procession with neither beginning nor end. Fabre expected the caterpillars to tire of their useless march and begin a new direction. After all, they had to eat, and an ample supply of their **favorite food** (pine needles) was close at hand, plainly visible at the center of the flowerpot but outside the immediate range of the circle (Rice and Tucker, 1986).

However, through shear force of habit, the living, creeping circle kept moving around the rim of the pot...around and around, keeping the same relentless pace for seven days and seven nights....And would have continued had it not been for **sheer exhaustion** and ultimate starvation, **death**.

These **processionary caterpillars** were blindly following instinct, habit, tradition, past expression, and standard practice. They were busily moving about but were unaware of the life or death crisis they faced. **Habitual activity** was stronger than starvation to these creatures. They got no place! They made no decisions for themselves, set no goals, had no interaction with the environment beyond the immediate path of movement, and used no resources except those required for continuous activity (Rice and Tucker, 1986).

Sometimes students **carry habits** of unbeneficial resource management from high school, community college, workforce, or family to the college experience. In a sense, some students may behave as the processionary caterpillars, following other students rather than the **written policies** and **procedures** of the college or university. Often, when this happens, professors and/or the university will be blamed for any mistakes the student is bound to make using this life pattern.

Human relations are **complicated** to the degree that each of us has different values, goals, and philosophies by which we operate in our daily lives. **Goals** compete and conflict for the limited resources. Life is a complexity of change with competing goals and resources. Even within a cohesive group, goals, and expectations differ from one individual to another. **Demands** and **resources** vary also. University environments are in constant states of change. If students ignore the need to change, they may not be so different from the processionary caterpillars observed by Fabre. The processionary caterpillars had so much "order" in their lives that they died from lack of a change in directions. Each of Fabre's caterpillars was free to choose a different direction. Each college student has been somewhat freed from parents, relatives, and others to pursue his/her own destiny, to choose his/her own directions. The directions chosen can be determined by philosophies and values held, goals set, and standards used to measure accomplishments. **Purposeful change** is one of the products of effective management.

Some people look at the management of resources as order, or a form of control. Other people operate from crisis to crisis, from brush fire to brush fire. Some students wait until the night before a test or paper is due to begin studying for the test or writing the paper. In some cases, the student performs well on the test, or gets a good score on the paper; however, this is a chance the student takes. It makes much better sense to prepare well in advance to avoid going in the wrong direction. Management is the purposeful use of resources to achieve desired goals.

Three purposes of management according to Rice and Tucker (1986) are to
1) maintain constructive order,
2) eliminate chaos,
3) produce change for more satisfying results for all within a living unit, without jeopardizing the management potential of others.

## VALUES AND PHILOSOPHY

Values shape management. **Values** are defined as those things that we cherish, which we feel worthy of possessing. Values are those things and ideas that are important to us. Values, goals, and philosophies underlie any management: time, stress, or financial. The relationship of values, goals, standards, and philosophies can be shown in a **triangular formation** according to Gross, Crandall, and Knoll (1980), Deacon and Firebaugh, (1986) Rice and Tucker, (1986). In this new millennium, it becomes important to include **philosophies** in this relationship. Values, goals, standards, and

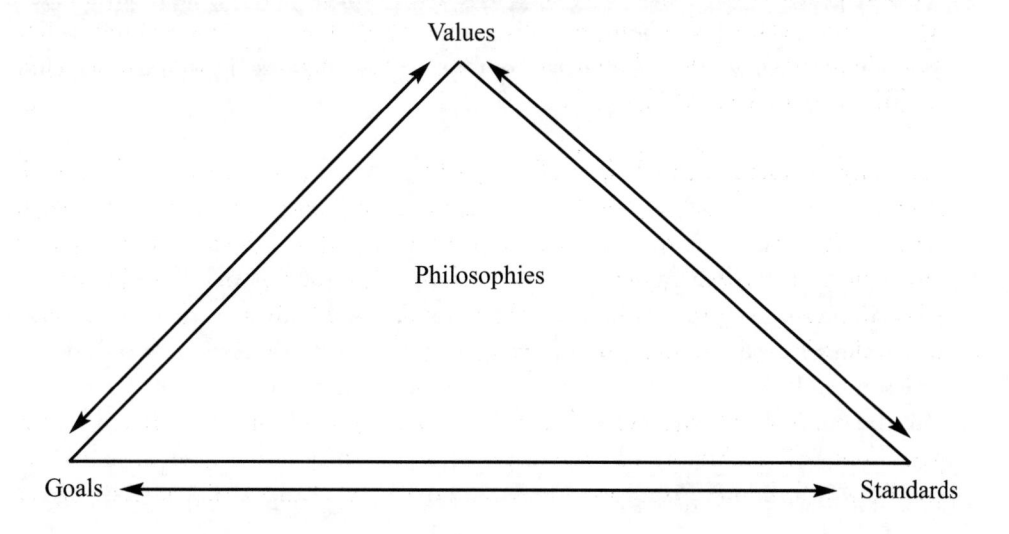

**Dimensions of Resource Management**

philosophies depicted in a triangular graph offer a more-thorough relationship of these components of management. A philosophy is your belief system.

Values function as the most important underlying force in directing managerial behavior, and thus are prime motivating forces in all resource management. Values will be changed or modified as a result of the resources available and of choices made in management. Values influence the means and ends of action and serve as a standard by which actions are evaluated. The statement that "men and women should have equal rights" is a statement of values. It establishes a desirable goal; it defines what should happen, regardless of whether it actually does happen. Values thus provide a frame of reference for choosing a course of action. If students believe that men and women should be treated equally, their actions are likely to reflect this value (Blanchard & Gothey, 2004; Frame, 2003; Peterson, 2004).

**Goals** are indicators of values. For example the goal of owning one's own home may be a concrete expression of the value of security. Goals are closely related to values, standards, and philosophies. Goals stem from values and are influenced by philosophies. **Standards** are specifications of value. Standards measure the degree of influence of a value and the limits within which one operates in working toward a goal. Goals are defined as those things one wishes to accomplish. **Goals** may be long-term or short-term. Long-term goals are set for periods three to five years from the date set, whereas short-term goals are set for periods six months to two years away from the date set (Marcorvitz, 2004; Mohn, 2004; Nwadei, 2004).

### *Characteristics of Goals*

- Goals must be stated clearly. The student must understand what he/she wants to accomplish.
- Goals must be attainable. The goal set must be something that the student's ability, resources, and potential will be able to accomplish.
- Goals must have a timeline for their accomplishment. Setting timelines will provide motivation to the student to get the job done in a timely manner. A timeline also allows a standard of measurement.
- Goals must be measurable. The student must be able to assess not only what was accomplished but also how well the job was done.

Use the goal example and write goals for yourself for a day, a week, a month. Check to see if your goals have the characteristics described for goals. Reward yourself if all of your goals follow the characteristics outlined in this chapter. If you did not include all the characteristics, review this section; then rewrite goals with the appropriate characteristics.

Goal Example: Joan will attain a 3.00 GPA for the fall semester during her first year at the university.

A **goal**, once achieved, may become a resource. Values are made concrete in goals. A goal is more easily defined and understood than a value. **Values** may be considered the source of goals and may also be looked upon as criteria against or by which goals are chosen.

Goals, values, and standards are all similar because each reflects what the individual or group considers important; also, they influence the use of scarce resources and hence may arouse conflict in their use. Marked differences, however, exist in relation to the degree to which one is conscious of them. An individual is less conscious of values than of standards and less conscious of either than of goals. A **variety of goals** may reflect the same value, and the same goal may stem from a different value or combination of values in different persons, or in the same person at different periods in his or her life.

## STANDARDS

A **standard** is a measure or model for comparison. Standards are affected by values, resources, and environment. If water in residence halls or the cafeteria is scarce or cut off for a time, one's standard of cleanliness, a value, may change. **"Situationality"** is an important attribute of a standard. This statement means that under different conditions or situations, different standards are used. There are quantitative and qualitative standards.

## RESOURCES

**Resources** are the means used to achieve goals and meet demands. The specific resources used will determine the solution. Anything that can help you reach a goal is a resource. For instance, your endurance and ability to think critically can help you succeed in college. Many resources come from within the individual or from relationships with others. These are called human resources and include ability, attitudes, time, people, and energy. Resources and processes are actions. Resources are classified as human, non-human or material, and natural.

## MANAGEMENT OF TASKS AND RESPONSIBILITY

**Time** is a resource like no other resource. Time is a human resource and is the only resource that is equal for each individual. Time has no respecter of race, gender, income level, geographical location, or occupation. Each of us has the same twenty-four hours in a day, seven days in a week, four weeks in a month, twelve months in a year, and fifty-two weeks in a year. No matter how much we desire to get yesterday back, it is gone forever, never to be returned. Time is a non-renewable resource; once it has expired, it is gone for good. So if everyone has the same amount of time, why do some people get a lot done and others so little in the same amount of time?

The phrase **time management** is actually a **misnomer**. Because we cannot alter the amount of time given, in general it is more accurate to use the phrase "managing responsibilities and tasks" rather than "managing time."

Time management, in part, determines the quality of one's life. What you do with the time you have each day can characterize the type of life you live, including the quality of your health and well being. The quality of time spent reading and doing assignments will show up in the quality of points you receive on your college transcript. The time you spend getting academic advisement can show up in your confidence in knowing that you are progressing as you should in your classes and are at the point that you should be at specified intervals. The time spent settings goals and standards will provide motivation to achieve even greater goals.

To be successful in managing tasks and responsibilities means that individuals **work smarter**, not harder. Explain this statement: "Effective time management means that individuals are aware that 'today' is all the time a person has to manage life and achieve goals." What is the relationship between one's skills and ability in respect to time?

## TIME MANAGEMENT

Again, time is a human resource that is equal for all persons, regardless of status in life. The amount of time is the same for the poor and rich, male and female, Asian or African, white or black, educated or noneducated. Time is a **quantifiable resource** because it can be measured using numbers. There are sixty seconds in a minute, sixty minutes in an hour, twenty-four hours in a day, seven days in a week, fifty-two weeks in a year, and 365 or 366 days in a year. It would appear that these units of time would allow an individual to get all the things done that need to be done. If we break the time down in smaller units, the picture is clearer. There are 1,440 minutes in a day; 10,080 minutes in week; 302,400 minutes in a month; and 3,628,800 minutes in a year. There are 168 hours in a week, 672 hours in a month and 8,064 hours in a year.

One's attitude toward time can determine how well one uses time to accomplish goals. Appropriate use of time leads to success. What is your attitude toward time and time use?

**What can you do in each of these periods of time?**

| | | |
|---|---|---|
| 1 second | 60 seconds | |
| 1 minute | 60 minutes | |
| 1 hour | 24 hours | |
| 1 day | 7 days | |
| 1 week | 30 days | |
| 1 month | 4 weeks | |
| 1 year | 12 months | 52 weeks |

Can you do more in four weeks than you can in one month? Explain your answer. Can you accomplish more in sixty minutes or one hour? Do you accomplish more in fifty-two weeks or twelve months?

Think about it. How do you spend your time? If time management determines in part the quality of one's life, why is it important to know how well you use your time? Take an inventory of the way you use (spend) your time.

What is your philosophy of time management?

What are your beliefs about time as a human resource?

## TIME ORIENTATION

The concept of time includes **orientation** to it. This comes from a person's ability to form representations of changes other than those perceived in the present–to see events and phenomena in a time relationship, reaching back to the past and progressing through and extending to the future. This ability is a very important faculty distinguishing humans from other living beings. It seems that all other animals live in a continual present. Awareness of distinctions between **past**, **present**, and **future** must have been the result of conscious reflections on the human situation.

An individual relates more fundamentally to the past, or to the present, or to the future. Each person is aware of each of the three orientations, but the set or predominant one varies in persons and especially in different cultures. Time orientations affect choices in life and thus have some relevance to resource use. If an individual is only concerned for himself or herself, using resources in the present would consume most of the time, whereas an individual concerned with the welfare of others first and then self would use resources to help others in the present and future, as well as to satisfy individual needs.

Although one cannot **save time** in a bank and use it later to accomplish a task, people do plan for the present and future and thus in doing so, envision the time it takes to perform various tasks. A student cannot put time for the first week of classes in a bank to use during the last week of classes; however, a student can plan time use for assignments due at the end of the semester to be accomplished at the beginning, middle, and end of the semester. A sense of the future enables the student to plan ahead.

Are you locked into one of the time orientations of past, present, or future? Do you think of performing as you always did in the past? Are you constantly thinking of the future and forgetting the past and present?

Take an inventory of the way you spend your time. (Draw a diagram.)

**Pareto's principle** theorizes that 80 percent of time expended usually produces only 20 percent of results, and 20 percent of time expended produces 80 percent of results (Rice and Tucker, 1986). This principle illustrates the importance of setting priorities. Priorities for long-term personal goals are usually based on importance to the individual's values, whereas work-related activities are often based on urgency or deadlines.

### Manage Tasks to Get More Out of Time
1. Set one-minute goals and accomplish them.
2. Learn to say no. Remember one person cannot do it all. Share responsibilities. Set priorities. What is important to you? What will it take for you to accomplish your goals?
3. Learn effective methods for jobs done often. Because you will spend a lot of

time studying, especially reading, learn speed-reading methods that work for you. Develop effective methods for writing papers. Learn how to use **information technology** in conducting research.

4. Make the best use of committed time. When you make an appointment to see an advisor or a professor, take along a journal article to read while you wait. Or write a letter to a friend or relative while you wait. **Balance** your checkbook. This practice may be used in any circumstance when you make an appointment for a specified period time.

5. Take an **inventory** of your use of time and work to improve your time utilization. One of the best ways to analyze time use is to determine how you currently use your time. Use the Inventory of Time Worksheet to determine how you use your time.

6. Learn the relevance of **Pareto's Principle** in managing tasks.

7. Overcome procrastination by making a **To-Do List** and following it. As you perform tasks on the list, check them off, thus providing motivation to finish other tasks on the list. Prevent putting tasks off; perform essential tasks first.

8. **Reduce** the number of **unnecessary tasks**. If it does not have to be done by you, let someone else perform the task. Some college students get caught up with doing other students' work and neglect their own in order to be popular or liked. The best rule here is, "Do your own work, and let others do theirs."

9. Learn effective ways to **organize paperwork**. Develop a filing system early on in your college years. Organize files by courses and assignments. Keep records of papers turned in, and keep a file of all returned papers. Keep all tests until you have received a grade on the transcript for the course. Blanchard and Johnson (1982) in the *One Minute Manager* discovered that managers spent a disproportionate amount of time (up to six hours a day) looking for things on their desks and in file cabinets. And one who has not learned to use computers effectively today may find himself or herself searching endlessly through a computer directory to locate a computer file of which the name is not remembered. Just think of what constructive work these managers could do in six hours (Rosen, 2004). Keep an electronic log of assignments and their evaluation scores. Scan graded papers into your electronic file.

10. Get rid of **effectiveness-killing emotions** (See diagram). The way one feels at the time he/she performs a task has a lot to do with the length of time it takes to complete the task and the quality of the work completed. Get rid of anger and jealousy before studying. If time could be measured as water in a vessel, effectiveness-killing emotions such as hate, jealousy, anger, and worrying would act as holes draining time away. Draw a diagram to illustrate this vessel.

11. **Eliminate clutter** and decrease the amount of time it takes to perform certain tasks. For example, clear your room and organize your desk, then observe how much quicker you perform tasks such as reading and writing papers.

12. Divide large tasks into smaller tasks for easier accomplishment.

13. Use **appropriate tools** to perform tasks. You would not use a sledge hammer to cut down a tree. In the language of the Information Age, you would not use an old-fashioned typewriter to type a 20-page paper that you'll have to revise several times; you'd use a computer with word-processing software.

14. Overcome the tendency to apply **Parkinson's Law**. Parkinson's Law states that a job expands to fill the time available to accomplish the task. This law illustrates the elasticity of some resources, even those as rigid as time. When time seems limited and people are busy, they tend to squeeze many activities into a

short timespan and seem to accomplish more than when they are under less pressure. The answer is to make less time available for given tasks, and they will be done more quickly.

15. Do difficult or complex tasks during your prime (best) time.

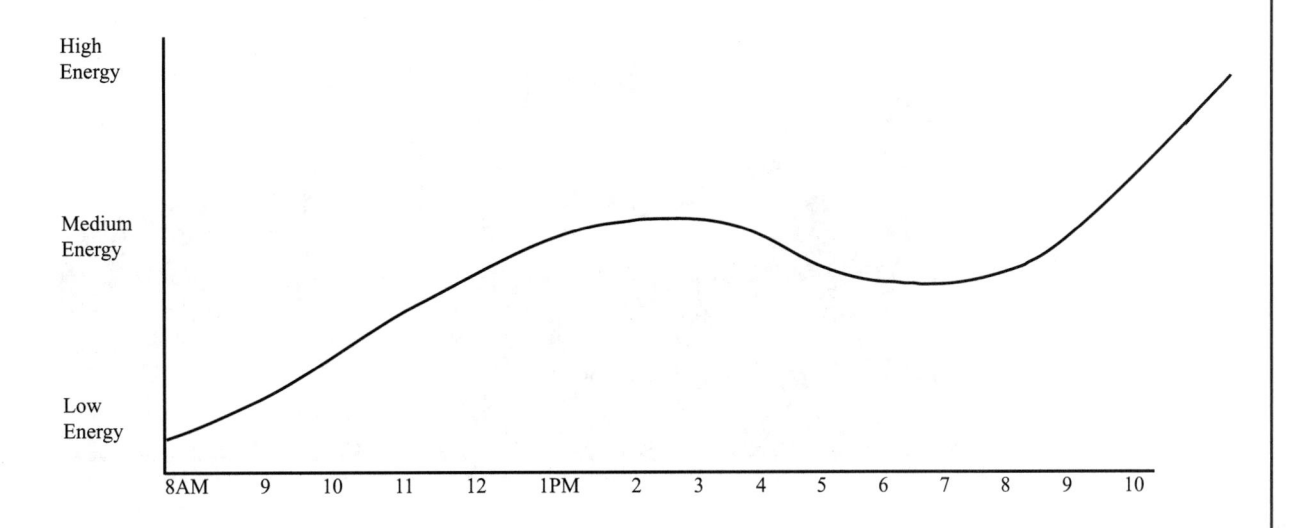

The graph above illustrates that this individual is not a morning person, because energy levels are very low in the morning, peak around noon, drop from 2-6, and pick up sharply between 7 p.m. and 11 p.m. Performing strenuous or complex tasks at times other than one's most productive times may be a source of stress.

## STRESS

Knowledge of stress draws from the field of physics, where it is referred to as pressure, strain, or force exerted on a mechanical system or structure. During the late 1920s, the concept of stress became increasingly applied in allied health fields to denote a measurable physiological condition that produces specific bodily responses in people.

Selye (1975), a physician and early pioneer in stress research, established that while almost any incident can create a stress response in someone, symptoms of stress are always the same. Blood pressure rises; heart beat speeds up; adrenaline and other hormones are produced; breathing rate increases; and blood and blood sugar are pumped faster into the body's extremities.

Stress can then be seen as an imbalance in the transaction between an individual and the environment, which can be tested by specific biological reactions. Energy is created, which the body can use to meet unexpected or threatening conditions.

Stress is the body's reaction to change, the rate of wear and tear on the body caused by living. Stress is understood from the subjective sensations it produces, such as being tired, feeling jittery, or experiencing illness. Stress has both physical and emotional causes (Atkinson, 2004; Casto, 2004; Civil, 2003).

Researchers, Selye, Angel, Koos, and Hill (1985), offer two classifications of stress: distress and eustress. **Distress** is harmful stress, and **eustress** is beneficial stress.

**Dimensions of Resource Management**

*Stress varies in intensity from hassles, which are bothersome but not disruptive, to crises, which may be incapacitating. The level of stress an individual experiences is related to how solvable he or she perceives the problem to be.*

However, too much stress of any kind can be harmful, particularly when it lingers.

The many changes experienced by students leaving home and going to college for the first time impact the biological organisms and thus can lead to stressful situations. Life circumstances–good or bad–have an impact on one's body. How the body reacts and responds to these circumstances will determine whether one suffers from distress or eustress.

Stress has been linked to a number of illnesses and diseases–from asthma, hypertension, and heart disease to ulcers and diabetes, to name some of the most common. Distress can disorganize routines and disrupt progression toward and accomplishment of goals (Civil, 2004).

## *Stress Management*

Not all stress is harmful. Stress provides a **stimulus** that can be positive as well as negative and can motivate people to accomplish tasks they might not otherwise undertake. Stress is a crucial, productive part of life. Good as well as bad stress occurs with such common occurrences as taking a test, getting a new teacher, losing a relative, not having enough money, getting married, and having children. Eliminating these occurrences or events would mean eliminating many of the common experiences of life (Casto, 2004).

Rice and Tucker (1986) reported that the ancient Chinese used two characters as a symbol for stress: **danger** and **opportunity**. Whenever persons are forced to function at a greater or lesser level than is usual or desired, the body experiences stress, but stress can also motivate some people toward actions far above their normal level of accomplishment.

## Stressors

1. **Stressors** are events, conditions, and demands that bring about a change in a student's life. Some students get married while in college; other students experience the death of parents, siblings, or other relatives during their college years. Some students even give birth and get divorced while in college. According to Selye (1975), these events carry very high numbers in the categories of stress, 50-100.
2. Stress affects the body **physically**, **emotionally**, and **psychologically**. Although the physical response is the same for everyone, emotional and psychological responses may vary. Good physical and emotional health is necessary for students to sustain a sense of **balance** through the challenges of college life and beyond.
3. Stress is not inherent in a **stressor** but is a person's response **to** the stressor. Therefore, the amount of change required by the stress factor determines whether it will produce stress in a person or family.
4. Some stress in life is beneficial and is called **eustress**. It is not the pressures of life but, rather, how people relate and react to stressors that make the difference in their feelings of well-being.
5. Stress varies in intensity from hassles, which are bothersome but not disruptive, to crises, which may be incapacitating and cannot be managed with the normal resources and routines of a system.
6. The **level** of stress experienced is related to the perception held toward the event, particularly its perceived solvability versus its perceived insolvability.
7. The degree of stress felt may be due to one's vulnerability to stress. The amount of time during which stressful events are anticipated, the frequency of potentially stressful events encountered, and the person's previous experience with stress management can all influence a student's vulnerability to stress (Atkinson, 2004; Civil, 2004).
8. The **degree** of stress encountered is related to the abnormality of the hardships it imposes. Hardships are either an inherent part of the stressors or advance conditions imposed by the stressors. For example, hardship of a parent or spousal death may mean disruption of a student's routine and a necessary change of roles to manage the rest of the student's workload.
9. It is important to manage stress because it can be both painful and dangerous—physically and mentally. **Chronic stress** can inflict real body harm.
10. Stress buildup is an accumulation, without resolution, of the individual stress responses. It is important to both prevent distress and also to manage distress once it has occurred (Allen, 003; Clark, 2003; Civil, 2004).

## FAMILY COPING TASKS FOR STRESS MANAGEMENT

Students and families can work on ways to manage stress so that satisfactory resolutions to stressors are found. The following steps will assist you:
1. Assessing the potential danger from the stressor.
    a. Identifying the source of stress.
    b. Assessing the hardships stress will likely cause.
    c. Estimating the potential changes it will make in family life.
    d. Discovering personal and family coping resources.
2. Coping with the hardships of the stressor.
    a. Setting new goals.
    b. Planning the coping process.

  c. Exploring and securing additional coping resources.
  d. Reorganizing routines to maximize resource effectiveness.
  e. Redefining role expectations and negotiating task responsibilities.
  f. Adjusting the level and standard of living.
 3. Regenerating the system.
  a. Reorganizing the system's roles, rules, responsibilities.
  b. Renewing family integration.
 4. Defining a new life plan.
  a. Balancing new courses of action.
  b. Becoming more individually self-assured.

## *Stressful Events for College Students*

- New class
- Lack of finances for college
- New faculty
- Roommate adjustment
- Tests
- New interpersonal relationship
- Field trips
- Jail term
- Academic probation
- Resources
- Part-time job
- Graduation
- Vacation
- Pregnancy
- Loss of job
- Lost or stolen wallet/purse
- Breakup of interpersonal relationship
- Death of family member
- Holidays

## *Ways to Avoid Distress*

- Set **realistic goals** for college, career, and beyond.
- Plan and organize tasks in order to utilize time wisely.
- Eat healthy foods and exercise regularly.
- Get appropriate amount of rest for your lifestyle.
- Learn to say no more often.
- Get rid of clutter.
- Go to class on time.
- Work on assignments early and proofread your work.
- Accept or decline invitations to a meal or social function.

## *Ways to Reduce Stress*

- Recognize the difference between distress and eustress.
- Recognize stressors that tend to put you in distress and avoid those.
- Simplify work by breaking large tasks into smaller tasks, eliminating steps, and rearranging work areas or study areas for more-effective studying or work.

- Be patient; learn to wait.
- Find humor in things and events.

*Ways to Relieve Stress*
- Reward yourself for accomplishments.
- Schedule some fun activities.
- Study in a group sometimes.

## MANAGING ECONOMIC RESOURCES

### Human and Non-Human Resources

**Economic resources** include money, credit, employee benefits, and wealth. The nature of economic resources determines to a degree the manner in which economic resources are managed. **Human resources**, such as skills and abilities, become more developed with use; however, non-human economic resources, when used or consumed, are risked in anticipation of gain. When money is spent on materials, supplies, or equipment, that money is no longer available for investing or saving, but other resources have been purchased in exchange for the money spent. Therefore, students must consider carefully how to use their money in order to get the most from the money. When **credit** is used, it expands current buying power but curtails future spending and increases risk. Tangible possessions, such as books, jewelry, clothes, cars, furniture, CDs and computers, can satisfy goals by providing for the needs, wants, and pleasures of living and can also start you on the path to establishing wealth. However, acquired in excess, these possessions can produce the opposite effect.

**Economics resources** are defined as the composite of financial assets and tangible possessions creating an individual's environment. Because money and credit are among the two most important economic resources during a student's college years and in work and family life, the focus in this unit will be on the management of money and credit as strategic for financial management. The information in this unit is designed to assist students in assessing potential lifelong income patterns related to career and work choices, to determine ways to align spending with **financial goals**, and to create satisfaction from the utilization of money and credit. An important point to remember about the management of money and credit is that you must apply the principles and strategies on a regular basis and over time in order to reap the benefits.

Some college students will for the first time be in total control of large sums of money from student loans, grants, or scholarships available to them. Other students will have managed their finances over the years, some successfully and others not successfully. Some students have had bank accounts in high school, whereas some will never have written a check or deposited money into a bank. Because of the diversity of students' financial experiences, this unit will provide very basic information, which can be used by all students to increase their **financial management skills**.

# FINANCIAL MANAGEMENT

**Definition:** Financial management is the purposeful use of economic resources to achieve goals that enable individuals and families to satisfy needs and wants across the life span, both short-term and long-term. It includes planning, evaluating, coordinating, facilitating, and implementing resources to achieve desired results.

As with any type of management, **goal setting** becomes very important in the initial phases of financial management. Financial goals are needed to enable students to maintain or improve their standard of living, cope with an emergency, lessen and prevent distress, save for unanticipated future expenses, and secure all the materials, supplies, and tools needed to perform well academically, emotionally, socially, and physically. Financial goals will vary with the students' understanding of philosophies of education. Financial goals will vary with the students' age and life circumstances. Financial goals will vary with the state of the nation and world economy. Financial goals will vary according to the students' attitudes, values, and standards.

Economic values determine the way you view money and wealth. Some common economic values students may hold include the following:
1. Money provides status and is an outward symbol of concern about prestige or appearance.
2. Money provides security and is needed to provide a sense of well being.
3. Credit is easy money and can be used to get all I want right now.
4. Money is to be used to better myself or my family.
5. Money is to be used wisely to avoid great indebtedness and a sense of embarrassment.
6. The government has plenty of money, so I don't have to repay my student loans.

Which of these economic values do you hold? Which of these values, if acted out in terms of an objective or a strategy, would cause damage or harm to an individual?

**Money borrowed** must be repaid, whether it is borrowed from a bank, another student, another person, a credit union, a church, or a family member. Studies consistently show that many disputes occur in families and between roommates over the fact that borrowed money was not paid back (Rice & Tucker, 1986; O'Neil & Brennan, 1997; Cummings, 2003).

Excessive use of credit can lead to tremendous indebtedness for college students. **Credit cards** may be sent to students via mail, even without a request for them. One common-sense rule about accepting credit cards is simply this: **no job, no credit card**. If you did not request it, do not accept it. Additional information on credit will be covered later in this unit.

## NETWORTH, ASSETS, AND LIABILITIES

Financial worth must be measured in order to accomplish good financial planning. You are probably worth more financially than you realize.

**Assets:** Those things that you own that have material worth or a dollar value.

**Liabilities:** Those things that have a dollar value which you owe to someone else or to some institution. Liability is another word for debt.

**Net worth:** Your assets minus your liabilities.

**Thus the formula: Net Worth = Assets - Liabilities**

If you are married, a separate net worth statement should be prepared for the family and for yourself. Since the net worth statement also serves as a financial inventory for future planning, the name of the owner of the asset/liability is important. Whose name is on the documents?

To determine the value of assets/liabilities, use current value, not what you would like something to be worth.

**Evaluating the worth of items:**
- Check with the product's dealer; see local papers for items similar to yours; and contact local retailers and antique dealers, etc.
- Jewelry: Check with a local jeweler.
- Cost of college education: See **Chronicle of Higher Education** or get information from specific colleges and universities.
- Other items: Use your best guesstimate, or use appraiser for items of real value.

Why is it advantageous for students to be concerned about their net worth?
- It can help you identify problem areas.
- It is essential for any financial planning—retirement, etc.
- It is the only way of estimating what will be available to pass on to your heirs or to give away.
- It is interesting to know.

Your **net worth** changes daily; it is a statement for one day in your life. This evaluation needs to be done on a regular basis, especially in times of rapidly changing economic conditions or when there has been a major change in your life that has had financial implications. Determine your net worth at least once a year. Prepare your net worth statement(s) using the worksheets provided.

Net Worth Assets (those things you own) - liabilities (those things you owe: debt). When assets are more than liabilities, what should be done?

Net Worth = Assets of $10,000 and liabilities of $10,000. What is the net worth?

Net Worth = Assets of $10,000 and liabilities of $5,000. What is the net worth?

## FINANCIAL GOALS

Financial goals will provide the student with
1. a plan to work toward.
2. a realistic look at his/her financial situation and a better use of income.
3. a motivation for sound financial management.
4. a sense of financial security and stability and a good feeling about him- or herself.

Goals fall into three categories. For the purpose of this text, the categories are defined thusly:
- Short-range: within a year
- Mid-range: two- to five-year timeline
- Long-range: beyond five years

Using characteristics of goals cited earlier in this chapter, write a **financial goal** for each of the categories listed above.

Priorities may need to be established. Short-term goals may become mid-term if resources are not available. Students as well as non-students have more needs and desires than resources; it is necessary to prioritize. One way of approaching financial goal-setting is to list all the items that are going to cost you money, and then check off those you "must have." The leftovers are those that you "would like to have." Immediate needs or desires may hinder long-term goals. If long-term or mid-term goals are important to you, find a way to eliminate something else much later.

Financial goals may be formed as you read through this unit. One major goal of this unit is for you to become financially knowledgeable and in control of your economic resources and economic power by the end of the sophomore year or the next two years (Hedges, 2002; Cummings, 2003; Wise, 2003; Peterson, 2004).

## THE BUDGET AND BUDGETING PROCESS

A **budget** is a plan for the allocation of available resources among various needs and wants. It includes income and planned expenditures.

It is very important for students to develop the habit of setting a budget and following it in order to manage finances wisely. Individual budget-setting will involve only the individual concerned. However, when budgets are made for groups, such as a student government association, a fraternity, a sorority, a class, a club, or a professional organization, the budget must be made by members of the group, with all the members participating in some phase of the budgeting process. The budget will then reflect what the group has determined as its standard criteria—the varied goods and services that reflect the values and philosophy of the group. Thus, the budget becomes a useable plan that defines the parameters for the group's use of economic resources.

**Budgets** list the items that are needed or wanted over a given period of time and an estimation of the cost of items needed, as well as the income or economic resources available to obtain the items or services needed. Practical budgets are based on identification of weaknesses in past spending and adjustments necessary to achieve desired goals. After a budget is planned, it needs to be implemented.

Many standard budgets have been developed by agencies. These are useful for making comparisons, but individual and group expenditures should not be expected to follow these plans too closely because of differences in values, goals, and other factors that direct individuals' lives.

## *Budgeting*

A budget is a **spending plan**. A budget must be workable and tailored for you or your group if it is to effectuate sound financial management.

**Steps in Budgeting**
1. Set your financial goals.
2. Determine your **income**.
3. Determine your fixed expenses (i.e., the same or similar amounts paid monthly or regularly).
4. Determine flexible expenses (i.e., those that occur at different times and in different amounts).
5. Make necessary adjustments.
6. Revise on a regular basis, as needed.

**Clues for Determining Expenditures**
1. Keep track of your daily expenditures for at least a month to get an idea of typical expenditures.
2. Look at last year's records for regular items, such as rent, insurance, medical bills, taxes, tuition, room, board, and transportation to determine how much was spent on each of these items.
3. Examine checkbook records, ATM records, and financial statements as a source of information on spending habits. Financial statements can be viewed online.
4. Keep receipts of labeled purchases in one place and refer to them in checking expenditures. Keep an electronic log of expenditures. Check out this website. www.microsheet.com.

**Writing Goals**
Using characteristics of goals in this chapter, write a financial goal for each category below.
- Short-range: within a year
- Mid-range: two- to five-year timeline
- Long-range: beyond five years

## *Budgeting Tips*

Many budgets are too restrictive, too tight, and **too unrealistic**. Make yours simple but effective. A budget is a management tool. It should assist you, not restrict you, in financial management and planning.

**Savings** should be a fixed expense. One of the major ways to accomplish your financial goals is through savings. Budget savings and pay into your savings account each month.

**Emergency Fund:** You should set aside an emergency fund equivalent to two months' income. This fund should be the first claim on your savings plan until the reserve is in place. Remember the big items that come due once or twice a year; i.e., insurance premiums, tuition, room, board–that must be included in your budget. Set aside money for these on a monthly basis.

**Estimating Income:** When estimating income, be **conservative**. If in doubt, put down the minimum. When estimating expenses, on the other hand, anticipate the maximum, but be realistic. If you are married, budgeting must be a family project. Remember to allow money for personal allowances for you and all members of your family.

**Two-Paycheck Families:** Who pays for what? Are all income funds pooled? Are there separate bank accounts? Even the experts don't agree on the answers. There are advantages and disadvantages to answers to each of these questions, which depend to a large degree on income, lifestyle, personality, etc. Both partners must make such decisions.

**Suggested Expenditures by Categories**

| Categories | Family | Student* |
|---|---|---|
| Savings | 5-10% | 3-5% |
| Housing | 25-30% | 15-25% |
| Food | 14-20% | 10-20% |
| Transportation | 11-16% | 3-5% |
| Clothing | 4-6% | 8-10% |
| Recreation | 4-6% | 2-4% |
| Education | 5-10% | 15-30% |
| Other | 10% | 1% |

*These percentages are based on expenditures for a college student who lives in a residence hall with no car.

These are suggestions that various **"experts"** have made. Use them only as checkpoints, not as absolutes. The "other" category may include items such as childcare, personal insurance, etc.

How would you change the percentages in each category to fit the budget you currently follow?

**Balancing Your Checkbook**

Your financial institution will send you a monthly, bimonthly, or quarterly summary of your checking account. This summary is called an **account statement**. This statement lists checks, deposits, charges, and interest earnings on the account.

When you receive an account statement, check it against your **check stubs** or register. The institution's record and your record should agree. This is known as **balancing** your checkbook (see Figure 2.1). All banks now have electronic account statements that you can access using a computer.

In most cases, the financial institution will enclose copies of canceled checks with the account statement. Some of your checks may not be returned because they had not been cashed when the statement was made. These are called outstanding checks.

Compare the **canceled checks** with those listed on the statement. Then compare them with your record of checks written. In your check register or on the check stubs, mark off the checks that have been returned to you (see Figure 2.2). Also mark off any **deposits** that are shown on the statement. If the financial institution has made any service charges, subtract them from the balance in your checkbook. Likewise, if you have **earned interest** on your account, add that amount to your checkbook balance.

Begin by double-checking your own addition and subtraction in your check stubs or register. Be sure you have not made an error before you question the financial institution about its statement.

Some financial institutions do not return canceled checks. However, the statements they issue will list each check by amount and check number. In this way, you will be able to tell which checks are still outstanding.

Balancing your checkbook **promptly** is always wise. Financial institutions can make errors. You should not depend completely on them to keep your account in order. The sooner you notice an error, the sooner it can be corrected.

*Balance your checkbook promptly to catch any errors made by your financial institution and avoid overdrafts and penalties.*

There is another good reason for balancing your checkbook promptly. People who neglect this task are more likely to write **overdrafts**. These are checks written when there is not enough money in the account to cover them. They are also known as checks that **bounce**.

Most financial institutions fine account holders for **writing overdrafts**. Many businesses also fine customers who write overdrafts in payment for goods or services. The total fines for an overdraft can easily exceed $40. Thus writing an overdraft can be costly, as well as embarrassing.

At this point, a little math will help you if your checkbook is not balanced. Most statements have a worksheet printed on the back to help you with the math. Complete the following steps in the space provided on the worksheet:
1. Write the closing balance shown on the bank statement.
2. List the deposits you have made that have not shown on the statement.
3. Add the amounts from Steps 1 and 2 and write down the total.
4. List by number and amount all outstanding checks. Add the amounts to find the total amount of money representing outstanding checks. Write down the amount.
5. Subtract the amount in Step 4 from the amount in Step 3. The difference will match the balance shown in your checkbook.

What should you do if your balance and the financial institution's balance do not match?

Dimensions of Resource Management

### When Income Is Too Low to Meet Expenses

Making the necessary **adjustments** when income is too low to meet expenses is a difficult task. Choosing between books and food is a difficult decision, but for some students, this choice must be made. Do not let **pride** get in the way of survival. If help is needed, see the Office of Student Affairs, Financial Affairs, your major department, or social service agencies in your community. Your local religious group or student organizations may be helpful, as well.

**Worksheets & Assignments**
Prepare your budget using the activity sheets for income, fixed expenses, and flexible expenses.

## CREDIT

Virtually everybody uses **credit** everyday. We live in an era of what seems to be abundant credit, which in turn allows people to spend more than ever before. Credit becomes a vicious cycle for many people. College students are often targeted by banks, savings-and-loan institutions, gas companies, and department stores. If caution is not exercised, one can easily get into financial trouble. Credit is expanding current purchasing power through deferred payments. Credit may also be referred to as **"renting money"** (Sohl, 1985, p. 37).

Using credit demands careful budgeting and planning. How much credit is safe? What should be the ratio of credit charges to salary? Experts say to use no more than **20%** of your take-home pay on credit. Students may find it helpful to observe some simple rules in using credit.

1. Use credit in emergencies.
2. Use credit when prices are rising on an item. If you wait until all the money is saved, it will cost you a good deal more.
3. Use credit for something you really need but cannot purchase with cash; then budget the payments.
4. Use credit when carrying checks or cash would not be advantageous.

Students may obtain credit from banks and **credit unions**, as well as through credit cards from gas companies and department stores. It has been stated that students who do not have jobs do not need credit cards. However, it is important for students–especially female students–to establish a **credit rating** in their own name. In most cases, you will not receive credit unless you have established a credit rating. For females, this is especially important, because even though women may marry or already be married, 85 percent of married females will at some time be widowed or divorced and will need their own credit. Establish a credit rating before the emergency or crisis develops.

*Using credit demands careful budgeting and planning. Experts say to use no more than 20% of your take-home pay on credit purchases.*

Get a part-time job and establish a savings account and checking account in your own name. Wait several months and then apply for a credit card through the bank. Or take out a small loan, using your savings account for collateral. Pay the loan back on the agreed-upon basis. You have thus established a credit rating and proved yourself **credit-worthy**. For most credit applications, you will need the net worth statement and income statement you worked through earlier in this chapter. Keep these statements up to date.

Female students who are married with credit cards in their husband's name may want to request a separate account in their own name for reporting to the credit bureau. Forms must be filled out with the exact name you want to use. Do not use Mrs. John Harris since that will not help the situation. You want to establish credit under your name. Students with no income of their own will have to get a **co-signer** in order to get their application processed.

**Tips on the Use of Credit Cards**
**Use one credit card** for items that you intend to pay over time. If you can get a small loan from a bank, do so, because the **interest rates** are less expensive. Use all other credit cards for items that you intend to pay off each month. Don't mix the two. If you pay your total balance each month, some credit card companies will not charge interest. Some banks, however, are beginning to charge interest from the date of purchase to the date of payment. The key to any credit is the interest rate charged. Interest rates and terms vary, so shop around to get the best buy. Read all the **fine print** on the application before you sign it. Ask questions if you do not understand the form. There is also an annual fee on some credit cards, ranging from $65 to $300.

For most people, the best deal is a card with a low interest rate and a 25-30 day grace period. To do comparison shopping, check with Bankcard Holders of America's Publications, including Women's Credit Right, How to Shop for a Bank Card, and Solving Your Credit Card Billing Questions at **Bankcard Holders of America**, 333 Pennsylvania Avenue, S.E., Washington, D.C. 20003; phone 800-638-6407 (out of the D.C. area) and 202-543-5805 (in the D.C. area).

No matter how much your income may be, it is unwise to overload yourself with too many credit cards. It can be hazardous to your **credit history**. Credit card debts count as debt on your credit file whether you use them to the maximum limit or not at all.

If you find that your credit is out of control, try talking to creditors and arranging a favorable repayment schedule. **Ignoring bills** will not make them go away. You must pay the debts owed to your creditors. Search for impartial counseling from someone or an organization that does not attempt to take advantage of your situation. You may want to contact the Consumer Credit Counseling Service, The National Foundation for Consumer Credit, 8701 George Avenue, Suite 507, Silver Springs, MD 20910. This is a nonprofit counseling service that offers counseling on areas such as budgeting, design of a debt repayment plan, and management of credit. You might find their local listings and locations in the white pages of your telephone directory. This credit website may also be helpful to you: www.consumer credit.com.

# GLOSSARY

**Assets:** what we own.

**Automated Teller Machine (ATM) Card:** a magnetic card used to access bank machines and to use in exchange for goods and services in place of money or credit cards.

**ATM Machine:** equipment that allows one access to checking and savings accounts and cash.

**Budget:** a spending plan consisting of income and expenses.

**Checks:** paper notes that instruct your financial institution to pay a certain sum of money to a person or company.

**Credit:** renting money. Credit is expanding current purchasing power through deferred payments.

**Credit Card:** a magnetic card used to purchase goods and services instead of cash or check.

**Credit Union:** a non-profit financial establishment owned and operated by members that functions as a bank with lower finance charges.

**Debt:** what you owe.

**Distress:** bad stress.

**Ecosystem:** organisms in relation to their environments.

**Expenses:** costs incurred from purchasing good or services.

**Goals:** what we want to accomplish.

**Human Resources:** resources over which an individual has control of use, such as time, human energy, and ability. Human resources come from within people.

**Income:** money earned from jobs or careers.

**Liabilities:** what you owe (debts).

**Macro-environment:** the community, school, church, fire station, and police departments that surround the family.

**Management:** the purposeful use of resources to accomplish goals. Management is working with and through individuals and groups to accomplish goals.

**Micro-environment:** the immediate surroundings of the family or organizational unit.

**Money:** a standard piece of gold, silver, copper, nickel, or paper used as a medium of exchange and a measure of value.

**Networth:** assets minus liabilities.

**Non-Human Resources:** resources that are not physically or mentally a part of a person. They include money, possessions, water, air, and clothes.

**Pareto's Principle:** theorizes that 80 percent of time expended usually produces only 20 percent of results, and 20 percent of time expended produces 80 percent of results.

**Parkinson's Law:** a job expands to fill the time available to accomplish the task.

**Phobia:** excessive, persistent fear.

**Philosophy:** one's belief about life, education, etc.

**Resources:** the human and non-human means to achieve goals.

**Savings:** money put aside or accumulated for future use.

**Standard:** a basis for comparison.

**Stress:** the body's reaction to change; the rate of the wear and tear on the body caused by life.

**Stressors:** conditions, events, and demands that bring about a change in an individual's life.

**Time Orientation:** refers to past, present, and future.
**Values:** what we believe worthy of possessing.

# REFERENCES

Adair, J. E., & Allen, M. (2003). *The concise time management and personal development* Thorogood.

Allen, D. (2003). Getting things done: *The art of stress-free productivity.* Penguin Putnam.

Atkinson, W. (2004). *Eliminate stress from your life forever: A simple program for better living.* AMACOM.

Bing, S. (2003). *The big bing: Black holes of time management, gaseous executive bodies, exploding careers, and other theories on the origins of the business universe.* New York: Harper Business.

Blanchard, K., & Gothey, S. (2004). *The on-time, On-target manager: How the last minute manager conquered procrastination.* William Morrow.

Blanchard, K., & Johnson, S. (1982). *The one-minute manager.* William Morrow.

Brown, T. (2004). *What mama taught me: The seven core values of life.* Quill.

Casto, M. L. (2004). *Get Smart! About modern stress management: Your personal guide to living a balanced life.* 1st Books Library.

Civil, J. (2004). *Stress Management.* Spiro Press.

Clark, J. (2003). *Stress: A management guide.* Spiro Press.

Cummings, S. (2003). *Simplified personal financial planning: A revolutionary approach to money management.* 1st Books Library.

Davis, S. J., Botkin, P. (1994). *The monster under the bed.* New York: Simon and Schuster.

Ellis, D. (1994). *Becoming a master student.* Boston: Houghton Mifflin.

English, M. (2004). *Real-time strategic management and simulations.* Inter-America Consulting.

Firebaugh, F. M., & Deacon, R. E. (1986). *Family resource management: Principles and applications.* Boston: Houghton Mifflin.

Fox, C. D. (1997) "Incorporating the parental problem-solving approach in the classroom," *Journal of Family and Consumer Sciences,* 89 (2).

Frame, J. (2003). *Managing projects in organizational ways to make the best use of time, techniques, and peoples.* New York: Jossey Bass.

Furrow, D. (2004). *Moral sounding: readings on the crisis of values in contemporary life.* Rowman and Littlefield.

Glueck, W. (1997). *Management.* Hinsdale, Illinois: Holt, Rinehart, Winston.

Gross I., Crandall, R., & Knoll, M. (1980). *Management for modern families.* New York: MacMillan.

Hedges, E. (2002). *Avoiding financial pitfalls: A practical guide to money management.* 1st Books Library.

Hersey, P., & Blanchard, K. (1982). *Management of organizational behavior: Utilizing human resources.* Englewood Clifts, New Jersey: Prentice-Hall, Inc.

Jackson, I. A. (2004). *Profits with principles: Seven strategies for delivering value with value.* Currency.

Knaub, P. K., Weber, M. J., Russ, R. (1994). "Ethical dilemma encountered in human environmental sciences: Implications for Ethics Education," *Journal of Family and Consumer Sciences,* 86 (3).

Marcovitz, H., & Synder, G. (2004). *Teens, religion, and values.* Mason Crest

Publishers.

Mohn, R. (2004). *An age of new possibilities: How humane values and an entrepreneurial spirit will lead us into the future.* Crown Publishers.

Nwadei, A. C. (2004). *The relationship between perceived values congruence and organizational commitment in multinational organizations.* Transaction Publishers.

O'Neil, B., & Brennan, P. O. (1997). "Financial Planning Education throughout the life cycle," *Journal of Family and Consumer Sciences,* 89 (2) 32-36.

Peterson, G. B. (2004). *The Tanner Lectures on human values, Vol. 24.* Utah: University of Utah Press.

Peterson, P., Fasbozzi, F. J., & Haebegger, W. D. (2004) Financial management and *analysis workbook: Step by step exercises and tests to help you master financial management and analysis.* New York; John Wiley & Sons.

Rice, A. S., Tucker, S. M. (1986). *Family life management.* New York MacMillan.

Rice, A. S., Tucker, S. M., & Siegel, J. G. (1991). *Family life management.* New York: MacMillian.

Rosen, A. (2004). *Effective IT project management: Using teams to get projects completed on time and under budget.* AMA COM.

Ross, J. (2004). *The original student calendar: Time management guide: August 16, 2004 - August 28, 2005.* Orca Book Publishers.

Selye, H. (1975). *Stress in health and disease.* Wobum, MA: Butterworth.

Shim, O. K., & Siegel, O.,G. (1991). *Theory and problems of personal finance.* New York: McGraw-Hill, Inc.

Smith, S. G. (2004). *Worth doing.* New York: State University of New York Press.

Sohl, J. (1985). *Managing our money.* Cincinnati: Services Center.

Swartz, T. (2002). *Easy ways to save and manage money: A money management system.* Leathers publishing.

Slack, R. A. (2003). *Beliefs and values: A Logical basis for personal ethics.* 1st Books Library.

Wise, J. (2003). *Five steps to financial management: Money management made easy.* Hensley publishing.

Worth, R. (2004). *Organization Skills.* Ferguson Publishing.

## WEBSITES:

www.consumercredit.com
www.microsheet.com
www.mvelopes.com

# ACTIVITY 1

## BUDGET FINANCIAL GOAL

*Write Your Financial Goal*

**Income**
Amount

Job/Salary _____

Gifts _____

Donations _____

Total _____

**Expenses**

Food _____

Housing (Residence Hall Rate) _____

Savings _____

Transportation _____

Clothing _____

Recreation _____

Education _____

Other _____

**Total** _____

1. Does the income exceed the expenses?
2. What is the dollar difference between income and expenses?
3. Do budget items appropriately reflect your financial goals?

Dimensions of Resource Management

# ACTIVITY 2

## BUDGET FINANCIAL GOAL

***Write Your Financial Goal:***

Income _____

Job/Salary _____

Gifts _____

Donations _____

    Expenses

    Fixed _____

    _____

    _____

    _____

    Flexible _____

    _____

    _____

    _____

Use information in Activity 1 to determine flexible and fixed income.

# ACTIVITY 3

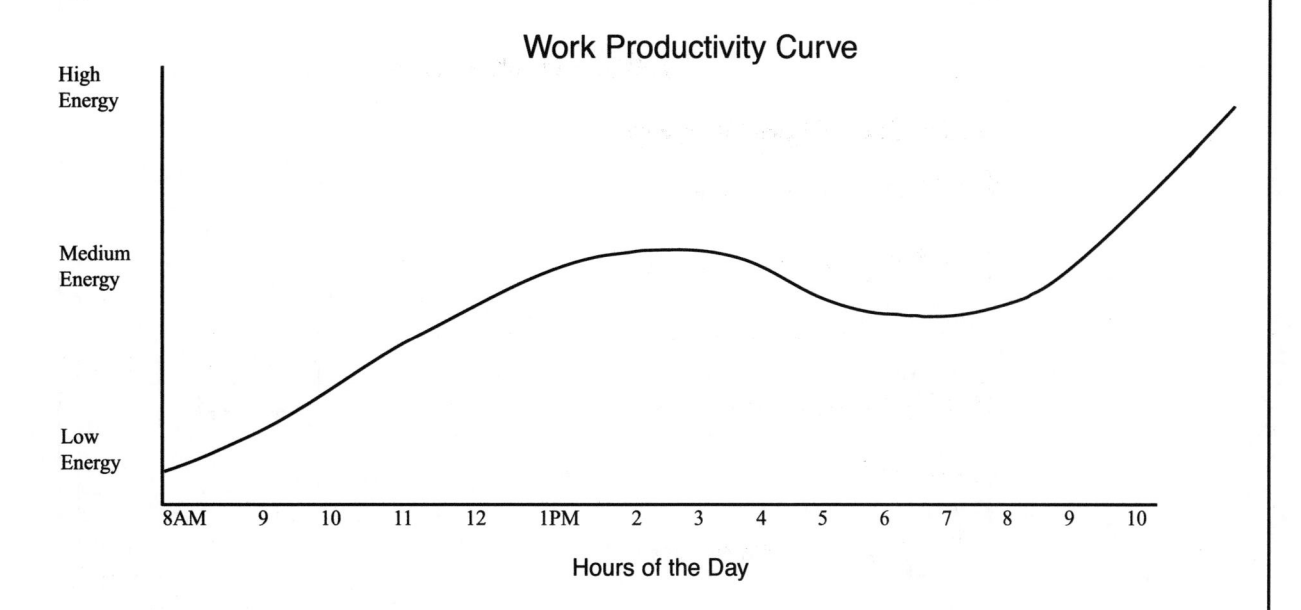

**Work Productivity Curve**

[Graph showing energy level (Low, Medium, High) on the y-axis versus Hours of the Day (8AM through 10PM) on the x-axis. The curve starts at low energy at 8AM, rises to medium energy around 2-3PM, dips slightly around 6-7PM, then rises sharply to high energy by 10PM.]

At what time of day is this person most productive? Explain your answer.

At what time of day is this person the least productive?

**Dimensions of Resource Management**

**Figure 2.1**

## Balancing Worksheet

Month   March 1-31, 2000

BANK BALANCE
shown on this statement        $ __174.11__

ADD +                          $ __420.48__

DEPOSITS made but
not shown on statement
because made or received
after date of this
statement                      _____

TOTAL                          $ __594.59__

SUBTRACT -

CHECKS
OUTSTANDING...                 $ __77.63__

BALANCE...                     $  516.96

The above balance should be the same as the up-to-date balance in your checkbook.

Checks Outstanding
(Written but not shown on statement because not yet received by Bank.)

| CHECK NO. | | |
|---|---|---|
| 778 | $ 30 | 00 |
| 779 | 27 | 63 |
| 780 | 20 | 00 |
| | | |
| | | |
| | | |
| | | |
| | | |
| | | |
| | | |
| | | |
| | | |
| | | |
| TOTAL | 77 | 63 |

**Figure 2.2**

March to April 2000
Record All Charges Or Credits That Affect Your Account

| Check Number | Date | Description of Transaction | Payment/Debit (-) | T | Fee (-) | Deposit/Credit (+) | Balance $143.38 |
|---|---|---|---|---|---|---|---|
| | 3-8 | Deposit | $ | | $ | $  81.50 | 81.50 |
| | | | | | | | 224.88 |
| 774 | 3-10 | New View Vision Center | 54.57 | | | | 54.57 |
| | | contact lens replacement | | | | | 170.31 |
| 775 | 3-13 | Edison Electric | 44.40 | | | | 44.40 |
| | | electric bill | | | | | 125.91 |
| 776 | 3-18 | Image Salon | 24.00 | | | | 24.00 |
| | | haircut | | | | | 101.91 |
| | 3-22 | Deposit | | | | 467.20 | 467.20 |
| | | | | | | | 569.11 |
| 777 | 3-28 | Sloane Realty | 395.00 | | | | 395.00 |
| | | rent | | | | | 174.11 |
| 778 | 4-2 | Alum Creek United | 30.00 | | | | 30.00 |
| | | offering | | | | | 144.11 |

110                                                                                     Chapter 4

# CHAPTER *five*

## Dimensions of Communication

### INTRODUCTION

**You cannot "not" communicate.** Communication is using messages to stimulate meaning in the minds of others. Messages flow from a sender to a receiver through words, tone, body posture, eyes, or other stimuli. Effective communication contributes to effective problem-solving and decision-making.

Communication is the basis of all human interaction and of all group functioning. The existence of groups depends on communication, on exchanging information, and on transmitting meaning. Effective communication can greatly assist students in accomplishing many goals.

*Messages flow from a sender to a receiver through words, tone, body position, eyes, and other stimuli. To effectively communicate, t's important to recognize how each of these dimensions combines to create your message in the receiver.*

### OBJECTIVES

The objectives of this chapter are to help students
1. articulate the communication process.
2. apply principles of the different types of communication to college courses and college life in general.
3. use several forms of non-verbal/verbal communication to communicate more effectively.
4. apply principles of conflict resolution in problem situations.
5. illustrate the function of telecommunication devices and equipment in the learning process.

### KEY CONCEPTS

1. We cannot "not" communicate.
2. Communication is the basis of all human interaction and all group functioning.
3. Communication is transmitted in verbal and non-verbal categories.
4. The communication process includes sending, encoding, decoding, and receiving messages.
5. One of the biggest stumbling blocks in communication with persons for whom English is not the first language is the anger that often comes from the frustration of not understanding or being understood.
6. Listening plus understanding equals communication.
7. Learning how to cope with different people is an important dimension of effective communication.

> 8. Four key principles of communication effectiveness are ethics, audience analysis, perceptual awareness, and the seven axioms.
> 9. Use correct administrative channels of communication on your campus and in your work environment to achieve success.
> 10. The ability to resolve conflicts successfully is probably one of the most important skills a leader or student can possess.

College students communicate with several groups: roommates, residents in residence halls, classmates, fraternity and sorority brothers and sisters, faculty, and community groups encountered through community service projects. Through communication, students share ideas, opinions, and facts with others. The massive availability of telecommunication devices and techniques, such as headsets, beepers, pagers, the Internet, cellular phones, electronic calendars, think pads, etc., make communication today both rapid and voluminous. Yet students and professionals find themselves spending several hours surfing the Internet, reading and answering e-mail messages, plugging numbers, names, addresses, and notes into their PDA, and answering pager messages. Technology does not solve the communication problem. Technology assists in delivering various forms of communication to us. We must take it upon ourselves to learn appropriate techniques that will result in effective communication skills (Cleary, 2004).

Effective communication is a skill students will use throughout their lives. It is based upon a mutual effort between people to understand one another. Speakers must try to make their messages relevant to listeners. At the same time, listeners must open their minds to the messages being sent.

All forms of communication–speaking, listening, reading, writing, paging, teleconferencing–can be grouped into two different categories. The first is verbal communication, which involves the use of words. Non-verbal communication is the second category; this involves sending messages without the use of words.

Excellent communication skills can do more to advance a promising career than almost any other factor. The object of communicating is to create some degree of accurate understanding among the participants (Worth, 2004).

The term "communication" stems from the Latin root word, *communicate*, which means to make common. When two people have the same idea in mind, they have communicated, by making common, their understanding. Accuracy is determined by the degree of commonality shared.

More than ever, one's ability to communicate well affects one's capability to thrive in today's organizations and professions. If a student could strive for excellence in but one competence, communication would be the wise choice. This fact is obvious as you consider this evidence:
- Ninety percent of those who work in careers and professions do so in organizations. Organizations involve groups that cannot function without communication.
- Most employees serve customers in their work. Customers cannot be served without communication.
- College professions are constantly creating new knowledge and information

breakthroughs. The results could not occur without communication. Agencies of government, religion, social action, and education could not accomplish their goals without communication. College students study, take tests, write reports, and conduct research. Without communication, none of this would be possible. While in college, students form relationships that last a lifetime through the communication process.

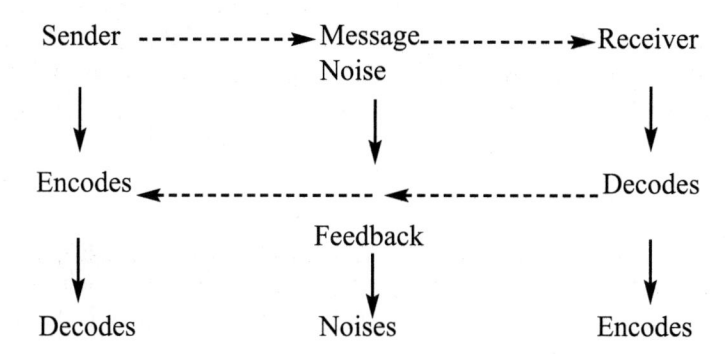

Business demands more participation and mental involvement from employees and associates at all levels. Companies no longer employ "hired hands" for routine mechanical tasks. They hire the whole person, including the brain. The "hired brains" convey ideas for better organizational success via communication. Progressive companies listen to the ideas of their people as well as customers and other stake holders. Listening is a crucial communication skill.

# THE COMMUNICATION PROCESS

```
Sender ----------> Message ----------> Receiver
                   Noise
   |                 |                    |
   v                 v                    v
Encodes <----------------------------- Decodes
                  Feedback
   |                 |                    |
   v                 v                    v
Decodes          Noises               Encodes
```

During the communication process, the sender encodes, then sends, a message. The message is received by the receiver, who decodes the message, then encodes a message back to the sender (called feedback), which can determine if the message sent was correctly interpreted by the receiver.

## *Sending Messages Effectively*

The first aspect of effective communication is the sending of a message. The three basic requirements for sending a message so that it will be understood are to phrase the message so it may be comprehended, to have credibility as a sender, and to ask for feedback on how the message is affecting the receiver. Our educational experiences in kindergarten, middle school, junior high, high school, and the university have taught us various aspects of sending and receiving messages (Worth, 2004; Van Der Merve, 2004; Cleary, 2004).

1. *Clearly "own" your messages by using first-person singular pronouns ("I" "my").* Personal ownership includes clearly taking responsibility for the ideas and feelings that one expresses. People disown their messages when they use phrases such as "most people," "some of our friends," and "our group."
2. *Make your messages complete and specific.* Include clear statements of all the necessary information the receiver needs to comprehend in the message.
3. *Make your verbal and non-verbal messages agree.* Every face-to-face communication involves both verbal and non-verbal messages. Usually these messages are

Dimensions of Communication

congruent. The person who is saying that he appreciates your help is smiling and expressing warmth in other non-verbal ways. Communication problems arise when a person's verbal and non-verbal messages are contradictory. If a person says, "Here is some information that may be of help to you" with a sneer on his face and a mocking tone of voice, the meaning you receive is confused by the two different messages being sent.

4. *Be redundant.* Sending the same message more than once and using more than one channel of communication (such as pictures and written messages, e-mail, as well as verbal and non-verbal cues) will help the receiver understand your message.

5. *Ask for feedback concerning the way your messages are being received.* To communicate effectively, you must be aware of how the receiver is interpreting and processing your messages. Be sure to continually seek feedback as to what meanings the receiver is attaching to your messages.

6. *Make the message appropriate to the receiver's frame of reference.* Explain the same information differently to an expert in the field, a novice, a child, an adult, your boss, and a coworker.

7. *Describe your feelings by name, action, or figure of speech.* When communicating your feelings, it is especially important to be descriptive. You may describe your feelings by name ("I feel like crying"), or by figures of speech ("I feel down in the dumps"). Descriptions help communicate your feelings clearly and unambiguously.

8. *Describe others' behavior without evaluating or interpreting.* When reacting to the behavior of others, be sure to describe their behavior ("You keep interrupting me") rather than evaluating it ("You're a rotten, self-centered person who won't listen to anyone else's ideas") (Johnson & Johnson, 1991, p. 110).

One of the most important elements in interpersonal communication is the credibility of the sender. **Sender credibility** refers to the attitude the receiver has toward the perceived trustworthiness of the sender's statements. Sender credibility has several dimensions:

1. The reliability of the sender as an information source—the sender's dependability, predictability, and consistency.
2. The sender's motives. The sender should be open about the effect he or she wants the message to have upon the receiver.
3. The expression of warmth and friendliness.
4. The majority opinion of others concerning the trustworthiness of the sender.
5. The sender's expertise on the topic under discussion.
6. The dynamism of the sender. A dynamic sender is seen as aggressive, emphatic, and forceful and tends to be viewed as more credible than a passive sender.

There is little evidence from the studies on sender credibility to suggest which of these dimensions is the most important. A highly credible sender is one who is perceived in a favorable light in *all* of these dimensions. A sender low in credibility, on the other hand, is one who is perceived in a negative light in *any one* of the dimensions. Unless we appear credible to a receiver, he or she will discount our message, and we will not be able to communicate effectively with that person. Sender credibility, in short, might be defined as the perceived trustworthiness of the sender (Johnson & Johnson, 1991, p. 111).

## Receiving Messages Effectively

Developing sending skills meets only half the requirements for communicating effectively; you must also have receiving skills. The skills involved in receiving messages are based on giving feedback about the reception and the message in ways that clarify and aid continued discussion. Receiving skills has two basic parts: 1) communicating the intention of wanting to understand the ideas and feelings of the sender and 2) understanding and interpreting the sender's ideas and feelings. Of the two, many theorists consider the first–communicating the intention to understand correctly, but not evaluate a message–to be the more important. The principal barrier to building effective communication is the tendency of most persons to judge or evaluate the message they are receiving (Johnson & Johnson, 1991, p. 111).

The specific receiving skills are paraphrasing, checking one's perception of the sender's feelings, and negotiating for meaning. Let's look at each of these skills in turn.

1. *Paraphrase accurately and non-evaluatively the content of the message and the feelings of the sender.* The most basic and important skill in receiving messages is paraphrasing–restating the words of the sender. Paraphrasing should be done in a way that indicates an understanding of the sender's frame of reference. The basic rule to follow in paraphrasing is this: *Speak for yourself only after you have first restated the ideas and feelings of the sender accurately and to the sender's satisfaction.* When paraphrasing, it is helpful to restate the sender's expressed ideas and feelings in your own words rather than repeating his or her words exactly. Avoid any indication of approval or disapproval, neither add nor subtract from the message, and try to place yourself in the sender's shoes to understand what he or she is feeling and what the message means.

2. *Describe what you perceive to be the sender's feelings.* Sometimes it is difficult to paraphrase the feelings of the sender if they are not described in words in the message. Thus, a second receiving skill is to check your perception of the sender's feelings simply by describing that perception. This description should tentatively identify those feelings without expressing approval or disapproval and without attempting to interpret them or explain their causes. It is simply saying, "Here is what I understand your feelings to be; am I accurate?"

3. *State your interpretation of the sender's message and negotiate with the sender until there is agreement as to the message's meaning.* Often the words contained in a message do not carry the actual meaning. A person may ask, "Do you always shout like this?" and mean, "Please quiet down." Sometimes, therefore, paraphrasing the content of a message will do little to communicate your understanding of it. In such a case, you must negotiate the meaning of the message. You may wish to preface your negotiation for meaning with "What I think you mean is..." If you are accurate, you then make your reply; if you are inaccurate, the sender restates the message until you can state its essential meaning (Johnson & Johnson,1996, p. 111).

What is effective communication? What is ineffective communication? **Effective communication** exists between two persons when the receiver interprets the sender's message in the same way the sender intended it. If John tries to communicate to Jane that it is a wonderful day and he is feeling great by saying, "Hi!" with a warm smile, and if Jane interprets John's "Hi!" as meaning John thinks it is a beautiful day and he is feeling well, then effective communication has taken place. If Jane interprets John's "Hi!" as meaning he wants to stop and talk with her, then ineffective communication has taken place.

**Dimensions of Communication**

The model of communication is typical of the applied approaches to interpersonal communication. In this model, the communicator is referred to as the **sender,** and the person at whom the message is aimed is the **receiver**. The **message** is any verbal or non-verbal symbol that one person transmits to another; it is subject matter being referred to in a symbolic way (all words are symbols). A **channel** can be defined as the means of sending a message to another person, the sound waves of the voice, the light waves that make possible the seeing of words on a printed page (Cleary, 2004; Owens, 2004; Worth, 2004; Rubin, 2004).

Because communication is a process, sending and receiving messages often takes place simultaneously: a person can be speaking and at the same time paying close attention to the receiver's non-verbal responses.

The process of communication between two persons can be a successful exchange. The model has seven basic elements.
1. The intentions, ideas, and feelings of the sender and the way he or she decides to behave lead him or her to send a message.
2. The sender encodes a message by translating his or her ideas, feelings, and intentions into a message appropriate for sending.
3. The sender sends the message to the receiver.
4. The message is sent through a channel.
5. The receiver decodes the message by interpreting its meaning. The receiver's interpretation depends on how well he or she understands the content of the message and the intentions of the sender.
6. The receiver responds internally to this interpretation of the message.
7. Noise is any element that interferes with the communication process. In the sender, noise refers to such things as his or her attitudes and frame of reference and the appropriateness of his or her language or other expression of the message. In the receiver, noise refers to such things as attitudes, background, and experiences that affect the decoding process. In the channel, noise refers to a) environmental sounds, such as static or traffic, b) speech problems, such as stammering, and c) annoying or distracting mannerisms, such as a tendency to mumble. To a large extent, the success of communication is determined by the degree to which noise is overcome or controlled (Johnson & Johnson, 1991, p. 107).

## DIVERSITY IN COMMUNICATION

Universities need to provide and structure learning experiences that enable students to speak, write, and read their culture into the curriculum and at the same time enable teachers to learn their way into the students' cultures. For students who do not or have not yet acquired non-verbal patterns of the mainstream, the communication and maintenance of their cultural identity within that stream is not a simple matter. When teachers cannot decode, read, and understand unfamiliar non-verbal communication behaviors of students who are culturally different from themselves, all kinds of labels can be attached to the students. A person's verbal communication skills are often judged solely by looking at or listening to that person. Cultural assumptions are made based on the language spoken, particularly for some African Americans, Hispanics, and Native Americans who speak from their own heritage.

The curriculum as a tool for socialization within the educational institution should provide instructional designs and methods for teaching language and literature as much as possible, through using the context that makes up various cultures. When the curriculum provides experience for students to speak, write, and read their culture into the curriculum, and teachers learn their way into students' cultures, then students of various minority ethnicities can be embraced and offered full access to all rewards available in society.

We face difficulties and frustrations on both sides of the language barriers that we face regularly in our multi-cultural society. We can also make mistakes in communicating with people for whom English is not the first language. Students will face this situation, whether it is with another student, a faculty member, or an administrator. The way a student handles himself or herself in the relationship will be very important. To cut off listening to a professor just because he or she speaks with an accent or dialect is not the way to manage this relationship.

The biggest stumbling block in communications with persons for whom English is not the first language is the anger that often comes from the frustration of not understanding or being understood. Remember, first seek to understand, then to be understood. Be patient and employ your listening skills. Ask simple questions to get clarification. Laughing at someone's struggle to speak English does not show the kind of maturity and respect we look for in college students (Thompson, 2004; Winnett, 2004).

## ACTIVE LISTENING

Active listening is more than hearing someone talk. It is a skill that involves putting aside personal feelings, concentrating on what is being said, and showing the other person that you are really trying to understand what he/she means.
Apply these rules and increase your listening power.
1. Calm down. You cannot listen when you are overheated. Back off and cool down. You will be better able to listen to the other person's side.
2. Try hard not to interrupt. Interrupting shows that you are more interested in voicing your opinion than in listening and understanding what the other person has to say.
3. Maintain eye contact. This may be difficult when you are upset, but looking up at the ceiling tells the other person that you aren't giving your attention to what is being said.
4. Be respectful. Good manners often keep a difficult situation from getting out of hand.
5. Watch your body language. A listener who shrugs, rolls his eyes, or taps his foot puts out negative vibes.
6. Avoid communication potholes. This maxim means concentrating on important matters and not getting sidetracked by non-essentials. Your purpose is to find out what the other person is really upset about so you can both work on a solution.
7. Encourage the other person to talk. Nod your head and say, "Tell me a little more" or "I didn't know you felt that way." These are encouraging moves.
8. When it is your turn to talk, speak in a calm, unexcited voice, and mention the other person's name. This is a positive way to show you are interested in hearing the other person's point of view.

9. Before you tell your side, repeat in your own words what you think the other person said. This action identifies you as a good listener.
10. Try to remember that everyone has an opinion and that everyone makes mistakes.

**Listening + Understanding = Communication**

# FOUR KEY PRINCIPLES OF COMMUNICATION EFFECTIVENESS

(Adapted from Timm, P. R., & Stead, I. A.'s model, 1996.)

1. **Ethics** is a system of moral philosophy that addresses issues of right and wrong. People who enter certain professions or work for certain employers automatically agree to assume certain moral duties as a part of their work. Doctors, attorneys, police officers, clergy, military officers, and public officials take oaths to save lives, uphold the public welfare, abide by rules of confidentiality, and fulfill the responsibilities of their professions in an honorable manner. In general, ethics define who people are. Ethical communicators persuade, but do not manipulate. Communicators who adhere to a high sense of moral values will ultimately be more successful than people whose ethics are "flexible" or "situational." In short, ethical communicators are more successful.

College students need to develop ethical character to obtain credibility. Communicating one's own work to faculty rather than plagiarizing others' work will make for a more effective student. Most of the reports and papers you write will have to be documented to show your sources of information. Documentation will communicate to your professor that you understand what it means to analyze a topic or an issue and give credit to those who communicated to you through the Internet, books, tapes, CDS, or in person.

Students can communicate ethically by doing their own work, giving credit to authors when their work is used, using appropriate words and phrases that do not offend or make others uncomfortable, and using the power of communication to enlighten rather than to deceive. Applying clear ethical standards will help students avoid the distortion, confusion, or ambiguous communication that damages credibility. Without strong credibility, the likelihood of communicating effectively is greatly diminished.

2. **Audience Analysis** is a process of making educated guesses about the audience and adjusting the message to best meet its needs. There are four approaches to discovering your audience members.

**Approach 1** -What does the audience need or want to know? You are in a class situation and you are giving a report. Is it what your classmates and the professor need or want to know?

**Approach 2** -What do they expect? Is the report relevant to the topic under discussion? Is it accurate, up to date, factual? Is it concise and to the point? People hear what they expect to hear, even if they have to distort a communicator's real message to make it fit what they anticipated.

**Approach 3** -What is the nature of the audience? When students come together for a particular class, there are certain objectives to be accomplished. A lot of what happens is information-sharing. In oral reporting in a class, classmates normally accept the role of a listener; they are quiet and listen to the speaker.

There is also interaction during the presentation. The alert receiver of the message carries on a mental dialogue with the sender and with his or her own thoughts. The alert message sender gets nonverbal feedback from listeners in the form of facial expressions, body movements, laughs, and grunts or groans. The reader creates mental impressions from the non-verbal aspects of a document (its appearance, tone, visuals, etc.).

Finally, there is interaction between the audience members when more than one person gets the same message. The listener who sees other students dozing off or becoming agitated or enthusiastic may be affected by these reactions. Whispered remarks or snickers among classmates can quickly degrade the effectiveness of a serious presentation. The reader may well ask others their reactions to a document before forming a conclusion.

**Approach 4** -What are the demographics? This approach to audience analysis gathers as much information as possible about key characteristics of the people with whom you are communicating. These characteristics may include age, gender, socioeconomic status, political philosophy, occupation, hobbies and activities, educational level, and so forth. From these data, the communicator can draw certain inferences about his or her audience.

The characteristics of age, gender, socioeconomic status (SES), etc., are not of themselves significant to the communicator. Their significance lies in the fact that these factors affect receiver values and attitudes, which, in turn, affect the way a receiver interprets messages. New incoming information is filtered through existing beliefs to determine if it makes sense. If it is deemed sensible, is it pleasant, neutral, or unpleasant to the audience? The result will be an audience that is either positive, neutral (disinterested), or negative toward the information you present.

When a communicator deals with hostile or excessively negative people, another problem arises. The person presenting information to such an audience should be aware that attitude changes come about slowly, and the message sender should be realistic about the goals for the communication effort. In dealing with a potentially hostile audience, the communicator may find it useful to establish some sort of common ground on which the audience and the sender can agree.

3. The third key to communication effectiveness is **perceptual awareness**. By this is meant that good communicators are sensitive to, and account for, the fact that people see the world differently. No two people perceive the same event in the same way. Images in peoples' heads are formed through the process of perception in which people take in, organize, and make sense of information from the world around them. Understanding this process can help the communicator adjust his or her message for maximum effectiveness. People perceive things according to their own fields of experience. The differences in peoples' perceptions are rational and inevitable. The communicator most likely to run into trouble is the one who has absolutely firm faith in

the "truth" of his or her own perceptions. Failure to recognize the complexity of human perception often results in failed communication.

Communication barriers arise from noise. Anything that detracts from a message can be seen as noise. "Noise" is a term used to refer to any kind of distractions or disruption of the communication process. Typographical errors, misspelling, enunciation, or an ambiguous sentence are examples of writer- or speaker-caused noise. Message receivers can also create noise by their bad reading habits, deficient hearing, weak vocabulary, or failure to pay attention to the ideas conveyed.

The sloppy appearance of an assignment can create noise by distracting the reader from what is said in it, just as the sloppy appearance of a speaker can cause a listener's thoughts to wander.

Barriers arise from lack of feedback. When accurately interpreted by a message sender, feedback can tell the sender how successful he or she has been. If the message does not seem to be getting across, the careful communicator will make readjustments (restate ideas, stress key points, adapt the message to the reader or listener to improve the chance of accurate communications).

Media choices affect the kind and quality of feedback you are apt to receive. Written messages allow little or no immediate reaction. Face-to-face conversations allow for a great deal of feedback, including direct questions, comments, and non-verbal reactions, such as a frown, a smile, or a nod of the head.

"Know your audience" should be the motto of anyone sincerely interested in being a better communicator. Efforts spent in careful probing analysis of your message receivers will pay handsome dividends in helping you communicate pertinently and purposefully. The need for audience analysis remains the same, despite any technological or environmental changes in professional communication.

### 4. Axioms of Communication Effectiveness
**Axiom 1:** Message senders with high credibility are more effective at getting ideas across. Credibility is a function of trustworthiness, expertise, and, to a lesser extent, dynamism and similarity. When people show themselves to be honest with you and to have no hidden motives that would benefit them at your expense, you are more likely to believe them. When people are seen as having expertise in the particular topic about which they are communicating, they are likely to be more persuasive. When people are seen as dynamic, sincere, and enthusiastic, they are often seen as more credible. Finally when people are seen as "like us," having similar standards, values, or interests, we are more likely to believe them.

On September 11, 2001, two airplanes with passengers and hijackers aboard ran into the Twin Towers of the World Trade Center in New York City. All passengers and hijackers were killed, and the Twin Towers were destroyed. Hundreds of people in the towers lost their lives that day also. A third plan crashed into the Pentagon and killed all passengers aboard, and several persons lost their lives who were in the Pentagon. Yet another passenger plane went down in Pittsburgh, PA, killing all persons aboard. How was the September 11, 2001, tragedy communicated to the nation? Whom did you believe?

**Axiom 2:** A well-organized message communicates effectively. Organizing ideas into comprehensible sentences, paragraphs, and documents or presentations makes the likelihood of success much greater. People hold certain expectations about how a message is likely to be or should be structured.

**Axiom 3:** Repetition helps people remember a message. Some redundancy is necessary for effective communication. You can expect to be misunderstood, so work to reduce the likelihood through repetition. If the person didn't hear a part of the first page, he or she will likely hear the message when repeated.

Even in written messages, some repetition is needed to reduce the likelihood of mistakes. Often, visual displays of information repeat and reinforce text. In some cases, speakers or writers use a lot of repetition to create a theme or aid in remembering. Recall the famous "I Have a Dream" speech of Dr. Martin Luther King, Jr. He consistently repeats the phrase, "I have a dream" as he builds the momentum of his message.

**Axiom 4:** Two-way communication creates understanding. Without two-way communication, you might as well be talking to yourself. It is important to know what listeners and readers are thinking and how the message has affected them.

**Axiom 5:** Attention or distractions can occur as messages flow from person to person. Something happens to information as it moves from person to person. The more people a message goes through, the more pronounced the distortions. Each person puts his own "spin on the message"; each interprets it in an individual way and rephrases it in a similarly unique way.

The number of links in a communicator transmitter determine the degree of distortion. When students play the game "Telephone," one person whispers something into the ear of another person, who in turn passes it to another player, and then another, until each one has received the message. This creates a serial transmission effect. After ten to fifteen players, the message that is announced aloud by the last player is different from the message started by the first player. You can reduce serial transmission distortion by
 A. reducing the number of links in the network.
 B. selecting communication media that are less susceptible to individual interpretation.

**Axiom 6:** Visual support helps people grasp a message. Most college students today have grown up in a time when video images have been everywhere. From earliest television to today's dazzling computer images, people have come to expect more information to be communicated via visuals, not just words. Such images are referred to as graphics.

Charts, pictures, graphs, and full-motion videoclips have become commonplace in college and professional communication. Graphics add clarity and interest to both written and spoken messages. Graphics complement the message by
- helping message receivers visualize complex data.
- emphasizing important points.

- breaking up the text to make a document easier to read.
- condensing and simplifying difficult concepts.

**Axiom 7:** Openness and assertiveness make people better communicators. Constructive disclosure builds stronger understanding. Self-enclosure is the degree to which individuals reveal their attitudes and feelings to others. Assertiveness means being pleasantly direct in expressing those attitudes and feelings. Healthy effective interpersonal relationships develop when there is constructive disclosure.

The more open you are with someone else, the more open the other person will tend to be with you. Giving and receiving feedback can lead people to better productivity and more useful relationships with each other. If you do not know how others feel and how much they are reacting to events, you will not be of much help to those people. Likewise, if you are too hesitant to disclose your own feelings, others may not be able to help you, and you may fail to gain the advantages of that closer relationship. There are limits, however. Few people are interested in the most intimate feelings or fantasies of others. The Monica Lewinsky and Bill Clinton scandal is one that polls showed most Americans did not want to know about. Also, it is usually a good idea for faculty not to express their negative feelings toward university administrators and management policies in the classroom. Be pleasantly direct, not rude.

Listening is more than hearing, as it involves sensing, interpretation, evaluation, and response, as well. Furthermore, it is through speaking and listening that students acquire knowledge, develop language, and increase their understanding of themselves. As students learn language, they learn to think; and the pervasiveness of language itself in the teaching of any subject suggests that the teaching of listening skills can be a primary strategy in the development of critical thinking skills. Some of the skills needed for effective critical listening are 1) evaluating the strength of the speaker's main ideas and the quality of supporting evidence; 2) recognizing the difference between fact and opinion; and 3) recognizing the use of loaded language, stereotypes, and/or emotional appeals. These skills can and should be taught in schools (Pickering, 2004; Rubin, 2004; Winnett, 2004).

When giving feedback, Charles Jung and associates (1973) stated that it is useful to describe observed behaviors, as well as the reactions they caused. They offer these guidelines: the receiver should be ready to receive feedback; comments should describe, rather than interpret; feedback should focus on recent events or actions that can be changed, but should not be used to try to force people to change.

One especially important kind of feedback for administrators is letting staff members know how well they are doing their jobs. Effective school leaders give plenty of timely positive feedback. They give negative feedback privately, without becoming defensive.

**"Paraphrasing."** Charles Jung and his colleagues (1973) stressed that the real purpose of paraphrasing is not to clarify what the other person actually meant, but to show what it meant to you. This may mean restating the original statement in specific terms, using an example, or restating it in more general terms.

**"Perception Checking."** Perception checking is an effort to understand the feelings behind the work. One method is simply to describe your impressions of another person's feeling at a given time, avoiding any expression of approval or disapproval.

**"Describing Behavior."** Useful behavior description, according to Jung and his associates, reports specific, observable actions without value judgments, and without making accusations or generalizations about motives, attitudes, or personality traits. "You've disagreed with almost everything he's said" is preferable to "You're being stubborn."

## COMMUNICATION THROUGH ADMINISTRATIVE CHANNELS

Get a copy of the university's organizational chart to find the channels of administrative communication on your campus. It is important to follow the channels beginning with the one closest to the problem or situation. For example, faculty report to department chairs, program directors, or deans. Deans report to the provost, vice chancellor or vice president for academic affairs, and the provost and vice chancellors/vice presidents report to the chancellor or president. Therefore, if you have a problem in the classroom you would communicate first to the classroom instructor, and if satisfaction is achieved, you need not go any further; however, if the problem is not resolved, you may proceed through the administrative channels until a resolution is reached. It is unwise to take problems directly to the top administrative channel without having gone through the other channels first.

*When you have a problem, it is important to follow administrative channels, beginning with the one closest to the problem or situation. It is unwise to take problems directly to the top administrative channel as a first option.*

On some small college campuses and some Historically Black Colleges and Universities (HBCU) campuses, particularly, chancellors and presidents have open-door policies and invite students to come in to see them regularly. Make use of this policy an exception rather than a rule. An abuse of an open-door policy will not find favor with chancellors and other administrators.

When you begin your own career, keeping the job may depend on your knowledge of the administrative channels and your ability to work within the confines of the set channels.

Effective leaders must work at developing conflict management styles. In any conflict situation, you may respond in one of several ways: by defusing, avoiding, negotiating, or confronting. Which of these conflict management styles you choose should depend on the nature of the situation, rather than your particular personality traits. Read the following descriptions to learn more about the styles and their applications (Owens, 2004).

## CONFLICT AND CONFRONTATION

The ability to resolve conflict successfully is probably one of the most important skills a leader or student can possess. Success in the practice of this skill depends on
- early recognition of impending conflict,
- avoidance of unnecessary and destructive discord,
- the capacity to use controversy creatively as a means of furthering understanding and bringing persons together in spite of differences,
- the courage to face the pain, tension, and anxiety of conflict in order to find the basic causes, and
- the willingness to keep open the lines of communication to make changes.

## Definition

Conflict may be defined as a clash of opinions and interests, usually involving a struggle to win. Controversy denotes a situation arising from expressions of opposing views, especially those based on value judgments.

## Conflict Resolution

For the leader, there are a number of possible responses to conflict situations, whether they involve individuals or groups within or outside the organization. An explanation of a range of alternative responses is given below. Conflict-resolution strategies are classified into three categories: avoidance, defusion, and confrontation (Dry, 1993; Owens, 2004).

## Avoidance, Defusion, Confrontation

1. Avoidance: Some people tend to avoid conflict by ignoring it, circumventing it, or escaping the situation entirely. This may be a short-range solution, but it rarely, if ever, leads toward satisfaction for all parties concerned.
2. Defusion: This tactic delays discussion and action on the central conflict. It may place emphasis on peripheral issues or promote confusion about what the central issues really are. This sometimes has value in allowing for a cooling-off period before moving into substantive discussion, but often it is used to avoid clarification of the real issues and, therefore, results in dissatisfaction and anxiety.
3. Confrontation: This response involves the direct encounter of conflicting persons or issues. Strategies include the use of power and/or negotiation.
    a. Power strategies utilize the power resources of an individual or group, such as money, affiliations, authority of position or other status, or ability to enforce decisions. The problem with this strategy is that it may cause damage to one or more parties involved in the conflict. However, there are times when the use of power is justified: e.g., in the struggle for women's rights. Women need to marshal all the power resources they can because of the overwhelming power held by those holding opposing views. It is very difficult to bargain from a powerless position, and women must recognize the power they hold and use it constructively to bring about changes (Aburdene, P., & Naisbitt, 1992).
    b. Negotiation strategies attempt to resolve the conflict with compromise or a mutually satisfactory solution.

*Confrontation is just one way to resolve a conflict. Other strategies involve avoidance and diffusion.*

# HOW TO COPE WITH DIFFICULT PEOPLE

### *Step 1: Assess the Situation.*

- Has the person acted differently in at least three similar situations?
- Are you reacting out of proportion to the situation?
- Was there a particular incident that triggered the troublesome behavior?
- Will direct, open discussion relieve the situation?

If your answer to at least one of these questions is yes, you are probably dealing with a problem you can solve, not a difficult person that you cannot change.

### *Step 2: Stop wishing they were different.*

- Stop blaming them; it won't change anything. Give up wishful thinking; unrealistic hopes lead to even more resentment.

### *Step 3: Get some distance between you and the difficult behavior.*

- Label with prototypes, not stereotypes. Stereotyping assumes all complainers are the same, and they are not. Seek to understand the person from the inside out.

### *Step 4: Formulate a plan for interrupting the interaction.*

- Negative interactions become even more negative. You can't change the other person, but you can change your response.

### *Step 5: Implement the strategy.*

- Timing–Select a time when you are not under great stress and have the energy to experiment. Preparation–Use mental rehearsal and role-play.

### *Step 6: Monitor and modify.*

- Expect that you will have to plan, experiment, and persist. Know when to give up; if necessary, create physical or organizational distance.

## SUMMARY

Each of us communicates all the time, whether or not we are aware of it. Communication is the basis for all group functioning. The massive availability of telecommunications devices and techniques makes communication today both rapid and voluminous.

All forms of communication can be grouped into verbal and non-verbal categories. More than ever, one's ability to communicate well affects one's capability to thrive in today's organizations and professions.

During the communication process, the sender encodes, and then sends a message. The message is received by the receiver who decodes the message, then encodes a message (feedback) back to the sender. Sender credibility refers to the attitude the receiver has toward the perceived trustworthiness of the sender's statement.

Cultural assumptions are made based on the language spoken, particularly for those who speak from their own heritage. When the curriculum provides experience for students to speak, write, and read their own culture, students of various minority ethnicities can be enhanced and offered full access to all rewards available in society. Active listening is putting aside personal feelings, concentrating on what is being said, and showing the other person that you are really trying to understand him/her. Listening plus understanding equals communication.

There are four key principles of communication effectiveness: ethics, audience analysis, perpetual awareness, and axioms.

When you begin your own career, keeping the job may depend on your knowledge of administrative channels and on your ability to work within the confines of the set channels.

## GLOSSARY

**Active Listening:** putting aside personal feelings, concentrating on what is being said, and showing the other person that you are really trying to understand what he/she means.
**Body Language:** the actions of the body to express meaning.
**Cellular Phones:** telephones without cords that may be used in transit as well as at home.
**Channel:** the means of sending a message to another person.
**Communication:** sending and receiving messages to convey ideas.
**Communication Barriers:** any elements that prevent a message from being received as intended.
**Communication (formal):** written or oral expressions that follow prescribed styles of writing, such as term papers, theses, research activities, etc.
**Communication (informal):** written and oral expressions that tend to be free-flowing in style rather than following a prescribed style.
**Communication (verbal):** the use of words and language to express a message.
**Communication (non-verbal):** the use of body language or other actions to send messages.
**Communication (oral):** spoken words.

**Communication (closed):** messages are sent and the receiver gets no feedback before decoding the message.

**Communication (open):** the receiver is able to probe the sender to get additional information in decoding messages.

**Conflict:** two or more ideas, people, things, trying to occupy the same space at the same time.

**Conflict Resolution:** coming to agreement on ways to work through problems.

**Conversation:** oral communication between persons.

**Decoder:** breaking down messages sent by receiver.

**Decibel:** the unit of measuring the intensity of sound.

**Empathy:** the ability to put yourself in someone else's place and experience his or her feelings.

**Encoder:** putting the language to the message.

**Feedback:** the receiver of the message decodes the message, then encodes a response to the sender.

**Hearing:** the act of perceiving sound: a purely physical activity by which acoustic energy in the form of sound waves is changed to energy the brain can understand.

**Language:** communication by voice, using arbitrary, auditory symbols in conventional ways with conventional meanings.

**Listening:** giving attention for the purpose of hearing, analyzing, interpreting, and responding. Psychological processes that allow one to attach meaning to the patterns of energy heard.

**Message:** any verbal or non-verbal symbol that one person transmits to another.

**Noise:** any element that interferes with the communication process.

**Pagers:** small electronic communication devices that operate as a telephone and message storage system.

**Receiver:** the persons to whom the message is sent.

**Sender:** the person that sends the message in the communication process.

**Sound:** the audible result of an utterance or something heard.

**Speaking:** uttering words and sounds with the voice: talking.

**Telecommunications:** the sending and receiving of messages (data) from one electronic device to another via computer networks and the information superhighway.

## REFERENCES

Aburdene, P., & Naisbitt, J. (1992) *Megatrends for women: From liberation to leadership!* New York: Random House.

Cleary, S. (2004). *The communication handbook: A student guide to effective communication.* Juta & Company.

Covey, S. R. (1990). *The seven habits of highly effective people.* New York: Fireside Books.

Geddes, D. S. (1995). *Keys to communication: A handbook for school success.*

Jerry, J., and Janice L. Herman (Eds.). *The practicing administrator's leadership series.* Thumond Oaks, CA: Cowin Press.

Johnson, D., & Johnson, F. (1991). *Joining together: Group theory and group skills.* Needham Heights, MA: Allyn and Bacon.

Johnson, E. (1998). *Brothers on the mend: Understanding and healing anger for African-American men and women.* New York: Pocket Books, Simon and Schuster.

Jung, C. (1973). *Interpersonal communication: Participant materials and leader's manual.* Portland, OR: Northern Regional Laboratory.

Owens, H. (2004). *Communication skills for effective management.* Palgrave Macmillan.

Pickering, M. J., Megas, K. (2004). *Creativity, communications and cultural values.* Sage Publishers.

Rubin, R. B. (2004). *Communication research; Strategies and sources with Infrotrac.* Wadsworth.

Smith, R. (2004). *Speaking secrets for the bored room. How to fire up your audience, turbo charge your career.*

Thompson, P. (2004). *Narrative and genre: Contexts and types of communication.* Transaction publisher.

Timm, P. R., & Stead, J. A. (1996). *Communication skills for business and professions.* Upper Saddle River, New Jersey: Prentice Hall.

Ury, W. (1993). *Geting past no: Negotiating your way from confrontation to cooperation.* New York: Bantam Books.

Van Der Merve, N. (2004). *How to deliver effective written and spoken messages.* Juta & Company.

Winnett, A. (2004). *How to build relationship that stick. The wonderful benefits of satisfying communication.*

Worth, R. (2004). *Communication skills.* Ferguson.

## WEBSITES

www.speakingforsuccess.net
www.calibratedcomm.com
www.speakingsmart.com

# ACTIVITY 1

## *Coping with Difficult People–A Quick Reference Guide*

| TYPE | CHARACTERISTICS | COPING TECHNIQUES |
|---|---|---|
| Hostile, Aggressive | Behavior: intimidating, abrupt, abusive, loud, indignant, sniping, explosive.<br><br>Underlying issues: strong need to be "right"; fear of weakness in themselves and others; need to be in control; suspicious of and quick to blame others. | If the attack is overt: Let them run down. Stand up to them. Don't argue. Don't return fire.<br><br>If the attack is covert: Bring it to the surface. Don't snipe in return. |
| Complainers | Behavior: whining, blaming, accusing; may complain to you about you, or may complain to you about others.<br><br>Underlying issues: feel powerless; need attention; want to view themselves as perfect and blameless. | If complainers blame you: Listen attentively. Acknowledge their complaint. Don't agree. Move into problem-solving.<br><br>If the complainers complain to you about someone else: Don't listen. Tell them to stop! Offer to pass on their complaints or to set up a meeting. |
| Silent, Unresponsive | Behavior: in response to your direct questions or statements, only silence, a nod, or a grunt; only a "Yes" or "No" when more information is called for.<br><br>Underlying issues: hard to generalize, but could be silent sniping, fear of your reaction to what they would say if they talked, or fear of their own feelings. | Ask open-ended questions. Use a friendly, silent stare. Don't fill up the silence. Make a direct observation: "I'm waiting for your answer, and you're not saying anything."<br><br>Help them overcome their fear: "Can you say anything about this?" or "How about starting in the middle?" |

**Dimensions of Communication**

| TYPE | CHARACTERISTICS | COPING TECHNIQUES |
| --- | --- | --- |
| Super Agreeable | Behavior: outgoing, sociable, friendly, quick to agree or give support; doesn't follow through with action.<br><br>Underlying issues: strong need to be accepted or liked; fear of conflict or of making you unhappy. | Help them feel accepted and appreciated. Make honesty non-threatening. Don't let them make unrealistic promises.<br><br>In conflict situations, propose win/win solutions. |
| Wet Blankets, Negativists | Behavior: regularly shoots down others' ideas or solutions, no matter what they are.<br><br>Underlying issues: often genuinely believe it is futile to try to change things; feel powerless; don't trust people in power. | Avoid getting drawn in. Don't take their comments seriously. Don't argue. Express your realistic optimism.<br><br>Use negative comments constructively: "How might we overcome that obstacle?" |
| Indecisive Stallers | Behavior: appear helpful and agreeable; postpone decisions, particularly ones that others may not like; beat around the bush.<br><br>Underlying issues: don't want to hurt anyone and therefore postpone difficult choices; genuinely concerned with quality over expediency; when confronted with practical problems, they stall until the issue "goes away" or it is too late to do anything. | Make it easy for them to be direct with you. Express their doubts for them: "You might be concerned that I won't like your answer... ?" Help them problem-solve.<br><br>Work with them to prioritize solutions. Give lots of support when they make a decision. Follow up to make sure they implement the decision. |

# ACTIVITY 2

## *Quiz on Presentation Skills*

How well do you present yourself when speaking in public? Rate yourself on a 1 to 5 scale. Where 1 is "not true at all about me" and 5 is "very true about me."

1. I use information well.  1 2 3 4 5
2. I organize information logically.  1 2 3 4 5
3. I solicit audience involvement.  1 2 3 4 5
4. I am an enthusiastic speaker.  1 2 3 4 5
5. I am poised and confident.  1 2 3 4 5
6. I use body language to connect positively with the audience.  1 2 3 4 5
7. I speak the language my audience understands.  1 2 3 4 5
8. I enjoy giving presentations.  1 2 3 4 5
9. I like to get audience reaction to my presentations.  1 2 3 4 5
10. I test AV equipment before giving the presentations.  1 2 3 4 5
11. I can adapt easily to changes in equipment or space.  1 2 3 4 5
12. I know and use microphone etiquette.  1 2 3 4 5
13. I have a variety of speaking styles.  1 2 3 4 5
14. I dress appropriately for speaking engagements.  1 2 3 4 5
15. I respond well to audience questions.  1 2 3 4 5
16. I address multi-cultural audiences appropriately.  1 2 3 4 5
17. I address and give complements to my audience before speaking.  1 2 3 4 5
18. I thank the audience for its attention before I sit down.  1 2 3 4 5
19. My presentations are usually rated as very effective.  1 2 3 4 5
20. Handouts prepared for the presentation are done well.  1 2 3 4 5

<u>Less than 80 points</u> -You need to learn and practice more. Read books and articles on public speaking. Attend public speaking seminars.

<u>80-100 points</u> Congratulations! You are poised and confident and have good strategies for speaking. Try building more interaction with audiences.

Dimensions of Communication

# CHAPTER *six*

## Dimensions of Computer Technology

### INTRODUCTION

Technology in the twenty-first century has expanded tremendously. We have picture phones, hand-held computers such as Personal Digital Assistants (PDAs), educational assistive technology, computerized adaptive testing, more versatile pagers, expanded Internet services and digital products that have totally revolutionized the way we do business, manage our personal lives, and even relax. Individuals are utilizing a wider variety of technology at a much earlier age. Recently, I watched a three-year-old turn on the television, change the TV from regular broadcast to Direct TV, change the station to Disney, switch over to the DVD mode, and put a DVD into the player. He then sat back and watched the movie. He did not pause once. He knew just what to do. It was amazing.

*Personal computers have changed the way we navigate through our busy and sometimes hectic personal, professional, and academic lives.*

Computers are being used by individuals of younger ages as well. Few technologies have touched our lives like the revolution in technology over the past 10 years. The personal computer, in particular, has revolutionized the way we instruct, learn, conduct business, and generally navigate our way through busy and sometimes hectic schedules. Daily, it is common to hear computer users say, "I could not make it without a computer," or "How did we survive before the personal computer?" This chapter is designed to acquaint you with computer technology and its many applications, to explore computer peripherals, to examine what you should know when contemplating the purchase of a computer and peripherals, and to introduce you to some other advancements in the field of technology.

### OBJECTIVES

The objectives of this chapter are to:
1. describe the parts of the computer and explain how they operate.
2. describe the various applications of the computer.
3. introduce basic computer terminology to explore other advancements in the field of technology.

> **KEY CONCEPTS**
>
> | | | |
> |---|---|---|
> | CPU | Internet | Library First Search |
> | WWW | OnLine Computer | J-Stor |
> | CD-ROM | Memory | Chat Room |
> | Hard Drive | DVD | Distance Education |

## PARTS OF THE COMPUTER

### *The Central Processing Unit*

The **Central Processing Unit** (CPU) is the "brain" of the personal computer. Presently, CPUs are running at speeds of several gigahertz (ghz) per second. Speed is especially important because software makers are producing huge packages that will not run efficiently on slower processors. The new AMD and Intel Quad 4 processors can produce outstanding graphics, 3-D images, and accelerate through complex statistical packages with ease. Basic computers today are stocked with sufficient CPU power to operate word-processing programs, connect to the internet, and plow through graphics and statistical packages.

### *Random Access Memory*

Essential to the efficient operation of the personal computer is the amount of **Random Access Memory (RAM)** it has. As the CPU carries out its functions and the user requests more of the computer, data are stored in memory chips. The more memory on board the computer, the faster one can access data. Most of today's software requires at least 512 megabytes of RAM, but most computers today are stocked with at least one gigabyte of memory, twice the minimum required.

### *Hard Drives, Floppy Drives, and Other Storage Media*

Though the Central Processing Unit is the "brain" of the computer, other components are necessary to the machine's operation. The hard drive, usually the "C" drive, stores data entered at the keyboard and software, such as word processing, database management, and graphics programs. Today, hard drives store **gigabytes** (billions) of keystrokes of data, and because computer technology advances so quickly, currently, one can purchase a 750 gigabyte hard drive, and it is likely that they will increase in capacity.

Computers also require a **floppy drive**. Currently, the floppy drive, usually the "A" drive, uses a 1.44 megabyte disk. This "A" drive is used to transfer software to the hard drive. The USB flash drive is quickly replacing the floppy drive. Whereas the "A" floppy only holds 1.44 megabyte of information, a typical USB flash drive hold two, four, and eight gigabytes of information.

### *Compact Disk-Read Only Memory (CD-ROM)/Digital Versatile/Video Disc (DVD)*

#### *(CD-ROM), Compact Disc-Recordable and Compact Disc-Rewritable*

One of the most important innovations in computer technology over the past ten years is the **Compact Disk-Read Only Memory (CD-ROM)**. The significance of the

CD-ROM is its holding capacity (600 megabytes of information). This device occupies a bay on the front of the computer. And because the CD-ROM disk holds so much data, software writers are able to store video, audio clips, graphics, and text. The CD player also accepts regular audio CDs, making it possible for users to enjoy their favorite musical selections while working on documents, playing games, or surfing the Internet.

What is also significant about CD-ROM technology is that it introduced the multimedia platform. With the use of a sound card (capable of producing high-quality sound), speakers, and a microphone installed onto the computer's motherboard, users have a platform that incorporates video, audio, graphics, and text. This technology could eliminate the need for a videocassette recorder (VCR), television, and sound device. A newer format that advances CD-ROM technology is the **Compact Disc-Recordable (CD-R) drive**. This device uses a blank CD and allows the user to record up to 650 megabytes of non-erasable data. Though used primarily as a data backup system, the CD-R also allows one to record audio CDs for playback in any CD player. A more recent format, the **Compact Disc-Rewritable** uses a blank disc that allows users to re-record up to 650 megabytes of data. The disc is erasable and is used in the same manner as a regular floppy disc.

*In 1995, after years of research, the Digital Versatile/Video Disc (DVD) technology was invented. By 2001, computer manufacturers were stocking their computers with the DVD drive that played standard DVD movies. DVD discs can store up to 4.7 gigabytes of information, or the length of a two-hour movie. Today's computers contain a combination CD-ROM and DVD-ROM drive, capable of recording and playing both compact disks and DVD disks.*

Computer manufacturers are striving to keep computer users in front of the computer screen with the introduction of several media formats for the personal computer. There is the television for PC and the FM radio for PC. Computer users can attach a cable TV connection to their computer and watch television or listen to the radio while working in documents.

## *Modem/Fax Board*

An important computer peripheral is the **modem/fax card**. This device is used by the computer to communicate with other computers around the world. It is connected to a telephone line, and users dial into other modems to access data. The modem is especially important today because it links computer users to the **World Wide Web** (the Internet). Modems transfer and receive information at baud rates equal to one bit per second. Today's modems carry data at relatively fast rates, up to 56,000 bauds per second. Most modems today are integrated with facsimile (fax) capabilities. The user can send and receive fax messages over the computer. The stand alone facsimile machine (not connected to a computer) continues to be used by many businesses. Manufacturers, however, have begun to make stand-alone fax machines that are multi-functional, capable of scanning images and text, copying images and text, and printing. The fax machine has a computer interface and is connected to the computer using a serial cable.

# USING COMPUTERS TO MAKE PRESENTATIONS

Today, college professors, salespersons, college presidents, and others use computers to make presentations. Several peripherals are used to project the image on the computer screen to a larger screen for viewing by large groups. One such device is the **Liquid Crystal Display Board**. A cable is attached to the input jack on the LCD board and to the output jack on the computer.

Another device used to project computer images on larger screens is the **Pocket Scan Converter**. This very small apparatus (about six inches long) uses a cable between the computer and the television. The image on the computer is then transferred to the television screen. The converter is an inexpensive way to project computer images to a larger screen. The cost for this six-inch device is about $120, the LCD projector is used to project images from the computer to a large screen or wall, whereas LCD boards range from $600 to $4,000.

## *Printers*

One of the advantages of the computer is that it allows the users to desktop publish. Desktop publishing replaces costly typesetting and printing that heretofore were done by professional typesetters and graphics gurus. Software packages can produce stunning texts and images, and today's sophisticated printers yield high-quality output. Two output technologies are used in most printers today. Laser technology produces the largest number of **dots per square inch** (**dpi**) on a page. The more dots used to print a single letter, the higher the quality. Laser printers for the average consumer can produce up to 600 x 600 dpi. This is book publication quality. The other technology is ink jet. These printers are less expensive, providing typically 1440x720 x 300 dpi. One of the advantages of ink jet printers is that they produce color as well as black ink. Some more-expensive ink jet printers may produce 1440 x 720 dpi, and up to 4800 dpi on special glossy paper.

## *Scanners*

One of the most useful computer peripherals today is the **scanner**. This device, which comes in three basic varieties: hand-held, sheet-fed, and flatbed, is used to scan text, photographs, and other images directly into the computer. The scanned data are converted to a digital format and can be loaded into word processing (most commonly), photo-manipulation, graphics, or most any other software program.

Scanners use **Optical Character Recognition** (**OCR**) software that can save the user time. It helps reduce the need to re-type documents; photographs can be scanned into brochures and newsletters; and any paper document can be scanned and manipulated as if it were typed on the computer originally.

## *Software*

Computer users today have hundreds of software packages from which to choose. As stated earlier, most computer users primarily employ **word-processing programs**. There are several packages on the market today; however, two manufacturers have the largest share of the industry. These two companies, Microsoft Corporation, makers of Microsoft Word, and Corel, makers of WordPerfect, are in stiff competition to gain

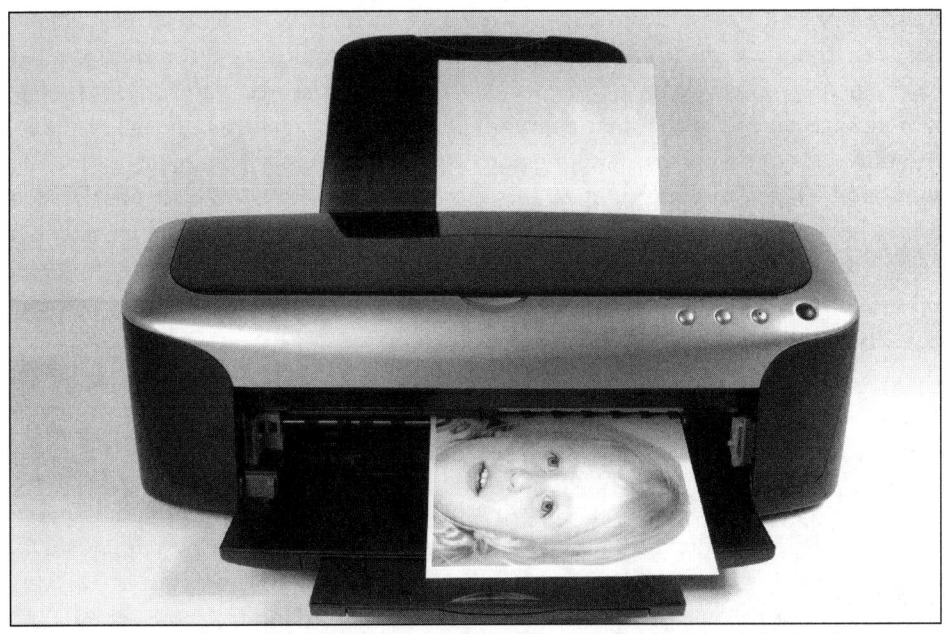

*Desktop publishing allows computer uses to create professional-quality documents and photos at home or work.*

the market edge, and so they continue to upgrade their products. Both of these packages have cut-and-paste capabilities, spell check, a thesaurus, loads of clip art, large first letters, graphics, presentations, Internet access, table creation, templates, and dozens of other word-processing tools.

Database management programs are useful to businesses, schools, professors, and students. These programs allow the user to create an electronic file. A person's name, address, telephone number, and other important data can be stored and retrieved, sorted, and modified. For example, a department on a university campus could keep an electronic file on all graduates. Newsletters, surveys, and requests for money could be sent to alumni. There are several database management programs on the market today, including, Microsoft's Access, PC-File, Clans Works, File Maker Pro, and Paradox.

**Spreadsheet software** has become an indispensable package in the business world today. This program calculates and plots data. Students are allowed to use a spreadsheet in some math classes. Popular spreadsheet programs include QuattroPro, Lotus 1-2-3, and Excel.

## THE ELECTRONIC PORTFOLIO

An **electronic portfolio** is a collection of student work that exhibits the student's efforts, progress, and achievement in a given area or areas. Electronic portfolios reflect a wide range of student work from the freshman to the senior year and may contain hundreds of pieces of work that do not easily fit into a traditional "notebook" type portfolio. Electronic portfolios are gaining wide acceptance by colleges and universities at undergraduate and graduate levels and by employers across the country.

Students who develop electronic portfolios have an opportunity to present themselves in the most favorable light, using text, graphics, sound, and video that can be dis-

**Dimensions of Computer Technology**

played over time, using **Electronic Portfolio's** Timeline features. The software allows the user to output the data in several media, including disk, audio recordings and videotape, and CD-ROM. Not only would students be prepared with additional marketable skills, but this innovative approach demonstrates high-level professional presentation skills during interviews for graduate studies, potential employment, scholarships, and fellowship opportunities. It is more convenient to send electronic portfolios rather than box up cumbersome booklets that would be costly to duplicate in a professional manner.

## THE INTERNET (WORLD WIDE WEB)

The **Internet** is one of the most important developments in information technology. It has revolutionized the way the world conducts business, delivers and accesses information, researches topics, and communicates globally. The World Wide Web, commonly referred to as the Web, is a network of thousands of computers sharing information in the form of text, graphics, video, and sound. Used by corporations, educational institutions, federal, state, and local governments, and businesses of all sizes, the Internet has become a major distributor of information in this "information age." The Internet is accessed through a direct network connection, usually by educational institutions and businesses, and through the use of an internal or external modem.

A service provider, such as America Online, Prodigy, CompuServe, and dozens of local companies are required to access the Internet. Web browser software is also needed to access the Internet, the most popular of which are Microsoft Explorer and Mozilla. Web browsers allow users to navigate the Internet through the use of menus, icons, images, graphics and buttons. These provide a link to the information requested on a page. The first page of an Internet site is referred to as the "home page." This **"home page"** has an Internet address that must be typed in or accessed through a **"bookmark"** that has been stored by the user. The "home page" contains the name of the site, the creator's name, contents and links to other pages within the document, and other Internet addresses.

## COMMUNICATIONS

### *Electronic Mail (e-mail)*

**Electronic Mail** or **e-mail** is another revolution in computers and information technology, in general. Electronic mail is a message sent from one computer to another via a server provided by an Internet company (provider). Not only can mail be sent, but files from favorite software programs can be sent as well. Users must have an address, usually a combination of letters in the first name, or any other letter or number combination that is not in use by another user. Many universities have free e-mail for enrolled students. Using any computer connected to the Internet, students can send and receive messages worldwide. Some professors have their courses on the Internet, and a student e-mail account allows a two-way exchange between students and professors.

In addition to university accounts, there are a number of Web sites that offer free e-mail. Two popular sites are *Hotmail.com* and *Yahoo.com*. First-time users log on to the Web page and fill out a questionnaire; within minutes, an account can be set up. E-mail can be sent and accessed from any computer around the globe that is connected to the Internet.

## News Groups, Chat Rooms, and Mailing Lists

The Internet is more than the World Wide Web and electronic mail. It is also a place where users can interact with other people around the world through news groups, mailing lists, and chat rooms. News groups (also referred to as Usenet, News groups, or just News) are an integral part of communication on the Internet. They allow users to participate in discussions on a wide range of subjects with millions of people around the world. There are literally thousands of news groups to which users can subscribe. A news group member logs on to the news group and posts a message that is related to the group's topic, and then waits for responses.

**Chat rooms**, on the other hand, are places on the Internet where people can interact by typing messages back and forth. It is essentially a conversation with dozens of people who are in the chat room. Some chat rooms provide guidelines on what can be discussed. Users log on using their screen name and then can join the live chat.

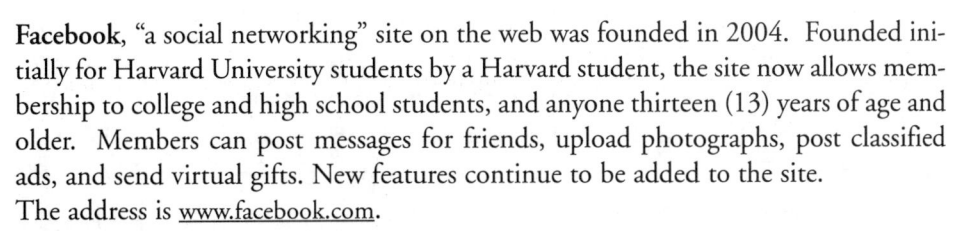

*E-mail, chat rooms, and mailing lists allow computer users to interact and communicate with other users and information sources on the World Wide Web.*

**Facebook**, "a social networking" site on the web was founded in 2004. Founded initially for Harvard University students by a Harvard student, the site now allows membership to college and high school students, and anyone thirteen (13) years of age and older. Members can post messages for friends, upload photographs, post classified ads, and send virtual gifts. New features continue to be added to the site. The address is www.facebook.com.

**Myspace** is also a community of worldwide users sharing photographs, videos, and other information about themselves and activities. Chat rooms, blogging, news, mail, and a wide range of activities are available at www.myspace.com.

A **mailing list** is an interest group to which users subscribe. There thousands of list groups on the Internet. One can find mailing lists for most of the academic disciplines. For example, individuals who subscribe to a psychology mailing list might share research interests with other members. Members also invite dialogue on a specific research area and pose questions that might spur debate. One can find list groups in sports, medicine, city, county and state administration, and hundreds of other areas. Communication in a mailing list occurs through e-mail. Members of some mailing lists might receive fifteen to twenty notifications daily.

## LEARNING AND TEACHING VIA THE INTERNET

### Research on the Internet

The Internet is an excellent source for researching nearly any topic. Using the Internet's powerful search engines, such as Lycos, Yahoo, Excite, Alta Vista, and others, users can find millions of pieces of information on thousands of subjects. Additionally, many college libraries can be accessed over the Internet. Books, articles, dissertations, theses, and other information can be accessed. Students can also research colleges and universities worldwide to find information on admissions, student services, costs per semester, listings of academic programs, and much more. Some colleges and universities even provide a virtual tour of the campus.

By far, one of the most comprehensive research sites on the World Wide Web is the **On Line Computer Library First Search. OCLC** allows users to research several databases, including WorldCat Books and other materials in libraries worldwide; an index of articles with text online or by e-mail; a Union List of Periodicals; Arts and Humanities; AGRICOLA (materials related to various aspects of agriculture); an index to AIDS and cancer research; applied science and technology; *Book Review* (digest of fiction and nonfiction books); *Books in Print; Dissertation Abstracts;* FactSearch (facts and statistics on topics of current interest); GEOBASE (worldwide literature on geography and geology); PapersFirst (an index of papers presented at conferences); ProCDBiz (a telephone listing of telephone numbers in the Yellow Pages across the nation); ProCDHome (a listing of residential telephones nationwide); and Worldscope (financial reports on companies worldwide and others).

## *Web Page Construction*

Web page construction has become more user-friendly over the past few years. While there are professional Web page construction companies that charge to set up and maintain Web pages for businesses, universities, and individuals, many software manufacturers have made it relatively easy for the average computer user to set up Web pages. Internet browsers, such as Netscape and Microsoft Internet Explorer, also allow users to create Web pages. The latest versions of Corel WordPerfect and Microsoft Word Suites also have Web page construction capabilities. One of the most popular page construction programs is Claris Home Page. This is a user-friendly software package that includes clip art images and templates and is so easy to use that one could build a Web page in just a few minutes. Claris also has an excellent online tutorial to navigate users from beginning to end in the construction of Web pages.

## *Distance Learning*

With the advent of the revolution in information technology, community colleges and four-year colleges and universities have begun to carry education beyond the walls of their respective campuses. **Distance learning,** or **distance education,** is an attempt by institutions to reach the traditional college-aged student, as well as an older population, without having them leave their homes. It allows these populations to earn college credits, associate, baccalaureate, and even master's degrees using the Internet, two-way television fiber optic technology, digital phone lines, and satellites.

Distance teaching and learning are also achieved by simultaneous communication between a teacher and students at several different sites, usually via satellite. Learning course material through a series of audio recordings and/or videotapes is also considered distance learning. In short, distance learning is a non-traditional way of delivering, conveying, and learning information via the Internet, the World Wide Web, the modem, satellite hookups, VHS tapes, cassette tapes, CD-ROM, and interactive multimedia courses.

## INTERNET ETHICS OR "NETIQUETTE"

The use of the Internet is a privilege, not a right, and abuse of any part could result in the revocation of access to the "Net." **Netiquette** is network etiquette, or the do's and don'ts of online communication. In many cases, there are no laws covering cyberspace, so personal responsibility and ethical behavior must rule in the absence of formal codes. Several organizations have emerged to help ensure that Internet users follow guidelines to protect the rights of all who venture into cyberspace. The National Computer Ethics and Responsibilities Campaign (NCERC) and its sponsor, the Computer Ethics Institute (CEI) have established "The Ten Commandments of Computer Ethics." (See information on Netiquette in Chapter 9).

**Ten Commandments of Computer Ethics**
1. Thou shalt not use a computer to harm other people.
2. Thou shalt not interfere with other people's computer work.
3. Thou shalt not snoop around in other people's computer files.
4. Thou shalt not use a computer to steal.
5. Thou shalt not use a computer to bear false witness.
6. Thou shalt not copy or use proprietary software for which you have not paid (or been given authority to do so).
7. Thou shalt not use other people's computer resources without authorization or proper compensation (includes using computers or telephones for personal business, or printing nonacademic materials with university-owned printers).
8. Thou shalt not appropriate other people's intellectual output.
9. Thou shalt think about the social consequences of the program you are writing or the system you are designing.
10. Thou shalt always use a computer in ways that insure consideration and respect for your fellow humans.

*(Computer Ethics Institute, June, 2006)*

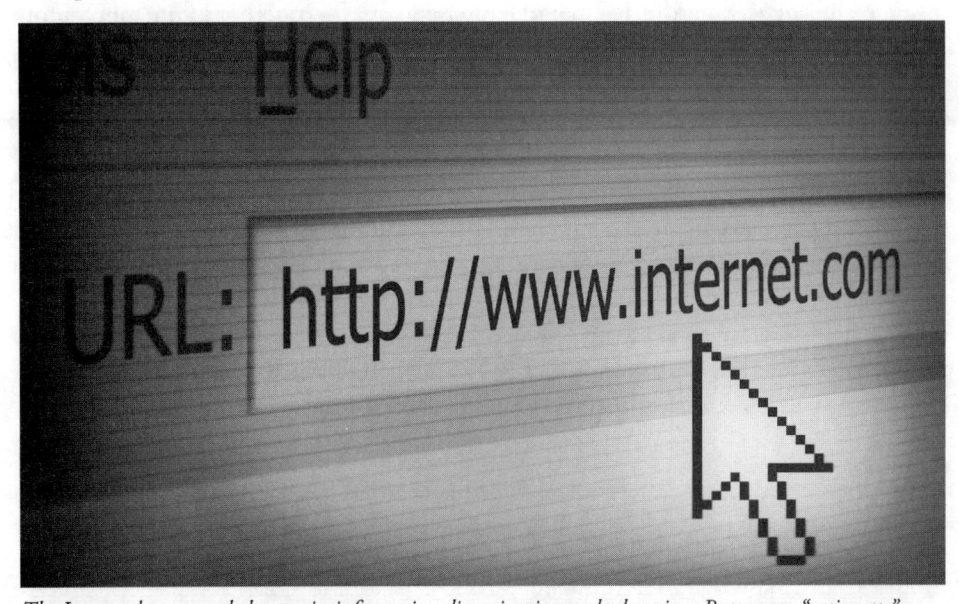

*The Internet has spurred changes in information dissemination and education. But proper "netiquette" should always be followed when communicating by computer.*

**Dimensions of Computer Technology**

## WHAT TO CONSIDER WHEN BUYING A COMPUTER

In this, the new millennium, it is likely that the personal computer will continue to be a major appliance in our lives. The computer is not a fad—an object that will fade into obscurity in a few years. Though prices for computers and computer peripherals continue to fall, for most people a computer purchase represents a sizeable investment. The most important questions one should ask before purchasing a computer are, "What is the purpose of buying a machine?" and "What am I going to do with it?" These questions will dictate whether or not an individual invests a small amount or large amount of money.

If the computer will be used primarily for word processing, the question is, "Do I need to buy a 2.33ghz machine, or should I settle for something much less?" One should also consider **expandability** and **upgradeability**. Expandability refers to the computer's ability to accept add-on features, like a scanner, television, or FM card. There should be a sufficient number (usually up to eight) of expansion slots on the back of the computer. Upgradeability refers to the unit's ability to accept another motherboard, CD-ROM drive, tape backup drive, or other devices. Make sure that the computer case has three to four bays on the front and that there are at least seven expansion slots on the rear of the machine.

There is also the issue of **proprietary** versus **non-proprietary** computers. A proprietary unit is one manufactured by the major computer companies, such as International Business Machines (IBM), Dell, and Hewlett Packard. These machines have components, in many cases, that are integrated into the motherboard. If any one device goes bad, that integrated component has to be replaced. Replacement could be costly. Additionally, a proprietary unit leaves little room for expansion and upgrade because it may be an "all-in-one" integrated machine.

A non-proprietary unit, on the other hand, is a custom-made machine put together by independent computer dealers. The customer can select the components that make up the entire machine, including choice of case (desktop, mini-tower, mid-tower, or full-tower), hard drive manufacturer and size, motherboard, memory, multimedia system, and more. The machine is more tailored to the needs of the user.

One should also keep in mind that computer and software technologies are advancing at an accelerated rate, and what is considered "cutting-edge" today may be "old" in six months to a year. It doesn't mean that the machine is obsolete. It is virtually impossible to keep up with the rapid advancements in computer technology. If the Internet is where you want to go and if Windows XP is your preferred operating system, then you are safe purchasing a computer with an upgradeable motherboard that will accommodate a 2.7ghz CPU and a case that has several bays and expansion slots. A 150-200 gigabyte hard drive, wireless internet or a network adapter, a 16X-24X CD-ROM/DVD multimedia kit, and at least 1 gigabyte of RAM are more than enough computing power for today's average user.

## GLOSSARY

**Address:** a way of identifying any location in the memory of the computer.
**Application Program:** software designed for a specific purpose (such as inventory, mailing list, etc.).

**ASCII:** the American Standard Code for Information Interchange. The most generally used format for representing and exchanging textual information among computers.

**Autoexec.bat File:** a file that is located by the operating system when you turn on a PC-compatible computer and that commands the operating system to perform specific tasks, such as loading other programs automatically.

**Basic:** a numbering system that uses only 1's and 0's which is used by computers to store information.

**Break:** an interruption of a transmission. The BREAK key tells the computer to stop what it's doing and wait for further instructions.

**Buffer:** an area in the computer's memory used to temporarily store information.

**Byte:** a sequence of eight bits that represent a single character.

**CAI:** Computer-Aided Instruction, which involves a two-way "conversation" between the student and the computer.

**Cache:** a separate area of RAM that stores frequently used instructions or data so the CPU can use them more quickly than if they were stored on a disk or in another area of the memory.

**Character:** a single letter, number, or other symbol represented by one byte (8 bits).

**Chip:** a generic term for an integrated circuit, a single package holding hundreds or thousands of microscopic electronic components.

**Computer Network:** two or more connected computers that have the ability to exchange information.

**Computer Program:** a series of commands, instructions, or statements put together in a way that tells a computer to do a specific thing or series of things.

**Cursor:** a position indicator on a CRT, usually a flashing rectangle.

**Debug:** to go through a program to remove mistakes.

**Display:** a method of representing information in visible form. The most common forms for micros are the CRT's and printed page.

**Documentation:** (1) the instruction manual for a piece of hardware or software; (2) the process for gathering information while writing a computer program so that others using the program are able to see what was done.

**Downtime:** any period of time when the computer is not available or not working.

**Dump:** to copy all information available from one form of storage to another.

**Edit:** to modify or add data to an existing document or program.

**Electronic Mail (e-mail):** a network communications program that allows users to send and receive messages.

**Execute:** to carry out an instruction or series of instructions.

**Expansion Slot:** a special connector inside the computer where you can plug in a circuit board to expand your computer's capabilities.

**Extended Memory:** memory above 640K that is used by the software.

**Fax Modem:** a communication device that allows a computer to exchange information with a fax machine via a telephone line.

**Garbage:** meaningless information.

**Graphics:** pictorial information in two dimensions.

**Hard Copy:** a printout of information produced by the computer.

**Hardware:** the physical part of the computer (such as the CRT, CPU, memory).

**High Level Language:** a method of programming that allows a person to give instructions to a computer in a form using letters, symbols, or English-like text rather than in the 1's and 0's that the computer understands.

**Impact Printer:** a printer that produces hard copy by physically striking a ribbon and paper.

**Input/Output (I/O) Port:** a plug where you connect a monitor, keyboard, modem, and other components to the system unit.

**Interactive:** describes a computer system where two conversations go on between the user and the computer.

**Interface:** a piece of hardware or software used to connect two devices that cannot be hooked together directly.

**Internet:** a worldwide network that links thousands of individual computer networks at universities, corporations, and government agencies, enabling the exchange of data and electronic mail among users of those networks.

**K:** symbol for 1000, but in computer language, 1024 bytes of memory since information is stored in multiples of 8 bits (1 byte).

**Laptop Computer:** a portable computer whose components all fit into a box about the size of a three-ring binder.

**Load:** to put data and/or programs into a computer.

**Log In:** (Noun) the account name used to gain access to a computer system not a secret as with a password. (Verb) the act of entering a computer system.

**Location:** a single, specific place within computer memory where a piece of data is stored.

**Machine-Language:** the "native language" of the computer.

**Memory:** circuitry and devices that hold the binary 1's and 0's the computer can access.

**Megahertz:** (abbreviated as MHZ) millions of electrical cycles (hertz) per second. Computer microprocessor speeds are measured in megahertz.

**Menu:** a named list of commands by which you control a program or graphical user interface. You display a menu by selecting the menu name, then choose a command by selecting its name from the menu.

**Microprocessor:** the central processing unit of a computer that holds all the elements for manipulating data and performing arithmetic calculations.

**Modem:** an electronic device that allows computer equipment to send and receive information through telephone lines.

**Network:** an interconnected system of computers and/or terminals.

**Operating System:** software that oversees the overall operation of a computer system (like MSDOS).

**Peripherals:** hardware that is external to the computer itself, such as printers, cassette-tape recorders.

**Printer:** an output device that produces a hard copy.

**Printout:** hard copy produced by a printer.

**Program:** (1) a set of instructions that tells a computer to do something; (2) to prepare the set of instructions.

**RAM (Random-Access Memory):** The main type of memory used in a microcomputer. Also known as read/write memory because data can be easily changed.

**ROM (Read-Only Memory):** Memory where information is permanently stored and cannot be altered.

**Software:** programs or segments of programs.

**Spreadsheet:** an electronic calculating tool used for financial planning, budgeting, and record keeping.

**Status Bar:** an area at the bottom of a document window that shows the current page number, cursor location, and other information about the document.

**Surge Protector:** a special power adapter that protects a computer and its components that is usually installed and replaced as a unit.

**System:** an organized collection of hardware and software that works together.
**Telecommunication:** transmission of data between two computers and a terminal in a different location; done with phone lines, satellites, radio waves, etc.
**Terminal:** a piece of equipment with a keyboard for input and an output device such as CRT or a printer used to communicate with the computer.
**Timesharing:** a process whereby the facilities of a single computer are shared by a number of users.
**User Name:** the name by which someone is identified on a computer network or online computer service.
**Virus:** a program that performs destructive or annoying actions on a computer, such as erasing or renaming files at random, and that copies itself from one disk to another.
**Window:** a graphical box on the screen that displays a document.
**Word Processor:** the entry, manipulation editing, and storage of text used in a computer.
**WWW (World Wide Web):** the whole constellation of resources that can be accessed using a variety of tools. WWW also refers to the universe of hypertext servers, which are the servers that allow text, graphics, sound files, etc., to be linked together.

## BASIC COMPUTER TERMINOLOGY

**access time**–the performance of a hard drive or other storage device–how long it takes to locate a file.
**active program or window**–the application or window at the front (foreground) on the monitor.
**alert (alert box)**–a message that appears on screen, usually to tell you something went wrong.
**alias**–an icon that points to a file, folder or application (System 7).
**apple menu**–on the left side of the screen header. System 6 = desk accessories System 7 = up to 50 items.
**application**–a program in which you do your work.
**application menu**–on the right side of the screen header. Lists running applications.
**ASCII (pronounced ask-key )**–American Standard Code for Information Interchange–a commonly used data format for exchanging information between computers or programs.
**background**–part of the multitasking capability. A program can run and perform tasks in the background while another program is being used in the foreground.
**backup**–a copy of a file or disk you make for archiving purposes.
**bit**–the smallest piece of information used by the computer. Derived from "binary digit." In computer language, either a one (1) or a zero (0).
**boot**–to start up a computer.
**bug**–a programming error that causes a program to behave in an unexpected way.
**bus**–an electronic pathway through which data is transmitted between components in a computer.
**byte**–a piece of computer information made up of eight bits.
**card**–a printed circuit board that adds some feature to a computer.
**cartridge drive**–a storage device, like a hard drive, in which the medium is a cartridge that can be removed.
**CD-ROM**–an acronym for Compact Disc Read-Only Memory.

Dimensions of Computer Technology

**chooser**–a desk accessory used to select a printer, or other external device, or to log on to a network.

**clipboard**–a portion of memory where the Mac temporarily stores information. Called a Copy Buffer in many PC applications because it is used to hold information which is to be moved, as in word processing where text is "cut" and then "pasted."

**clock rate (MHz)**–the instruction processing speed of a computer measured in millions of cycles per second (i.e., 200 MHz).

**command**–the act of giving an instruction to your Mac either by menu choice or keystroke.

**command (apple) key**–a modifier key, the Command key used in conjunction with another keystroke to active some functions on the Mac.

**compiler**–a program the converts programming code into a form that can be used by a computer.

**compression**–a technique that reduces the size of a saved file by elimination or encoding redundancies (i.e., JPEG, MPEG, LZW, etc.)

**control key**–seldom used modifier key on the Mac.

**control panel**–a program that allows you to change settings in a program or change the way a Mac looks and/or behaves.

**CPU**–the Central Processing Unit. The processing chip that is the "brains" of a computer.

**crash**–a system malfunction in which the computer stops working and has to be restarted.

**cursor**–the pointer, usually an arrow or cross shape, which is controlled by the mouse.

**daisy chaining**–the act of stringing devices together in a series (such as SCSI).

**database**–an electronic list of information that can be sorted and/or searched.

**data**–(the plural of *datum*) information processed by a computer.

**defragment**–(also -optimize) to concatenate fragments of data into contiguous blocks in memory or on a hard drive.

**desktop**–(1) the finder. (2) the shaded or colored backdrop of the screen.

**desktop file**–an invisible file in which the Finder stores a database of information about files and icons.

**dialog box**–an on-screen message box that appears when the Mac requires additional information before completing a command.

**digitize**–to convert linear, or analog, data into digital data that can be used by the computer.

**disk**–a spinning platter made of magnetic or optically etched material on which data can be stored.

**disk drive**–the machinery that writes the data from a disk and/or writes data to a disk.

**disk window**–the window that displays the contents or directory of a disk.

**document**–a file you create, as opposed to the application that created it.

**DOS**–acronym for Disk Operating System–used in IBM PCs.

**DPI**–acronym for Dots Per Inch -a gauge of visual clarity on the printed page or on the computer screen.

**download**–to transfer data from one computer to another. (If you are on the receiving end, you are downloading. If you are on the sending end, you are uploading.)

**drag**–to move the mouse while its button is being depressed.

**drag and drop**–a feature on the Mac that allows one to drag the icon for a document on top of the icon for an application, thereby launching the application and opening the document.

**driver**–a file on a computer that tells it how to communicate with an add-on piece of equipment (like a printer).

**Ethernet**–a protocol for fast communication and file transfer across a network.

**expansion slot**–a connector inside the computer which allows one to plug in a printed circuit board that provides new or enhanced features.

**extension**–a startup program that runs when you start the Mac and then enhances its function.

**fibre channel**–as applied to data storage and network topology -link to FC Glossary.

**file**–the generic word for an application, document, control panel, or other computer data.

**finder**–the cornerstone or home-base application in the Mac environment. The finder regulates the file management functions of the Mac (copying, renaming, deleting, etc.)

**floppy**–a 3.5 inch square, rigid disk that holds dat. (so named for the earlier 5.25- and 8-inch disks that were flexible).

**folder**–an electronic subdirectory that contains files.

**font**–a typeface that contains the characters of an alphabet or some other letterforms.

**footprint**–The surface area of a desk or table that is occupied by a piece of equipment.

**fragmentation**–The breaking up of a file into many separate locations in memory or on a disk.

**freeze**–a system error that causes the cursor to lock in place.

**get info**–a Finder File menu command that presents an information window for a selected file icon.

**gig**–a gigabyte = 1024 megabytes.

**hard drive**–a large-capacity storage device made of multiple disks housed in a rigid case.

**head crash**–a hard disk crash caused by the heads coming in contact with the spinning disk(s).

**high density disk**–a 1.4 MB floppy disk.

**highlight**–to select by clicking once on an icon or by highlighting text in a document.

**icon**–a graphic symbol for an application, file, or folder.

**initialize**–to format a disk for use in the computer; creates a new directory and arranges the tracks for the recording of data.

**insertion point**–in word processing, the short flashing marker that indicates where your next typing will begin.

**installer**–software used to install a program on your hard drive.

**interrupt button**–a tool used by programmers to enter the debugging mode. The button is usually next to the reset button.

**K**–short for kilobyte.

**keyboard shortcut**–a combination of keystrokes that performs some function otherwise found in a pulldown menu.

**kilobyte**–1024 bytes.

**landscape**–in printing from a computer, to print sideways on the page.

**launch**–start an application.

**Measurennents** (summary)

   *a bit = one binary digit (1 or 0) * "bit" is derived from the contraction b'it (binary digit)

   \> 8 bits = one byte

   *1024 bytes = one kilobyte

   *K = kilobyte

**Dimensions of Computer Technology**

*Kb = kilobit
*MB = megabyte
*Mb = megabit
*MB/s = megabytes per second
*Mb/s = megabits per second
*bbp = bits per second
i.e., 155 Mb/s = 19.38 MB/s

**MB**–short for megabyte.
**megabyte**–1024 kilobytes.
**memory**–the temporary holding area where data is stored while it is being used or changed; the amount of RAM a computer has installed.
**menu**–a list of program commands listed by topic.
**menu bar**–the horizontal bar across the top of the Mac's screen that lists the menus.
**multi-finder**–a component of System 6 that allows the Mac to multi-task.
**multi-tasking**–running more than one application in memory at the same time.
**nanosecond**–one billionth of a second (or, the time between the theatrical release of a Dudley Moore film and the moment it begins to play on airplanes ).
**native mode**–using the computer's original operating system; most commonly used when talking about the PowerPC can run software written for either the 80x0 systems, or the Power PC's RISC code.
**NuBus**–expansion slots on the Mac that accept intelligent, self-configuring boards. NuBus is a different bus architecture than the newer PCI bus, and the boards are not interchangable.
**operating system**–the system software that controls the computer.
**optical disk**–a high-capacity storage medium that is read by a laser light.
**palette**–a small, floating window that contains tools used in a given application.
**partition**–a subdivision of a hard drive's surface that is defined and used as a separate drive.
**paste**–to insert text, or other material, from the clipboard or copy buffer.
**PC**–acronym for personal computer, commonly used to refer to an IBM or IBM clone computer that uses DOS.
**PCI**–acronym for Peripheral Component Interchange -the newer, faster bus architecture.
**peripheral**–an add-on component to your computer.
**point**–(1/72") 12 points = one pica in printing.
**pop-up menu**–any menu that does not appear at the top of the screen in the menu bar (may pop up or down.)
**port**–a connection socket, or jack, on the Mac.
**Power PC**–a processing chip designed by Apple, IBM, and Motorola (RISC-based).
**Power Mac**–a family of Macs built around the PowerPC chip.
**print spooler**–a program that stores documents to be printed on the hard drive, thereby freeing the memory up and allowing other functions to be performed while printing goes on in the background.
**QuickTime**–the Apple system extension that gives one the ability to compress, edit, and play animation, movies, and sound on the Mac.
**RAM**–acronym for Random-Access Memory.
**reset switch**–a switch on the Mac that restarts the computer in the event of a crash or freeze.
**resize box**–the small square at the lower right comer of a window which, when dragged, resizes the window.

**RISC**–acronym for Reduced Instruction Set Computing–the smaller set of commands used by the PowerPC and Power Mac.
**ROM**–acronym for Read Only Memory–memory that can only be read from but not written to.
**root directory**–the main hard drive window.
**save**–to write a file onto a disk.
**save as**–(a File menu item) to save a previously saved file in a new location and/or with a new name.
**scroll**–to shift the contents of a window to bring hidden items into view.
**scroll bar**–a bar at the bottom or right side of a window that contains the scroll box and allows scrolling.
**scroll box**–the box in a scroll bar that is used to navigate through a window.
**SCSI**–acronym for Small Computer System Interface.
**SCSI address**–a number between zero and seven that must be unique to each device in an SCSI chain. Fast and Wide SCSI devices will allow up to 15 SCSI Ids (hexidecimal); however, the length restriction (3 meters) is such that it is virtually impossible to link 15 devices together.
**SCSI port**–a 25-pin connector on the back of a Mac (native SCSI port); used to connect SCSI devices to the CPU. Some SCSI cards (like the ATTO) have a 68 pin connector.
**SCSI terminator**–a device placed at the end of an SCSI chain to complete the circuit (some SCSI devices are self-terminating, or have active termination and do not require this plug).
**serial port**–a port that allows data to be transmitted in a series (one after the other), such as the printer and modem ports on a Mac.
**server**–a central computer dedicated to sending and receiving data from other computers (on a network).
**shut down**–the command from the Special menu that shuts down the Mac safely.
**software**–files on disk that contain instructions for a computer.
**spreadsheet**–a program designed to look like an electronic ledger.
**start up disk**–the disk containing system software and is designated to be used to start the computer.
**surge suppressor**–a power strip that has circuits designed to reduce the effects of surge in electrical power (not the same as a UPS)
**System file**–a file in the System folder that allows your Mac to start and run.
**System folder**–an all-important folder that contains at least the System file and the Finder.
**32 bit addressing**–a feature that allows the Mac to recognize and use more than 8MB of memory.
**title bar**–the horizontal bar at the top of a window that has the name of the file or folder it represents.
**upload**–to send a file from one computer to another through a network.
**Uninterruptible Power Source (UPS)**–a constantly charging battery pack that powers the computer. A UPS should have enough charge to power your computer for several minutes in the event of a total power failure, giving you time to save your work and safely shut down.
**UPS**–acronym for Uninterruptible Power Source.
**vaporware**–"software" advertised, and sometimes sold, that does not yet exist in a releasable form.

**virtual memory**–using part of your hard drive as though it were "RAM."
**WORM**–acronym for Write Once-Read Many; an optical disk that can only be written to once (like a CD-ROM).
**zoom box**–a small square in the upper right corner of a window which, when clicked, will expand the window to fill the whole screen.

## REFERENCES

Beekman, G. & Quinn, M. (2007).Tomorrow's technology and you. New Jersey: Prentice Hall.

Grabe, M. & Grabe, C. (2006). (5th Ed.) Integrating technology for meaningful learning. New York: Houghton Mifflin.

Pitler, H., Hubbell, E. R., & Kuhn, M. (2007). Using technology with classroom instruction that works.

Roblyer, M. (2005). Integrating educational technology into teaching. (4th ed.). New Jersey: Prentice Hall.

Stamatellos, G. (2007). Computer Ethics: A global perspective. New York: Jones & Bartlett.

## ACTIVITY 1

**Directions:** Complete the following tasks and respond to the statements below. Obtain an e-mail address from the computer center and give the address to your instructor. Then explore the process by sending mail to others.

1. What steps did you take to obtain the e-mail address?

2. Explain why you think that you were cautioned to secure your e-mail password and account number.

3. How did you feel sending mail over the information highway versus using an envelope and a stamp?

4. How secure is the Internet for sending and receiving personal/confidential mail?

5. What specific concerns or difficulties are you experiencing in using the e-mail procedures?

## ACTIVITY 2

**Directions:** Use the electronic mail to retrieve an assignment from the instructor. Send the completed assignment back to the instructor.

1. What steps did you take in retrieving the assignment?

2. What steps did you take to return the completed assignment?

3. Did you like this process better that turning in a paper-and-pencil test? Why or why not?

4. List three advantages and three disadvantages to using electronic mail.

_____

_____

_____

Dimensions of Computer Technology

## ACTIVITY 3

Many campus libraries have inter-library loan privileges, often referred to as the Inter Library Network. Obtain a library network card from the library. Then attend a session on how to use the Library Network. Use the On-line Computer Library First Search (OCLC) to research a topic. Identify one current source for each of the following: journal, article, book, website. Illustrate below how to document three different websites on the Internet.

1. _____

2. _____

3. _____

## ACTIVITY 4

**Directions:** Access the university's web page. Print out the requirements for your chosen major or the major you are considering. Remember that the requirements extend beyond the list of courses. Also review the requirements of a major in a related area. Now review the information carefully and answer the following questions.

1. What are the possibilities of a second major, minor, or concentration?

2. Did you learn of majors that you had not considered? If so, explain.

3. If your major was undeclared when you stated this process, do you now have some thoughts on the matter?

4. What are the career options in the alternative major?

5. What are the career options in your major?

# ACTIVITY 5

**Directions:** Use the Internet to obtain information about the university's Chancellor or President. Write a brief description about his or her professional contributions. Where did he/she attend school? Major achievements? Have you met the Chancellor or President? Too busy? Maybe send him/her an e-mail.

_____

_____

_____

_____

_____

_____

_____

_____

_____

_____

_____

_____

_____

_____

_____

_____

_____

# ACTIVITY 6

**Directions:** Visit the distance learning lab and view a demonstration of how distance learning works. Write a brief essay on your views about distance learning as a major learning resource. Include advantages and disadvantages. Do you think distance education would work for this class? Why or why not?

_____
_____
_____
_____
_____
_____
_____
_____
_____
_____
_____
_____
_____
_____
_____
_____
_____
_____

# CHAPTER *seven*

# Dimensions of Research

"*Everywhere our knowledge is incomplete and problems are waiting to be solved. We address the void in our knowledge and those unresolved problems by asking relevant questions and seeking answers to them. The role of research is to provide a method for obtaining those answers by inquiringly studying the facts, within the parameters of the scientific method*" (Leedy, 2004 et al., p. 3).

## INTRODUCTION

This chapter is designed to guide you through the research process, from selecting the problem to be studied, to writing the results of the study. You will be provided with activities and assignments that will assist you in successfully completing a mini research project. Remember that your ultimate goals are 1) to gain a basic understanding of practical research techniques and 2) to learn how to effectively use the general tools of research.

*Research is purposeful investigation that involves the study of relationships, variables, facts, and principles that often lead to more questions.*

A glossary of terms has been provided at the end of the chapter. Refer to the glossary as new **concepts** are introduced. These concepts should become a vital part of your vocabulary as you execute a professional research study. In addition to the glossary, references have been identified that will help you to better understand the nature of the research process.

It would be most beneficial to use the following techniques in working through this chapter:
- Step 1: Scan the entire chapter by examining topics and sub-topics to get an overview of the content.
- Step 2: Read thoroughly each dimension of research. Define all new terms and concepts and read for understanding.
- Step 3: Recite or discuss what you have read with your instructor and others.
- Step 4: Complete all of the activities and assignments.
- Step 5: Review what you have read as you think of related examples.

## OBJECTIVES

The objectives for this chapter are to
1. help students understand the nature and process of effective research;

2. help students understand and use both quantitative and qualitative research tools;
3. equip students with new skills and methods, sharpening their analytical powers and heightening self-awareness;
4. enable students to find resolutions for problems using more analytical and scientific methods;
5. motivate students to utilize critical-thinking skills in solving problems through effective research.

## KEY TERMS

| Research | Variables | Quantitative methods |
| Reliability | Validity | Scientific method |
| Data | Construct | Data analysis |
| Hypothesis | Concept | Qualitative methods |

## *Definition of Research*

The term **research** has been loosely used to describe a variety of tasks that do not always represent an accurate description of the research process. These activities may be referred to as library skills, the gathering of information, or even documenting information and events, but they are not descriptive of basic research or pure research in its truest form. Research, then, is not merely the search for, or discovery of, information or the transferring of facts from one situation to another.

Research is entirely different from the above tasks. There are many definitions of research. According to Gerring (2008) research is defined as an investigation that is purposeful. Other popular definitions relevant to this discussion include the following:

Research consists of the systematic study of the relationship of **variables** (Gay, 2008);

Research is a scientific study that can be systematically controlled, is **empirical**, and involves a critical investigation of hypothetical propositions about relationships among natural phenomena (Johnson, 2007).

Research is diligent inquiry or examination; a process of seeking facts or principles; an experimental investigation (Webster, 2008).

Leedy, et al. (2004) defined research as, "a procedure by which an attempt is made to systematically find, and support, with demonstrable fact, the answer to a question or the resolution of a problem." From these definitions, we can say that research is the process of generating knowledge and insight through the careful and systematic application of research tools and processes. Often, the end result of research is not an **absolute answer**, but one or more plausible explanations for phenomena we observe. Research may even lead to **more questions** rather than more answers. So, how do we do research?

# THE RESEARCH PROCESS

Research may be conducted using either a quantitative approach in which empirical studies are done to determine the meaning of data in the form of numbers or a qualitative approach focused on the narrative stories or insights of research respondents. Quantitative researchers have been viewed as "number crunchers." The focus of this chapter will be quantitative in nature; however, another approach that has been growing in popularity over the last 20 years or so has been qualitative research, also known as ethnographic studies or interpretive inquiry. This is an approach to research that provides an in-depth understanding of phenomena, events, and experiences from the perspective of those being studied. The constraints of the scientific method are not a factor here, although there are procedures and processes to be followed. The researcher, through this approach, often seeks to identify and analyze rich, complex themes surrounding events and experiences. Researchers using this approach had been referred to as "storytellers." Examples of qualitative research include **phenomenology**, **hermeneutics**, **ethnography**, **grounded research**, and some forms of **action research** and **participatory action research**. The richest results have often been based on the combining of quantitative and qualitative procedures through a process called **triangulation** (Johnson, 2007).

*Research is orderly, systematic, based on a theoretical framework, and replicable, cyclical, and performed in six stages.*

Based on these definitions, one may conclude that research is orderly, systematic, based on a theoretical framework, and replicable. Leedy et al. further described the research process as cyclical and as inclusive of distinct characteristics outlined in the following six stages (Figure 1). First, research begins with a problem to be investigated. This is an unanswered question in the mind of the researcher and is the focus of inquiry. Secondly, a clear statement of the problem describes the goal of the research study. This problem often gives rise to a **research question** that will guide the study. Thirdly, the research subdivides the problem into sub-problems that outline a specific plan or procedure. In the fourth stage, the tentative solutions to the problem or **hypotheses** are described to further direct the researcher in the process. Hypotheses are reasonable guesses about the occurring event(s) or facts and possible relationships between or among these events or facts. Facts are collected and organized in the fifth stage. The final stage is the interpretation of the facts that lead to either a resolution of the problem, particularly in the natural or physical sciences or compelling explanations or discoveries in the social sciences. The researcher, based on the research process, then confirms or rejects the hypotheses.

Having reviewed the process and the findings, the researcher may consider alternative solutions to the problem, and the process starts over again. In research, all six stages are employed each time the process is used. Therefore, the process could be viewed as a spiral effect in which the results of the initial research could actually create more problems than they resolve, leaving the researcher to replicate the study many times over. Thus, research begets research.

## *Characteristics of a Researcher*

Given the steps required in the research process, what characteristics must the researcher possess? The researcher must be
- diligent,
- open-minded, creative, and innovative,
- objective,
- willing to discover the truth,
- compelled to satisfy his/her curiosity,
- faithful, courageous, humble, and self-directed,
- persistent,
- exact in observation,
- systematic in recording evidence and collecting data,
- free of preconceived notions,
- free of personal biases, and
- one who finds pleasure in self expression and in making a discovery beneficial to others.

Above all, a researcher must realize his or her ethical responsibility to follow the scientific method without tampering with the appropriate process or the results. What other characteristics do you think may be important for a researcher to possess?

One may ask the question, "Why is all of this so important? Do we not already know everything that we need to know about why things happen? Why must the researcher possess so many of these qualities?"

It is critical to our very existence that we continuously research phenomena, problems, and issues. Scientists and researchers do not know all that there is to know to enhance our quality of life. Thus, research will always play a major role in our lives. The major purposes of research are to
1) develop new knowledge;
2) expand existing information;
3) validate past information;
4) help us find answers to our problems;
5) help us interpret ideas, facts, etc.; and
6) better understand issues or determine new uses for existing or new goods and services.

It is, therefore, imperative that researchers are reliable, dependable, and trustworthy in both processes and procedures in order to draw meaningful conclusions from the data analysis.

## *Sources of Knowledge*

Knowledge about problems, phenomena, and issues that are used to develop theories and hypotheses are derived from a variety of different sources. Knowledge is gained from **experience** and the observations made from repetitious behavior. Information is also gained by studying **history**. The past is prologue to the future. People in

**authority** often provide expertise in a wide variety of areas. Such a group might be **The Internal Review Board (IRB)** or **Committee** at an institution or agency. This board is designed to review the validity and practically of the research plan. This committee often does not need to be consulted unless human subjects are involved. Some educational and research institutions require that research regarding animals be reviewed by the IRB committee as well.

**Deductive reasoning** (start with general knowledge and predict a specific observation) and **inductive reasoning** (from particular experiences to general truths) either assist in setting the premise on which research is based or provide a set of generalizations from which conclusions may be drawn. Try to recall the detailed discussion on inductive and deductive reasoning in the chapter on critical thinking.

The scientific approach, often referred to as the **scientific method**, is a combination of the inductive and deductive methods. This approach was developed by Charles Darwin in his quest to develop his theory of evolution. Darwin found that inductive reasoning alone led to isolated bits of knowledge that did not explain all of the facts.

According to Ary, Jacobs, and Razavieh (2005), the mixing or interweaving of the inductive and deductive processes formalizes the scientific method and consists of five steps:
- Step 1: Defining the problem.
- Step 2: Hypothesizing as to the cause of the problem.
- Step 3: Deductive reasoning.
- Step 4: Collection and analysis of data.
- Step 5: Confirmation or rejection of hypothesis.

There are, however, limitations of the scientific approach. Subject matter in the social sciences is often very complex, and it is often difficult to collect data using traditional methods. It is sometimes difficult to observe human beings in a variety of natural settings or to simulate the natural setting. Although research should be replicable, it is sometimes quite challenging to repeat a study following the same procedures. This is particularly true in duplicating studies in which the researcher is attempting to measure or analyze the emotions and feelings of human subjects.

Despite the difficulties in using the scientific method, the advantages to its use significantly outweigh the limitations.

List three advantages of using the scientific method.

1. _____

2. _____

3. _____

As we continue in our discussion of the various steps, you will actually work through a mini research problem. After each step or dimension of the research process, you will be presented with sample items to work through, followed by an opportunity to complete that step of your own research project.

Your instructor may require individual or small-group projects. As a member of a research team, it is important to complete your assigned task as quickly and as efficiently as possible so that the group will obtain a resolution to the problem under study.

Take a moment to consider three possible areas or topics that you may want to research. While keeping in mind that the project should be manageable within the specified timeframe, select a topic that is of interest to you. Consider these topics as we discuss the development of the research problem.

### *Selecting the Research Problem*

There are basically two types of questions asked in educational research: theoretical and practical. The theoretical questions are very fundamental and focus on issues of how, why, or when. These types of questions are oriented toward developing theories or expanding knowledge for knowledge sake. Practical questions are applied and are designed to solve specific problems. For example, the application of a question may be to determine the effectiveness of something or the effect of one **variable** on another.

One must, however, examine practical questions in relation to actual problems and under the conditions in which they are found. An example of this approach would be to study the impact of stress stemming from the terminal illness of a family member on families that are actually experiencing this situation.

**Statement of the problem, problem statement, or purpose of the study** are all the same: a clear statement of what the researcher wants to do. It is important to remember that research is the process of testing, rather than proving. Thus the problem statement should imply objectivity. Leedy (2004) and Ary, et al., (2005) both stated that if there is no statement of the problem, there is no research. One must ask the question, "Is the problem researchable?" But how does one determine whether the problem statement is sound and researchable?

*Good research begins with a clear problem statement that defines the researcher's purpose and the problem to be determined or solved.*

There are specific characteristics of well-developed research problems. According to Leedy (2004) and Ary, et al. (2005), a good statement of the problem has the following characteristics:
1. Problem statements must state exactly the researcher's purpose and the problem to be determined or solved. It is not necessary to attempt to address all of the issues related to a topic at one time. The researcher is much like the ant bringing his grain of sand to the ant hill: small contributions of significant information contribute greatly to a definitive body of knowledge. A research question may guide the study.
2. Statements are written in the past tense.
3. Scope of the study is restricted to a specific question.
4. Philosophical issues and value judgments are avoided.
5. Problems should be written so well that anyone, anywhere, should be able to read and react to them without the benefit of your presence.
6. Problems are stated in grammatically correct sentences.
7. Yes or no questions are not researchable.
8. Comparison problems are not researchable.

In addition to characteristics, there are questions that must be answered in the affirmative in order to consider the research problem appropriate.
1. Is the problem significant? Would the solution to the problem make a difference in theory or practice? Is the answer to the problem already available?
2. Is the research on the problem feasible? Does the researcher possess the necessary skill to carry out the study?
3. Will the researcher have the necessary resources (time, money, physical support) to carry out the study?
4. Are pertinent data accessible?

## *Identifying Variables*

The discussion of the statement of the problem would not be complete without identifying the variables under study. A variable expresses a **concept** or **construct** and may take on different values (i.e., height, social class, gender, age, etc.). Your study will be primarily concerned with how variables relate to one another.

There are different types of variables. **Categorical (group) variables** include items such as occupations, languages, and religions. **Dichotomous variables** have only two classes and include items such as male/female and pass/fail. **Continuous** variables are infinite, such as the case with scores, age, height, and weight. **Dependent** variables are a consequence of, or are dependent upon, antecedent variables. The dependent variable is usually the phenomenon under study or investigation; what is being measured or examined. Independent variables are antecedent to the dependent variable. The independent variable is measurably separate and distinct from the dependent variable but may relate to the dependent variable. Examples of the independent variable may include personal characteristics, such as age, gender, race, or intelligence.

Variables may be directly manipulated by the researcher, as in testing procedures, teaching methods, or grading. Variables may also be attributes that cannot be manipulated, as in the case of age, gender, race, or grade level. In some instances, it is difficult to tell which is which. This kind of situation is not suitable for experimentation but is more suitable for **correlational studies**.

The following examples illustrate the use of independent (underlined) and **dependent variables** (bold).
1. The effect of computer-based drill on **math achievement**.

2. The effect of testing procedures, classroom grouping, and grading on **motivation**.

3. The effects of social class, age, gender, and uniform worn on **job performance**.

4. There is no significant difference in the **marital attitudes** of adolescents from divorced families and those from intact families.

## FORMULATING THE HYPOTHESES

The next step in the research process is to formulate hypotheses for the study. A hypothesis is a tentative answer to the problem or question under study. Ary, et al., (2005) offers characteristics of usable hypotheses that must be met prior to empirical testing.

Hypotheses must
- have explanatory power. The explanation offered by the hypothesis should be a possible explanation.
- state the expected relationship between variables. The relation between the variables should be plausible and not completely out of the ordinary. Thus, the tentative explanation should be consistent with known facts and theories.
- be testable. The variables must be clearly defined and capable of being measured. The hypothesis should be stated in such a way that it can be tested and found to be probably true or probably false.
- be stated in the simplest form.
- avoid value statements and judgments.

### *Types of Hypotheses*

Research hypotheses state what the researcher expects to find and may be directional or non-directional. Directional hypotheses tell whether the expected findings will be in a positive or negative direction, as in the following example: "There will be a 50% increase in the students' scores on the math final exam." Non-directional hypotheses do not indicate whether the findings will be positive or negative as in the following example: "There will be no difference in students' performance on the math final exam." Although research hypotheses cannot be statistically tested, they are very important in that they often help researchers formulate the research methodology.

Another type of tentative explanation for an occurrence or event is the null hypothesis. The null hypothesis is a totally objective statement that does not indicate what the researcher expects to find, but does state that there is "no relationship" or "no difference" in the two (or more) variables under study.

An example of the null hypothesis is, "There is no significant difference in the students' performance on the math final exam."

The null hypothesis is particularly useful when the researcher wishes to determine the probability or chance of getting similar results or findings if the study was repeated. Another use to denote a null hypothesis is "no effect."

Not all research projects require hypotheses. Such studies should have clearly stated objectives of the study. These objectives provide direction to the study, as do the hypotheses. While hypotheses are not always used in research studies, in general, any research activity has a stronger impact when hypotheses are used. Refer to earlier information presented on the research question.

## *Inductive and Deductive Hypotheses*

Inductive hypotheses are based on the concept of inductive reasoning. This statement means that generalizations are made based on observed relationships. For example, the teacher observes various acts and determines that the student has a behavior disorder. The thought process moves from specifics acts to a conclusion or generalization of the behavior. However, deductive reasoning, the basis for deductive hypotheses, is structured in the reverse, starting with a generalization and then stating specifics. For example, all students have good study skills. Thus, Cathy has good study skills. Sheila has good study skills. Harold has good study skills.

## *Reviewing the Literature*

A major component of the research design is the review of related literature. This review is an attempt to examine what is already known about the subject, what is still unknown, and what remains untested.

A thorough review of the literature will prevent the duplication of what has already been done; it will possibly identify data-gathering instruments, outline the design of previous studies, identify the variables and populations of previous studies, and identify major issues and recommendations made by other researchers.

When presenting an overview of the literature, share the findings as if you are telling a story. In this regard, remember to sequence the events. All foundational studies should be reported early in the discussion. Report earlier studies before studies conducted later. Discuss similar studies and their findings together. Studies that build on each other should be presented in that manner. A thorough review of the related literature will conclude with a summary of areas of agreement and disagreements in the findings. This review will be particularly helpful as you attempt to relate the findings of your study to the current literature.

## *Tools of Research*

How should one start the literature review? One of the general tools of research that permits all researchers, regardless of their discipline, access to such information is the library and its resources (Leedy, 2004). In the past, before the easy accessibility of microcomputers, the manual search through journals, newspapers, books, and other sources was the most frequently used method. However the microcomputer, a second important tool, has revolutionized the search for related literature. Access to the World Wide Web (Internet) has reduced the number of trips one physically makes to the library and allows one to roam through online library systems with a few strokes of the keyboard.

The microcomputer also allows for quick and convenient access to global knowledge. Compact Disk-Read Only Memory (CD-ROM), for example, provides indexes of information worldwide that was once only available through books in the library.

Computerized access such as this permits researchers even in remote areas to continue their work.

A third tool of research is using and understanding the language. A working knowledge of the terminology will assist the researcher in interpreting other studies and activities and in designing the current research project. The two remaining tools as described by Leedy (2004) that also help in the interpretation and design of research projects are 4) techniques of measurement, and 5) statistics. These five general tools are used in various combinations through the course of the research project. A thorough review of the literature is dependent on these tools.

### *Conducting Your Literature Review*

It is now time to conduct a review of the literature related to your research project. Although you are aware of the importance of conducting an exhaustive review of the literature, time may not allow for a thorough review for this mini research project. Therefore, review enough published studies to get a feel for the general findings of the literature.

## COLLECTING AND ANALYZING DATA

The next step in the scientific approach is to collect the data. Therefore, a data-gathering instrument must be developed. At this point, you have already determined that the data are accessible. **The Test and Measurement Yearbook** is just one collection of numerous data-gathering devices that have been evaluated for **validity** and **reliability**. There is little need to recreate the wheel if an instrument already exists and has acceptable levels of reliability. Most often, information on how to obtain a copy and permission to use are readily available in the **Yearbook**.

*The microcomputer has revolutionized the search for relevant research literature. Access to the World Wide Web makes library access available, both locally and internationally, with just a few strokes of the keyboard.*

Instruments that have not been previously validated must first be pilot-tested. The style of data-gathering device used will depend on the research problem being investigated. Remember to consider the audience in regard to the length and construction of the instrument. Some of the important steps in collecting and analyzing data are discussed below.

### *Sampling*

A major factor in developing the instrument is the characteristics of the population to be observed. In most cases, only a portion or sample of the total population is studied. A sample is a small group that is observed when it is not feasible to observe the entire population. It is very important that the sample have similar characteristics to the total population.

According to Howell (2007), there are many benefits of sampling:
1. Total characteristics of the population can be achieved in a shorter time.
2. Properly designed samples may reduce the cost of the study.

3. Money saved by proper sampling may be used to study the sample more intensely or repeat the study.
4. More attention can be given to each return, thus increasing the accuracy of the analysis.
5. Sampling significantly reduces the size of the group.

**Steps in Sampling**
1. Identify the population:
    a. target pop.–group you really want to say something about,
    b. accessible pop.–population at your disposal. The sample will come from the accessible population.
2. Determine the "sampling unit." The basis for this may be geography, social group, family or dwelling, individuals, events, behavior, etc.
3. Decide which sampling method is best for a specific study.

**Principles in Designing a Sample (Howell)**
1. Assure accuracy of sampling estimate so that it approximates the true figure.
2. Reasonable precision for the purpose of the study (size and representativeness of sample).
3. Adequacy of sampling procedure so that the probability of selecting each unit of the population is known.
4. Limited number of sub-classifications.
5. Cost effectiveness.

**Questions to Ask Prior to Sampling**
1. What is the purpose of the study?
2. What is the population to be studied?
3. Is a complete list of the individual elements of the population available?
4. Which types of sampling would be most appropriate?
5. Is the plan economically feasible?
6. What size of sample is desired?
7. How widely scattered is the population?
8. What are the means of communication?
9. Are the persons working with you trained in sampling techniques?

# SIZE OF SAMPLES

Large samples are more nearly accurate than are small samples. However, a sample representative of the population is more important than the size. Ideally, the sample is a replica of the population. As the sample size increases, sampling error decreases. Remember that several samples can be drawn from the same population, resulting in various ways of examining the data.

Samples can be contaminated or result in untrue data and a large degree of error if the proper procedures are not followed. Such gross errors could result in a **biased sample**. A biased sample may be the result of errors made either in designing the study, in identifying the population to be used, or in the actual collecting of data. However, sample size alone does not result in a biased sample. In fact, large samples are no more successful than small ones if there are problems in how the research study was structured initially or if the data collector used irregular procedures in determining who would and would not participate in the study. An example of irregular procedures would be selecting only persons that you like personally.

Sampling is most appropriate when:
1. the groups are very large; and
2. when the groups are similar or homogeneous.

**There are 2 basic categories of sampling:**
1. **Probability Sampling**–sample selection in which elements are drawn by chance procedure, (i.e., every element has an equal chance of being chosen. Types: random, cluster, stratified)
2. **Non-probability Sampling**–used when probability sampling is not feasible. It is more convenient and more economical. (Types: accidental and purposive)

## *Pilot Testing the Instrument*

It is best when using a newly designed instrument to try it out on a few people who closely resemble your sample. Often four to six people will be enough to pilot test the instrument to determine errors in concepts or wording and points that need clarification. This "dry run" will provide the researcher some assurance that most of the "snags" have been eliminated.

These are very basic guidelines. Your instructor may suggest others unique to your study.

## *Analyzing and Interpreting Data*

There are different types of data to be collected. Before discussing alternatives for data analysis, let us examine Steven's Scales of Measurement. Measurement refers to a process through which observations are translated into numbers and figures, finding out how much. There are four types of measurement scales:
1. **Nominal Scale:** used to merely identify the members of a category. This is very basic, and there is no empirical relationship between the items in the categories. The separation is based on qualitative differences rather than quantitative differences (i.e., gender, religion, race, age, occupation, disease, nationality). The mode is the appropriate statistical procedure used here.
2. **Ordinal Scale:** represents the identity of numbers or individuals of a category but does not indicate the distance apart, for example, numbers on football player's jersey. Another example would be ranking something on certain characteristics. Differences in more or less allow for ranking (i.e., greater than, less than, equal to, sergeant, corporal, private, president, vice president, chancellor). The median is the appropriate statistical procedure used here.
3. **Interval Scale:** provides equal intervals from a point of origin. Ratios between the numbers on an interval scale are meaningless. On this scale, both the order and the distance relationships among numbers have meaning. There is no zero point (i.e., as on the thermometer). Most statistical methods are appropriate here.
4. **Ratio Scale:** the highest level and provides a true zero point and equal intervals. Ratios can be between any two given values, as on a yardstick. Multiplication or division can be done with each value without changing the properties of the

scale (i.e., pints, quarts, gallons, pounds, weight, height, time). All statistical methods can be applied since one score can be multiplied or divided by the other.

Once the data are collected, the researcher will need to analyze the data in a manner that will test each hypothesis. There are many different types of statistical formulas that may be used to test hypotheses. Your instructor may discuss in detail procedures for various statistical analyses.

However, for this discussion and project, you will be only introduced to two types of statistics: descriptive and inferential.

**Descriptive statistics** are methods of handling quantitative information in such a way as to make that information manageable. Furthermore, descriptive statistics help us to
1. organize, summarize, and describe observations;
2. determine how reliably we can infer that those phenomena observed in a limited group or sample will occur in the unobserved larger population; and
3. evaluate studies conducted by others.

**Inferential statistics** help us in inferring or predicting future results of similar situations. The indices (plural) most commonly used in inferential statistics are
a. **The t-test**, which is used to find whether the difference between two sample means is statistically significant.
b. **Analysis of variance**, which is used to compare the means of two or more samples used to test the null hypotheses.
c. **Chi-square**, which is an index employed to find the significance of difference between proportions of subjects, objects, events, etc., that fall into different categories, by comparing observed frequencies and expected frequencies.

Please note that there are other measures to test for significant differences. However, this mini project will be limited to a discussion of these measures.

## *Percentages and Frequency Distributions*

Some of the data that you have collected may be analyzed in regard to how many, how much, or how often. Simple division will indicate the percentage of subjects who responded to a particular item. Frequently, distributions indicate how many people responded to a particular item or event. Frequency distributions are determined by using tally marks for each time a specified response is given. Counting the tally marks results in the actual number–not percentage–of the individuals who responded in the identified manner.

## *Interpreting the Data*

It is very important in interpreting the data for the researcher to remain objective and report what really is and not what one would like to see. The researcher's ethical responsibility is to make reasonable assumptions about the results, based on the data only.

There may also be a section in the reporting of the results, entitled, **Discussion**. This section allows the researcher to offer plausible explanations as to why certain findings may have appeared and not others. It also provides a chance to compare the findings of this immediate study with those examined in the review of literature.

## *Writing Styles and Manuals*

Writing styles vary from discipline to discipline. Five of the most commonly used writing manuals are *American Psychological Association (APA)*, *Chicago Manual of Style*, *Kate Turabian*, *Strunk and White*, and *Modern Language Association*. It is important to know the style manual used by your field of study. Consult with your advisor regarding the style option used in your discipline.

Following is a list of style manuals commonly used by various disciplines:

### The Sciences

Council of Biology Editors. *CBE Style Manual: A Guide for Authors, Editors, and Publishers in the Biological Sciences, 12th ed.* Bethesda: CBE, 2005.

Dodd, Janet S., Ed. *The ACS Style Guide: A Manual for Authors and Editors.* Washington: American Chemical Soc., 2006.

American Institute of Physics. *AIP Style Manual, 11th ed.* New York: AIP, 2007.

Rubens, Philip, Ed. *Science and Technical Writing: A Manual of Style.* New York: Holt, 2004.

### English/ The Humanities/Journalism

Gibaldi, Joseph, and Walter S. Achtert, *MLA Handbook for Writers of Research Papers*, 10th ed. New York: Modern Language Association of America, 2004.

Associated Press Staff. *Associated Press Stylebook and Libel Manual.* Reading, MA: Addison, 2006.

### Government Documents

Gamer, Diane L. *The Complete Guide to Citing Government Information Resources: A Manual for Writers and Librarians, Rev. ed.* Bethesda: Congressional Information Service, 2006.

United States. Government Printing Office. *Style Manual.* Wastington: GPO, 2008.

*The Bluebook: A Uniform System of Citation.* Compo. editors of *Columbia Law Review*, et al., 15th ed. Cambridge: Harvard Law Review, 2005.

### MATHEMATICS

American Mathematical Society. *A Manual for Authors of Mathematical Papers, Rev. ed.* Providence: AMS, 2008.

### MUSIC

Holoman, D. Kern, Ed. *Writing about Music: A Style Sheet from the Editors of 19th-Century Music.* Berkeley: U of California P, 2008.

### Psychology and Social Sciences

American Psychological Association. *Publication Manual of the American Psychological Association, 9th ed.* Washington: APA, 2007.

*Writing styles vary from discipline to discipline. To ensure your research is received well in your field of study, it is important to know the style manual used by your profession.*

**Style Manuals–General Notes**
1. Carefully read the style manual most appropriate for your discipline. Familiarize yourself with what is located in each chapter. Use tabs to mark various frequently used places.
2. The style requirements in the publication manual are intended to facilitate clear communication. The requirements are explicit, but alternatives to prescribed forms are permissible if they ensure clearer communication.
3. Scientific prose has a different purpose than does creative writing. Therefore, avoid setting up ambiguity, inserting the unexpected, omitting the expected, and suddenly shifting the topic, tense, or person.
4. Say only what needs to be said.
5. Short words and short sentences are easier to comprehend than long ones. Avoid wordiness.
6. Avoid the use of personal pronouns: I, he, we, she, they, them, those. Use formal, not informal, language.
7. Write from an outline.
8. Read your paper aloud to yourself and also to a colleague.

## SUMMARY

The process of conducting research is spiral in nature. It is a systematic cycle of steps that often results in creating new problems to be solved. It is very exciting to explore new territory and revisit old perspectives in an attempt to validate the findings or discover new meaning of knowledge. Research actually allows one to employ all of the thinking skills introduced in the chapter on critical thinking.

*Thorough research employs a battery of critical and systematic thinking skills, including inductive and deductive reasoning, mind mapping, graphic organizing, and moral reasoning.*

The problem-solving framework is built on a hierarchy of thinking, such as, but not limited to, inductive and deductive reasoning, mind mapping, graphic organizers, and moral reasoning. Such thinking skills are essential from the start—defining the initial problem to be investigated stated in as clear terms as possible to developing a scientifically sound plan of action to testing the hypotheses—to collecting and analyzing data—to interpreting such data in a quantitative or qualitative fashion that leads to a resolution of the problem. The more practice you have in thinking critically and systematically in evaluating situations, the easier you will find the problem-solving process in your everyday life.

## GLOSSARY

**American Psychological Association:** a writing style manual used as a guide for technical papers and reports.
**Analysis of Variance:** statistical procedure used to test the difference between two or more means.

**Bias:** an unequal or unfair advantage or disadvantage.
**Chi Square:** a statistical test used to find the significant differences among the proportions of subjects, objects, and events that fall into different categories.
**Chicago Manual of Style:** a writing style manual used for writing technical papers and reports.
**Correlational Studies:** a statistical technique for determining relationships between pairs of scores.
**Data:** plural for pieces of information, such as observations.
**Datum:** a single observation or piece of information.
**Descriptive Statistics:** serve to describe and summarize observations.
**Hypothesis:** a tentative proposition suggested; a solution to a problem or an explanation to a phenomena; sets a clear goal for research.
**Inferential Statistics:** the science of making reasonable decisions with limited information.
**Inquiry:** search for knowledge.
**Issue:** refers to the periodic time. An example is a monthly journal published by issues.
**Kate Turabian:** a writing style manual used for writing technical reports.
**Knowledge:** facts and theories that enable one to understand phenomenon (an occurrence) to solve problems.
**Null Hypothesis:** no difference, no association, no relationship, and is tested statistically. Results of statistical analysis indicate the probability of chance and/or error.
**Paged by Volume:** the first issue may be pages 1-200, the second 201-400, and so forth with the third and fourth issues. A continuation of page numbers, although volumes change.
**Research Hypothesis:** usually stated to indicate what the researcher expects to discover. Also referred to as the substantive hypothesis. Research hypotheses cannot be tested by available statistical procedures.
**Survey:** an instrument used to collect data for analysis.
**t-Test:** statistical procedure used to test the differences between two means.
**Theory:** summarizes and puts in order the existing knowledge in a particular area; it provides a provisional explanation for observed events and relationships; it stimulates the development of new knowledge.
**Variables:** express or relate a concept or construct. Variables take on different values.
**Volume:** refers to the year.

# REFERENCES

American Psychological Association. (2007). *Publication manual of the American Psychological Association* (5th ed.). Washington, D.C.: Author.

Ary, D., Jacobs, L. C., & Razaviech, A. (2005). *Introduction to research in education.* (7th ed.). New York: Holt, Rinehart, and Winston.

Campbell, W. G., Ballou, S. V., & Slade, C. (2008). *Form and style: Theses, reports, term papers* (6th ed.). Boston: Houghton Mifflin.

Creswell, J. W. (2005). Educational research: Planning, conducting, and evaluating quantitative and qualitative research.

Gay, L. (2008). Educational research. (9th ed.) California: Pearson.

Geering, J. (2008). Case study research: Principles and practices. Mass: Cambridge University Press.

Howell, D. (2007). Fundamental statistics for the behavioral sciences. New York: Wadsworth.

Johnson, R. B. & Christensen, l. B. (2007). Educational research: Quantative, qualitative and mixed approaches. (3rd ed.) California: Sage.

Leedy, P. D., Ormrod, J. E., & Ormrod., J. E. (2004). *Practical research: Planning and design.* New York: Macmillian.

Simmons, H. (2008). Doing case study research. California: Sage.

Slade, P (2005). Form and style. New York: Houghton & Mifflin.

Strunk, S. & White, L (2007). *The elements of style.* (4th ed.). Nevada: Coyote Canyon Press.

## WEB SITES

Links on Style Manuals:
A Guide to Citing Internet Sources (University of Puget Sound)
Documenting Sources (Princeton University)
Resources for Faculty (Eastern Connecticut State University)
MLA Style (Modern Language Association)
Resources for Teachers of Writing (University of Illinois)
Style Manuals and Citation Guides (Duke University)
Theses and Styles Manual Guide (James Cook University)
Style Manual and Sources Documentation (Concordia College)
Style Manual List (West Illinois University)
Links to Qualitative Research Web Sites:
- Bibliography for Qualitative Research
    http://kerlins.net/bobbi/research/qualresearch/bibliography/
- Qualitative Research Journals
    http://www.slu.edu/organizations/qrc/QRjournals.html
- Links to Qualitative Research from the University of Saskatchewan
    http://www.usask.ca/education/coursework/edres845/links.htm
- Computer Assisted Qualitative Data Analysis Software
    http://caqdas.soc.surrey.ac.uk/
- The Ethnograph Web Site: Software for Qualitative Research
    http://www.qualisresearch.com/

- Qualitative Research List of Internet Resources
    http://library.curtin.edu.au/research/resources/resres.html

**Electronic DataBases**
Refer to Chapter 6–Dimensions of Computer Technology–for additional electronic resources that may be used in conducting research (i.e., electronic data bases, social indexes, etc.)

# ACTIVITY 1

## *Evaluating Statements of Problems*

**Directions:** Now, having thoroughly reviewed the characteristics of a well-developed problem statement and important questions to ask, review the following statements. If you deem that the statement is incomplete, rewrite the statement in the space provided. You may want to refer to the discussion on the characteristics of well-developed problem statements.

A. The study was undertaken to determine what effect preschool experiences have on the socialization of children entering kindergarten.

B. The purpose of the study was to discover possible changes in the food habits of Korean immigrants currently living in southern California and to describe factors that may have influenced any changes in their food habits.

C. The purpose of the study was to (a) report and describe the foods consumed by Asians prior to the invasion by European races, (b) to list the nutrient content of the foods, and (c) to describe the food habits that might have had a bearing on the health of ancient Hawaiians.

How well did you do? All of the problem statements in Activity 1 are appropriate statements of the problem. If you found this to be true, you have done well! If you had difficulty, perhaps you should review the statements again.

Now you are ready to narrow the topics you have been considering for your personal research project in Activity 2.

# ACTIVITY 2

## *Developing the Research Problem*

**Assignment:** First, select one topic to be investigated. Using two to three sentences, briefly describe the situation or issue.

Issue:

_____

_____

_____

Now, write what might be a statement of the problem for the issue described. Remember the characteristics of well-developed research problem statements.

Statement of the Problem:

_____

_____

_____

_____

The third step in this process is to evaluate the problem statement that you have written. Refer to the list of characteristics and important questions. Does your statement of the problem meet these criteria? If not, please modify the statement.

_____

_____

_____

_____

# ACTIVITY 3

## *Identify Variables*

Do you think it is possible to have two or more dependent variables or two or more independent variables? Write two research statements or problems in which you underline the dependent variable once and the independent variable twice.

_____

_____

_____

_____

_____

_____

_____

_____

Now examine the statements that you have written and circle any continuous variables that you may have used. Draw a block around any categorical variable included in the statements that you have written.

# ACTIVITY 4

## *Evaluating Hypotheses*

**Directions:** For each of the following hypotheses, underscore the independent variable once; underscore the dependent variable twice; and indicate if the hypothesis is directional or non-directional.

_____ 1. There will be a significant difference in the language development of children of single-parent families and children of dual-parent families.

_____ 2. There is a significant relationship between the age of persons and their attitudes toward death and dying.

_____ 3. There is a significant relationship between a child's SAT scores and the mother's educational level.

_____ 4. There will be a significant effect on the development of HIV for individuals who participate in unprotected sex.

_____ 5. There is a significant difference in the grades of students who take math in the morning and those who take math in the evening.

_____ 6. There will be a significant difference between buying habits and socioeconomic status.

_____ 7. Family social status will have no effect on the consumer behavior of Native American women.

_____ 8. Air pollutants will have a significant effect on the absence of children from school.

_____ 9. There will be a significant difference in the marital attitudes of adolescents from divorced and those from non-divorced family structures.

_____ 10. There will be a significant difference in learning achievement between students taught by parents at home and those taught by teachers in a regular school setting.

# ACTIVITY 5

## *Formulating Hypotheses*

**Directions:** Refer to the problem statement that you developed for your mini research project. Write that statement in the space provided below. Now develop one research hypothesis and two null hypotheses to be tested.

**Statement of the Problem**

_____

_____

_____

_____

**Research Hypothesis**

_____

_____

_____

_____

**Null Hypotheses**

_____

_____

_____

_____

# ACTIVITY 6

## *The Review of Related Literature*

**Directions:** Conduct a review of the literature related to your mini research project. If you are working in a group, be sure to include everyone in the process and convene regularly to share your findings. This activity is designed to assist you in planning and completing the review of literature. Various forms of searches have been identified. Assign a component to each group member. Briefly summarize the findings. Use additional paper as needed.

See chart below.

| Activity | Person Responsible | Summary of Findings |
|---|---|---|
| Go to indexes and abstracts. | | |
| Review government publications. | | |
| Make as many copies of the bibliographic materials as needed. | | |
| Conduct an online search for libraries locally, nationally, and worldwide. | | |
| Make copies of relevant articles. | | |
| Search for data-gathering devices. | | |
| Review CD-ROMs on the subject. | | |
| Search the Internet for information on the topic. (Be sure to record or bookmark addresses for easy reference.) | | |

# ACTIVITY 7

## *Thinking It Through*

Let us take a moment to consider your mini research project. On a separate sheet of paper, answer the following questions regarding sampling techniques for your research project. Discuss your answers with the instructor.

1. What is the target population for your study? This is the group about which you really want to say something.

2. What is the accessible population for your study? This would be those individuals of the target group at your disposal.

3. What is a reasonable size for your sample? How did you arrive at this figure?

4. What type of sampling procedure will you use? Why?

Once the sample size has been identified, the researcher will need to design an instrument (i.e., questionnaire, survey, interview) to be used to actually collect the data. Such an instrument is also necessary for your project. Consider the type of information that you would like to collect and determine the best strategy for collecting the information. Here are some tips for designing data-collection tools:

- Always consider the age, experience, and educational level of the subjects or respondents.
- Keep the instrument short. Fifteen to 20 minutes should be long enough for your first project.
- The items should be brief and concise.
- When not using open-ended questions, always consider all of the possible answers to the item.
- Directions should be placed on each page.
- Reconsider the hypotheses that you have developed to be tested. Can you determine which items on the instrument or data-collection device will give you the information needed to test each hypothesis? Modify the instrument as needed.

## ACTIVITY 8

### *Developing an Instrument*

Decide the best method for collecting information about the problem that you are investigating. A common, though certainly not only, approach is the *survey*. Develop a survey that will yield the answers to the hypotheses, objectives, or questions. Be sure to remember the tips stated earlier in this discussion of the instrument.

## ACTIVITY 9

### *Analysis of Data*

The method used to analyze the data depends on the type of data collected and the hypothesis, objectives, or questions under study. Your mini project should not require the use of complex data analysis. Two common methods used to report the data are percentages and frequency distributions, or rather, the number of responses to each item (i.e., 40–or 82%–of the freshman class scored 90 or above on the midterm exam). Discuss with your instructor the best method to analyze the data.

## ACTIVITY 10

### *Style Manual*

Obtain a copy of the style manual and determine how to perform the steps below in your final report:
1. format the page margins;
2. number pages;
3. create tables, charts, and graphs;
4. hyphenate words and phrases;
5. use personal pronouns; and
6. use attributes such as italics, bold, underline, and centering.

Prepare a formal paper using an approved style manual.

# ACTIVITY 11

## *Formal Presentation*

Make a formal presentation to your class about your research project. Use the presentation checklist below as a guide. Having completed the presentation, reflect on the various steps of the project. Discuss your self-rating with your instructor.

<u>Oral Presentation Rating Scale</u>

Score (1-10 pts.)

1. Presenter is poised and professionally dressed. _____

2. Presentation content is organized. _____

3. Delivery of content is clear, brisk, and concise. _____

4. Information is accurate. _____

5. Presenter encourages active involvement of the audience. _____

6. Visuals, handouts, and printed materials are content-specific. _____

7. Materials are neat and legible. _____

# CHAPTER *eight*

## Dimensions of Diversity

### INTRODUCTION

This is a self-assessment exercise. Answer Yes or No to the questions posed. Then, use this information to write autobiographical information and a profile. Next, exchange your profile with three other classmates and answer the two questions at the end of this activity.

**Are you**
(Answer yes or no in the space provided.)
_____an American?
_____a descendant of an American immigrant?
_____a descendent of a slave?
_____a recent immigrant?
_____an International student?
_____an American woman?
_____a mother?
_____an American man?
_____a father?
_____physically or mentally disabled?
_____a full-time college student?
_____from a rural area?
_____from an urban area?
_____from the South?
_____from the North?
_____from the East Coast?
_____from the West Coast?
_____from the Heartland of the United States?
_____from another country?
_____single?
_____divorced?
_____widowed?

1. What do you have in common with your classmates?
2. How do you differ from your classmates?

You are probably wondering why you were asked to do the self-assessment exercise and whether the assessment has anything to do with your culture. Aspects of one's culture are endless, and we rarely analyze our culture. Questions pertaining to culture are thought-provoking. Take the time to find answers to questions pertaining to culture will help us to analyze our feelings and our views about the world.

We do not choose our culture. It is chosen for us before we are born. At birth, culture forms the group to which we will belong. If you are a little skeptical, let's examine a birth certificate. The birth certificate puts you into specific categories that define your social identity: race, gender, date, place, and time you were born, your type of birth–single, twin, triplet, etc., parents' names, ages, and birthplaces. How do you think the categories you were placed in at birth affect the kind of person you are now?

Before forming the conclusion that you are who you are because of culture and you've had little if anything to do with the kind of person you are, let's explore the context of culture. Culture is transmitted from one generation to the next and is created through people interacting with each other (Popenoe, 2000). Culture is found in various locations and settings–sometimes right next to us, across the street from us, or in a far away country.

The ways we view and define culture have changed. Before the twentieth century, culture referred to the ways of the rich, elite, and powerful. It was thought that only people who were refined and knowledgeable in the fine arts, classics, and history possessed culture. Today, culture is not so narrowly defined. Culture is not based on just one person's individual feelings. Rules, standards, and norms for the entire world are not set by only one culture.

Culture is a mighty past that we move forward in. Therefore, it is now a good time for you to confront your own views of culture. As a college student, you are in a unique position to discover that you are part of a complex world, capable of recognizing differences and open to learning different ways of thinking and doing things. While in college, you will examine who you are as you emerge in a world of very diverse racial, ethnic, gender, spiritual, regional, personality, and other human characteristics. Continuous learning and growth require continuous attention to how you relate to human beings who are like you and who are unlike you.

The purpose of this chapter is to help you—as you encounter people from other cultures—to avoid letting your culture overshadow the similarities and the richness of the different cultures. After studying the material in this chapter, you will be better prepared to do just that.

## OBJECTIVES

The objectives of this chapter are to
1. discuss the components of culture,
2. express an appreciation for the diversity among individuals, groups, and cultures,
3. show an appreciation for diversification in learning and teaching styles among individuals and groups,

4. adapt to the culture of higher education and the workplace,
5. explore the issues surrounding culture and means of addressing those issues, and
6. discover how effective interpersonal, inter-group, and inter-organizational skills in dealing with diversity can promote consensus, cooperation, and conflict management so that the values of constructive social change and justice may be accomplished.

### KEY CONCEPTS

- Culture
- Symbol
- Change
- Norm
- Ethnocentrism
- Multi-culturalism
- Macroculture
- Microculture
- Culturally literate
- Outliners

## COMPONENTS OF CULTURE

The first objective in learning through diversity is to identify, appreciate, and develop skills in intercultural relations. Culture is the portal through which we come to understand ourselves and extend our skills in dealing with others.

**Culture** is the deposit of knowledge, experience, beliefs, values, attitudes, meanings, hierarchies, religion, timing, roles, spatial relations, concepts of the universe, and material objects and possessions acquired by a group of people in the course of generations through individual and group striving (Berko, Rosenfeld, & Samovar, 1994, p. 9). The definition for culture is inclusive.

- Culture is shared.
- Culture is learned.
- Culture is reinforced.
- Culture is transmissible.
- Culture resists change.
- Culture is symbolic.

Through the process of social interactions, culture is shared and learned. For example, you learned to speak a certain language because it was the language your family spoke. Rules of proper conduct and behavior, as well as your gender roles, were learned through social interactions, first with your family and then reinforced through others in your environment. People in your culture reinforced the same messages and behaviors that the dominant culture deemed to be important.

"Culture dictates who talks to whom, about what, and for how long" (Berko, Rosenfeld, & Saovar, 1994, p. 8). You have been taught to think, feel, communicate, and strive for what your culture considers appropriate. What you learned promoted a kind of thinking that is category responding, that mirrors your culture. You respond to and evaluate other people by applying the standards of your culture. This is a natural phenomenon, but one that restricts and prejudices your view.

Culture is also transmissible, from person to person, group to group, and generation to generation. Both content and patterns of one's culture are transmissible through spoken language, sign language, and symbols. For example, American Sign Language (ASL) is a gesture-based visual language used by Americans who have hearing disabilities. Sign languages of other countries such as India, Italy, and Britain are quite different and distinct from ASL, the same way spoken languages are different.

Symbolism is transmissible, and the existence of culture depends on a person's ability to create and use symbols. A symbol is something used to represent something else whose meaning is shared and recognized by groups of people. Language is symbolic.

Languages are words (arbitrary letter combinations) that stand for or represent something. Words have no meaning in themselves. Let's examine a few words to illustrate the idea that language is symbolic. The words sandwich, pizza, potato chip, and banana are not edible nor are the words soda, tea, water, coffee, and milk drinkable. These words do not connect logically with what they mean. The relationship between the symbols and their symbolism is arbitrary, agreed upon by the people who use the symbol. Therefore, a component of learning a language is learning the rules for how meanings and symbols are connected. Words are given meaning by the people who use the words and not in the words themselves. The specific meaning given to words will reflect something about who you are and your culture. The effectiveness of the meanings between the words and symbols will depend upon the degree of consistency of meanings between the sender and the receiver. There will be very little differen-

*A symbol is something used to represent something else whose meaning is shared and recognized by groups of people. Language is symbolic in that it uses words to stand for ideas or objects, just as these illustrations do.*

tiation of meanings if the cultures are homogeneous. On the other hand, cross-cultural interactions create conflict if symbolic messages are incorrectly interpreted.

Symbols that have common or shared meanings within a culture help us:
- to understand abstract concepts such as God, justice, and patriotism. The words "liberty," "justice," and "equality" define a belief system that links Americans together.
- to respect ideas. For instance, the idea of every doctor's goal is represented in the Hippocratic Oath. The meaning attached to clothing also reflects who we are. For example, in America, a person wearing designer clothing and expensive jewelry and driving a prestigious car is showing symbols of success and status.
- to convey a certain attitude toward what is represented. An example is the Rainbow Coalition and inclusion. The Statue of Liberty conveys freedom.

When people of one culture come in contact with people from other cultures, conflict and change are inevitable, and people are forced to adapt. How rapid the change will occur depends on how deep-rooted the structural culture is. Deep-rooted cultural structures resist **change** and may take several generations before the cultural change is accepted as the **norm**.

Out of necessity, Japan and the United States were forced to change some of their basic commerce practices in the early 80s. When Americans started to purchase more Japanese- made cars than those made in the U.S., American automobile makers adapted Japan's quality-control methods. Japan, on the other hand, borrowed America's marketing practices.

Mexicans who migrated to America during the 1980s were also forced to make a change in a cultural practice. Mexicans changed their use of time when they entered the workforce. In their own country, it was customary for Mexicans to work hard, long hours, taking an extended lunch period during the middle of the day to rest. In America, the lunch period, as well as the workday, is much shorter than what the Mexican workers were used to. While the Americans, Japanese, and Mexicans were forced to adapt to new cultures, similar changes did not occur in deep-rooted cultural structures. It is doubtful that the Japanese or the Mexicans would change their view of the family or their notion of obligation.

## DIVERSITY AMONG INDIVIDUALS, GROUPS, AND CULTURE

Understanding individual culture begins with understanding cultural influences. The dominant culture in the United States stresses the importance of being identified as an individual. The focus is on the individual, and "I" is used more than any other word (Berko, et al., 1994, p. 34). You are told by people in your culture that:
1. you are an individual;
2. you are in control of your life;
3. you can be anything you want to be.

People in the macroculture reinforce the "I" concept, providing means of identifying that assist us in assuming conventional identities. **Macroculture** refers to people who make up the dominant culture. In the United States, European Americans are the dominant culture.

*Your individuality is based on traits and values learned as part of your ethnic origin, religion, gender, age, socioeconomic status, primary language, geographic region, place of residence, and abilities or exceptional conditions. As such, individuals are often members of more than one microculture.*

Yet, in the United States there are many distinct cultural groups (microcultures). A **microculture** is the culture of a group that includes aspects of the dominant culture, while having distinctive cultural characteristics of its own. Your individuality is based on traits and values learned as part of your ethnic origin, religion, gender, age, socioeconomic status, primary language, geographic region, place of residence, and abilities or exceptional conditions (Gollnick & Chinn, 2001, pp. 13-14). Being a member of one microculture often conflicts with the interests of another microculture. We learn to strive for what the macroculture considers appropriate. As you become aware of your interactions with the various microcultures and the dominant culture, you will begin to answer the question, "Who am I?" in very diverse ways.

Different cultures place different emphases on how much importance is given to defining ourselves. In America, the emphasis is on the individual. If you were Asian, emphasis would be on the group. If you were Japanese, you would be judged by your company affiliations. In China, the macroculture stresses the importance of how others feel about you. There is an old Chinese proverb, "If you know the family, you need not know the person." This proverb illustrates the high value the Chinese culture places on using others to define self (Berko, 1994, p. 37).

## DIVERSIFICATION IN LEARNING AND TEACHING STYLES

Let's go back to the self-assessment exercise you completed at the beginning of the chapter. Where are your classmates from? Are they from urban cities, the suburbs, the District of Columbia? More than likely, your classmates represent many geographical locations across America. What about the gender and racial makeup of your classmates—are there more females than males; more representation of one ethnic group? The data that you just provided were easily obtained. There are other characteristics about your classmates that will only emerge through interactions and over periods of time. Some of those characteristics are listed below.

1. There are various ability levels, including physical, emotional, and mental exceptionalities among your classmates.
2. All of your classmates have varied learning needs, based upon experiences and experiential development.
3. Various socioeconomic, racial, and ethnic backgrounds with corresponding advantages and disadvantages are represented.
4. Arrays of religious preferences are practiced.
5. Your classmates come from various family structures, including nuclear families, single parents, stepparents, same-gender parents; and parents whose primary language may not be English.

This may be a good time to pause and reflect on how diverse our society is to determine why it is important to value diversity.

You and your classmates learn in various ways (Learning Styles–Chapters 1), at various times, and through various instructional approaches (Chapter 2). Earlier in this text, you were exposed to different learning styles, and you probably identified your learning preferences. You may have discovered that you learn best by looking at the big picture before tearing it apart or by:
- looking at the parts and then creating a whole.
- being in a highly structured, teacher-orientated environment (lecture method), or by participating in student-directed activities.
- using deductive rather than inductive cognitive processes.
- seeing things (visually) or hearing things (auditory) or using a hands-on approach (kinesthetics).
- working independently or collaboratively.

Having viewed your own profile and your classmates, do you think all of you should be taught the same way or viewed in the same manner? Of course you do not. There is no single approach that can be used to teach all students in all situations, thus our dilemma when interacting with different cultures. The United States is a multicultural nation representing
- people who themselves or whose ancestors once lived in another nation.
- different classes, religions, and native languages.
- people who differ because of gender, sexual orientation, age, or physical, emotional, and mental abilities.

*Your view of a culture and how you interact with each group to learn from each other will be determined, to a great extent, by your professors and your collegiate experiences.*

## STEREOTYPES

Our macroculture exposes us to a social curriculum that portrays the positive and negative differences of the microculture through various media, such as radio, television, videos, newspapers, magazines, family, friends, and community attitudes. Over-simplification of one's microculture often leads to distorted stereotyping. You have probably heard that
- men are inferior to women.
- African Americans love soul food.
- females are weak.
- people with disabilities are helpless.
- the homeless are dangerous.

Dimensions of Diversity

Stereotyping is problematic for many reasons. Stereotypes ignore individual characteristics. They are neither true nor false because they are based on statements that were possibly true at some point in time or place, or with at least one group of people. Stereotyping often occurs along with first impressions. Impressions are formed from a name, a handshake, or clothing. Stereotyping is applied when the message conveyed fits a preconceived idea. Sometimes stereotyping is the result of an over-generalized composite representing statistical norms for particular roles and status. Stereotypical views about groups of people are broad generalizations that neglect the individuality within these groups (Gollnick & Chinn, 2001).

Stereotypes do not explain the wide range of variability that occurs within a given role or status. Decisions that we make as individuals, teachers, employers, politicians, and neighbors will be based solely or in part on misconceptions. We must overcome ethnocentrism. **Ethnocentrism** exists when we evaluate someone else's culture based upon our own cultural patterns and decide that our culture is superior. Being educated in **multiculturalism** means that you will learn to value diversity, have a positive view about diversity, and think critically about racism, sexism, ageism, etc.

With each passing decade, the United States is becoming more diverse. By 2010, it is predicted that the European American population will decrease to 68%, the Asian and Hispanic American populations will grow by 5%, the African American growth rate will be 1.3%, and the Native American population will grow by .8% (U.S. Bureau of the Census, 2001; U.S. Department of Commerce, 1996, as reported in Lasley & Matczynski, 2002). Therefore, we now turn our focus to issues of diversity. Your view of a culture and how you interact with each group to learn from each other will be determined, to a great extent, by your professors and your collegiate experiences.

The world is shrinking; your preparation to enter a global society will include how well you understand and interact with diverse ethnic and social groups. Before we continue, let's look at the demographics on your college campus. Think about the student body population on your campus. Hypothesize, make an educated guess, about the student population or student demographics on your campus. Were you surprised by your findings? More than likely you were. Maybe even more revealing are the number of events or lack of events that support diversity on your campus. Your professors will require you to attend many of these events and interact in a variety of ways with diversity. You cannot become culturally literate by attending a few events, listening to a lecture, or attending a workshop. The goal is for you to be able to function effectively in the context of cultural differences.

## CULTURAL LITERACY

To be **culturally literate** means that you will know how to effectively respond to the unique needs of individuals whose cultures differ from yours. Your university will give you the opportunity to become culturally literate by providing :
- an atmosphere that supports cultural awareness and sensitivities among all students, including students with disabilities, various sexual orientation, women, religious, and or linguistic differences.
- activities that will help students to rise above differences, to understand one another, and build bridges between cultures.

- a valuing of diversity, recognizing that the strength of any institution lies in its diversity.
- a community where all students will be given the opportunity to use their abilities to the fullest.
- an environment where all students will feel comfortable in discussing diversity issues and evaluating decisions using the standards of the culture under review.

Learning about and understanding other cultures means you will acquire respect for the differences and accept the many ways of viewing the world. By virtual definition, culture is broad. "Culture is the cumulative results of experience, values, religion, beliefs, attitudes, meanings, knowledge, social organizations, procedures, timing, roles, spatial relations, concepts of universe and material objects and possessions acquired or created by groups of people, in the course of generations, through individual and group effort and interactions" (Moore & Woodrow, 1998, p. 1). Culture is who we are, our language, expressions of behaviors, and a model of our daily activities. Culture is the cohesion of people living together in a society. When we think of culture, we think of ethnic groups, tribes, clans, regional subcultures, and neighborhoods. Almost simultaneously, we think about group differences from within and outside the dominant culture. Within these groups, there is an array of differences: different religions, ideological persuasions, professions and educational backgrounds, different family cultures, differences between men and women, and organizations (Moore & Woodrow, 1998).

So, are you beginning to see why it is so difficult to study and understand another culture? There are many cultural variables and significant variations within cultures. How, then, do we make any predictions about how a particular group or a person from a particular group within a culture will respond to various situations? Sure, we know that specific traits, patterns, and behaviors are unique to certain groups of people. Many research studies document the core cultural variables: ethnicity, education, gender, socioeconomic status, and religion (Anderson, 1988; De La Rosa & Maw, 1990; Dunn, 1993; Enright, 1987; Hale-Benson, 1986; Hansen, 1984; Herring, 1989; Howe, 1994; Loftin, 1989; Soldier, 1985; Tooker, 1983; Yu & Bain, 1985). It has been convenient and more simplistic to study group behaviors and make generalizations. The fallacy of using this method does not take into account individuals living within that culture who have different points of view. These individuals are called "outliners" and they exist in every culture. "**Outliners** are people who vary significantly from the norm. While still contained within the range of their culture, their views and behaviors differ significantly from those of their peers and may even look similar to other cultures. For instance, a businessman or an engineer from a developing country who was educated in England may have more in common with his peers in Europe than with his fellow countrymen" (Moore & Woodrow, 1998, p. 2).

Therefore, it is imperative that we refrain from making generalizations and predictions about how people from a specific culture will think or behave. We know from painful experiences the issues associated with profiling and making erroneous generalizations about people based upon predetermined group criteria. Cultural literacy includes:
- keeping an open mind.
- recognizing myths and inaccurate stereotypes.
- using problem-solving techniques.

- knowing who you are and what your principles are.
- knowing how you will react in intercultural situations.
- reflecting.

## CULTURAL VARIABLES

Individual differences in our society are not valued. Right away we begin to think, "Something is wrong with me. I am not normal." At first, we try to fix it. If medicine and therapy doesn't fix it, then society teaches us to accept it. We learn to cope, or we learn how to conceal our differences. This practice is deeply rooted and has changed very slowly over time. Cultural training, recognizing individual differences, and being tolerant have done very little to change attitudes. Because of the way individual differences are regarded in our cultural, there are several cultural errors embedded in the core cultural variables that impede cultural literacy.

Society teaches us that our gender plays a major role in determining our aptitude toward performance in school, in work, and in our personal lives. We are socialized to believe that girls should behave one way and boys another. For example, "girls are the weaker sex and should play with dolls so they will grow up to be caring, nurturing individuals. Men are breadwinners; therefore, boys must be taught self-sufficiency." We would like to think that we have overcome this way of thinking and that gender equity laws have dispelled this myth. Yet, we know that laws have not changed the practice. Numerous studies continue to document the disparity in pay between men and women, even when women make up approximately 50% of the workforce and many of them are the only source of income for their families. Additionally, achievement gaps continue to exist between genders. Girls may perform better than boys in some subjects, and boys may perform better than girls in some subjects.

*It is imperative that we refrain from making generalizations and predictions about how people from a specific culture will think or behave. Cultural literacy means keeping an open mind and recognizing myths and stereotypes that may play a part in our perceptions of other people.*

Why do these differences still exit? Many researchers believe that this is still true today because we accept it as "normal." Is this suppose to happen? Are genetic differences gender specific? (Joyce, Weil, & Calhoun, 2003; Berko, Rosenfeld, & Saovar, 1994; Gollnick & Chinn, 2001; Lasley, Matczynski, & Rowley 2002.)

Your finding from previous research in this chapter probably revealed your examples of gender-attributed stereotypes. You may want to review the data and develop personal strategies and awareness goals to help you change and to help others change their ways of thinking.

As a college student, you will interact with people from many different socioeconomic backgrounds. As you work with the various groups, remember to employ the strategies you learned from Chapter 2. Use the tools of multiple intelligences and learning styles that will bring about changes in the way we perceive and interact with others.

*Welcome opportunities to work with diverse groups. The diversity of thought and characteristics found in such groups can enhance learning.*

Your challenges are 1) to abandon, to let go of the stereotypical views of gender, wealth, racism, and cultural differences as determining factors of various abilities, especially academic abilities; 2) to study human behavior; and 3) to learn how social behaviors and social interactions can enhance learning. Welcome opportunities to work with diverse groups. You may find the following guidelines helpful.
- Use the cooperative learning strategies discussed in Chapter 2.
- Choose a meeting space that is warm, inviting, and promotes social interactions.
- Use different ways of knowing the materials (learning modalities).
- Provide time and space for thinking and personal reflecting.
- Rotate the various tasks among group members.
- Use strategies that promote growth and encouragement.
- When possible, use and accept people-orientated examples and situations.
- Role play, demonstrate, model.
- Develop personal relationships.
- Help each other to place academic context within the context to be studied.

## THE CULTURE OF HIGHER EDUCATION AND THE WORKPLACE

A new set of demands is being placed upon schools to produce and provide a workforce that meets the demands of an international society. As an individual in this society you will need to
- value diversity, in your microenvironment and macroenvironments, both with primary characteristics of diversity and diversity of thought.
- be willing to continue to learn and grow throughout life.
- engage in and value collaborative, team-oriented work relationships.
- function in consensus-reaching structures, rather than hierarchical, bureaucratic structures.

- learn to focus on relationship-oriented behavior by which individuals are empowered in the decision-making process.
- think globally in the use of knowledge, skills, and attitudes.
- exhibit knowledge and the use of various forms of technology (computers, videotapes, distance learning, etc.) to communicate, learn, and work.
- function in a more personal, rather than formal, manner in interactions with others.
- energize others through charisma, knowledge, and conviction.
- empower others to function in creative and innovative ways to perform work and/or discover new ways of doing things (Lasley & Matczynski, 2002).

## SUMMARY

American citizens fail when it comes to embracing diversity. Most of us feel inadequately prepared to address the diverse nature of the United States. America is in the midst of this transformation. **Transformation** is a process that brings about change in society's values, in views of reality, in political, economic, and social structures, in incorporation of people, and in ways of conducting business. A vivid illustration of this transformation is the affirmation that we are a diverse society. America is home to over 700 nonconventional religions. We have the greatest variety of multi-ethnic households in history. In Los Angeles, alone, 80 languages are taught in the schools. Americans are changing the social, educational, and political paradigms. Americans are learning to live and work together to create the vibrant tapestry that embodies the meaning and strength of our American way of life.

America is not a melting pot. In 1997, President Clinton appointed a national board to study racism in America. When President Clinton called for a "colorblind society," the chair of his board, Dr. John Hope Franklin, reminded him that the best way to reduce racism was to acknowledge it. A colorblind society concept would not foster the uniqueness of the microcultures that exist in America.

## GLOSSARY

**American Sign Language (ASL):** gesture-based, visual language used by Americans who have hearing disabilities.

**Acculturation:** process by which a minority individual or microculture tries to blend in and take on the cultural characteristics of the macroculture.

**Assimilated:** absorbed into the dominant culture.

**Culture:** deposit of knowledge, experience, beliefs, values, attitudes, meanings, hierarchies, religion, timing, roles, spatial relations, concepts of the universe, and material objects and possessions acquired by a group of people in the course of generations through individual and group striving (Berko, Rosenfeld, & Samovar, 1994, p. 9).

**Cultural Literacy:** being able to effectively respond to the unique needs of individuals.

**Customs:** traditions, long-continued habits.

**Ethnocentrism:** evaluating someone else's culture based upon your own cultural patterns and deciding that your culture is superior.

**Macroculture:** the dominant culture within a culturally diverse society.

**Microculture:** the culture of a group that includes aspects of the dominant culture, while having distinctive cultural characteristics of its own.

**Mores:** strongly held social norms that provide the moral standards of a social system and are strictly enforced (Popenoe, 2000, p. 565).

**Multicultural Education:** a strategy that uses cultural backgrounds to design and determine instructions and activities.

**Norms:** what is accepted, expected.

**Symbol:** something used to represent something else whose meaning is shared and recognized by groups of people.

**Transformation:** a process that brings about change in society's values, views of reality, political, economic and social structures, incorporation of people, and manner of conducting business.

## REFERENCES

Adams, M., Blumfield, J., Ccastaneda, R., Hackman, H. W., Peters, M. L., Zzuniga, X. (2000). *Readings for diversity and social justice: An anthology on racism, antisemmitism, sexism, heterosexism, ablesism, & classism.* New York: Routledge.

Berko, R. M., Rosenfeld, L. B., & Saovar, L. A. (1994). *Connecting.* Fort Worth, TX: Harcourt Brace.

Ellis, D., & Toft, D. (2002). *Becoming a master student* (10th. ed.). Boston, MA: Houghton Mifflin.

Gollnick, D. M., & Chinn, P. C. (2001). *Multicultural education in a pluralistic society* (6th ed.). Englewood Cliffs, NJ: Pearson Prentice Hall.

Joyce, B. R. Weil, M., & Calhoun, E. (2003). *Models of teaching* (7th ed.). Needham Heights, MA: Allyn & Bacon.

Lasley, T. J., Matczynski, T. J., & Rowley, J. B. (2002). *Instructional Models Strategies for teaching in a diverse society.* Belmont, CA: Wadsworth/Thomson.

Moore, C., & Peter, W. (April, 1998). Mapping cultures–strategies for effective intercultural negotiations. *Track Two,* 7(1), 1-12.

Popenoe, D. (2000). *Sociology* (11th ed.). Englewood Cliffs, NJ: Prentice Hall.

Samovar, L. A., & Porter, R. E. (2004). *Communication between cultures.* Belmont, CA: Wadsworth.

## WEB SITES

http://www.casanet.org/library/culture/competence.htm
http://www.diversityhotwire.com
http://www.diversityinc.com
http://www.dtcc.edu/policy/Diversity/Vision.htm
http://equality.monster.ie/articles/diversity/print/
http://www.inform.umd.edu/EdRes/Topic/Diversity/
http://www.mcreview.com/Spring04/spr04-feature3.html
http://www.mediate.com/
http://www.twofrog.com/diversity.html
http://zzyx.ucsc.edu

# ACTIVITY 1:

## *Photo Journal Essay*

Develop a photo essay journal that identifies you and the common threads and the experiences you share with other Americans. You may use the examples provided or create your own.

**A Self Portrait**
I am:
    a freshman, from New York, attending an HBCU, majoring in Business Administration, independent, dancing to the beat of my own drum.

**Things You Enjoy**
I enjoy:
    reading, sports, singing, playing golf,
    being with people, working with my hands,
    sharing my experiences with my family and friends.

**Challenges You Face**
I am looking for ways to:
    improve my self-esteem,
    improve my grade in chemistry,
    get to know my instructors.

**When I Get Up in the Morning, I:**
Stand on carpet made in _____.
Brush my teeth with a toothbrush made in _____.
Put my jeans on made in _____.

Dimensions of Diversity

# ACTIVITY 2:

## *Challenges Americans Face*

Make a list of the cultural challenges you believe college students face. Why do you view the items you listed as challenges? Compare your list with the lists of three of your classmates. Combine the items to make one list. How is the community addressing the challenges? Check community bulletin boards and events to answer the question. Write the community events beside the challenge. Use a presentation packet, such as PowerPoint or WordPerfect presentation to graph your group findings. Share the group's graph with the entire class.

**Cultural Challenges**                **Resolution to Challenge**

1. _____             1. _____

2. _____             2. _____

3. _____             3. _____

4. _____             4. _____

5. _____             5. _____

6. _____             6. _____

7. _____             7. _____

8. _____             8. _____

9. _____             9. _____

10. _____             10. _____

# ACTIVITY 3:

## *The Generation Gap*

**Directions:** Make a list of ten words that are ethnic-specific to your generation. Write down what the words mean. Find a symbol that expresses the word meaning. Show the list of words **only** to three people from different cultures. Ask each person to define each word. Then ask each person to choose a symbol and match it with a word and its definition.

**Words and Word Meanings**

1. _____
2. _____
3. _____
4. _____
5. _____
6. _____
7. _____
8. _____
9. _____
10. _____

**Words and Symbols:** Match the symbols with the words.

**Discussion:**

11. How did the words and symbols take on meanings that were different from their original meanings (your definitions)?

12. What language difficulties did you encounter?

13. How did you overcome the communication barriers?

Dimensions of Diversity

# ACTIVITY 4:

## *What Does it Mean to be an American? A United States Citizen?*

1. Read the poem *On the Pulse of Morning* by Maya Angelou. What thoughts come to mind about our identity as a people?

2. Analyze a song of your nationality. Underline words and phases that illustrate your culture. Underline words and phases that illustrate the dominate culture. What is the relationship between your culture and the dominate culture? Are your interpretations different from or similar to that of your peers? What predictions can you make to account for the differences and the similarities?

# CHAPTER *nine*

## Etiquette, Professional Protocol, and Ethics

### INTRODUCTION

During your college years, you will meet a variety of people: people from different **cultures**, from different backgrounds, and from different religious ideologies. An individual learns from the environment in which he or she is reared. **Socialization** takes place early in life, and many of those very early experiences are lasting ones. The behavior one exhibits outside the privacy of the home can and will affect those with whom one comes in contact. Because what we do can influence the behavior of others, as well as ourselves, it is important to set the best example that we can both in the private and the public domain.

*Professional protocol can make or break professional relationships. Knowing the right thing to do and the right time to do it will give you a competitive edge in career opportunities.*

### OBJECTIVES

The objectives of this chapter are to help students
1. analyze professional protocol and ethics for school, business, workplace, and international situations;
2. gain the competitive edge in career opportunities by obtaining knowledge of etiquette and practicing proper and appropriate professional protocol and ethics;
3. recognize the role of professional protocol, ethics, and etiquette in the life of a college student;
4. understand why dressing for success really works; and
5. understand the role of proper dining etiquette.

### KEY CONCEPTS

1. Rules of conduct and behavior are important in all kinds of social gatherings.
2. Professional protocol can make or break professional relationships.
3. The manner in which we meet and greet others can greatly influence the kind of relationship we establish with them.
4. Knowing the right thing to do and the right time to do it will enable one to function more effectively when working with others.
5. Knowing how to conduct yourself in a luncheon interview may determine whether or not you get the job.

6. Exercising proper conduct when in the presence of an international delegation can contribute to improved international relationships.
7. Professional protocol begins the freshmen year in college.
8. Ethics at home, school, work, and church can define one's character and the environment in which one lives.
9. Dressing for success is directly related to achieving job success.
10. The behavior expected in formal social gatherings is very much prescribed. It is important to know these expectations before embarking on a formal social gathering.

## ETIQUETTE AND SOCIAL BEHAVIOR

Etiquette is the **set of rules** that govern social behavior. Webster's Dictionary defines etiquette as "the practices and forms prescribed by social convention or by authority" (*Webster's Dictionary*, 1985, p. 467). In the late 1960s and the 1970s, various movements suggested that social etiquette no longer had a place in the lives of most American citizens. The Women's Liberation Movement brought adverse attention to the governing rules of etiquette. The Movement questioned whether etiquette resulted in female subservience to males. Other questions were derived from opponents of etiquette: What is the importance of etiquette in educational settings? What good is it to act politely and still not get what you want?

Protocol can be associated with etiquette and is defined as "etiquette as it relates to affairs of state, especially to diplomatic exchange" (Webster's Dictionary, 1985, p. 468). The definition indicates the relationship between **protocol** and **etiquette. Protocol** goes beyond social etiquette in that it links cultures and countries by creating a common means of communication between people of various lands and political viewpoints. Various decisions have been made about heads of state through an examination of their behavior. How would the president of a country be perceived if his or her picture were flashed across television screens in the following characterization? The **president** is dressed sloppily with no attention to color combinations or style, is eating foods with fingers that should be eaten with appropriate utensils, is resting his elbows on the table when eating, and is talking louder than all of the other guests.

**Social protocol** suggests that there are rules that must be followed to govern the behavior of each of us when we are in the company of others. Just a simple "hello," "good morning," or "good afternoon" will certainly do more to get you off to a good start in the mornings than not greeting classmates, family members, professors, or the staff as you begin your day.

*Social protocol suggests there are rules that should govern the behavior of each of us when we are in the company of others. It includes behavior such as greeting others warmly and sending a proper thank you for time spent in meetings or interviews.*

There are reasons for learning **rules** of etiquette; for example, knowing the right thing to do and the right way in which to do it will make you appear more comfortable and more at ease in social gatherings. The impression that you give when you first meet someone will last a lifetime; therefore, it is imperative for you to practice proper etiquette both at home and at the university (Brennan, 2004; MacFarlane, 2004).

## *Successful Dress for Men and Women: Gaining the Competitive Edge*

**Business clothes** refer to those clothes worn in job settings that blend into the environment without distraction or interference with work performance. Rules for business attire relate to color, fabric, style, and accessories. The **basic rule** for dress is conservative color, style, and fabric. The color in business clothes should be basic natural browns, navy blue, black, and gray. **Natural fabrics** such as silk, wool, cotton, silk wool blends, or cotton wool blends are the better choices in fabrics. Styles are basic straight lines in the cut of the suit. For the most part, suits for men should be regular or Italian style. An overly long jacket will be a distraction from your talents if you are in an interview. Shirts that are very bright in color will be distractive, and pants sagging around the hipline will not gain acceptance in the professional world. Pant legs should fit neatly and gently touch the top of the shoe (Brennan, 2004; MacFarlane, 2004; Purdy, 2004; Post, 2004).

**Shoes** should be clean and shined. Dark trousers require dark socks, shoes, and belt. Black shoes may be worn with any color suit or pants; however, brown shoes should not be worn with black or gray suits. There should be a continuous **color flow line** from the shoe to the trousers. In an interview, you should try to avoid wearing neckties with diagonal lines or busy designs. Very busy designs tend to confuse people who have to stare at the design for periods of time. Sometimes persons who fix their eyes on very busy designs will tend to become dizzy. You would not want your interviewer to become ill or disoriented.

Men and women must be very careful when it comes to **fragrances**. Very sweet or very strong odors must be avoided in social gatherings. Many people are allergic to the various odors found in colognes, shaving lotions, and perfumes. It may be best to go without any fragrance, but if you do wear a fragrance, wear it sparingly. **One rule** of thumb is that if you can smell it, you are wearing too much. You do not want your cologne, perfume, or shaving lotion to arrive in a room minutes before you do. Neither do you want your fragrance to remain in the room minutes after you have gone.

There are three basic requirements of business hair for men and women: hair must be clean, neat, and shaped or styled. For men, it is important to have a neat haircut that is complementary to the face. Women must also have hair styled or cut to complement the face. **Habits** of slinging hair out of the face, and back and forth, are very distracting and annoying to those constantly observing this behavior.

Although **earrings** are very popular now for men and women, men may want to think twice before wearing earrings to a business or job interview. Women's jewelry must also be restricted. Bangles on the wrists will create annoying sounds, so try to avoid distracting the interviewer from the conversation. Long necklaces worn by women to an interview may be dangerous, as well as distracting. **Long necklaces** may get caught in items in the room, on the secretary's desk, or in your interviewer's office. You will not want anything to impact negatively on your interview; therefore, your competitive edge will be to follow proper rules of etiquette as they relate to dressing and dining out.

**Women's clothing** for the job interview must also be conservative in color, style, fabric, and length. **Natural colors** will blend in with the natural colors and tone of the face: blacks, navy blues, browns, tans, and grays. **Suits** are preferable for women in business endeavors and interviewing; however, certain types of dresses may be worn. **Dresses** with low-cut necklines are not appropriate, since they may be distracting and may make the wearer uncomfortable. A simple A-line dress, such as a pleated skirt with the hemline just below the knee, would be appropriate for interviewing. In addition to avoiding **low necklines**, avoid dresses or skirts that are too short (above the knee) or too long (more than halfway down the leg). **Shoes** for women must be conservative, with the toes and heels closed in. If you are not accustomed to wearing **high heels**, this is not the time to begin. Wear shoes that are comfortable for you in terms of the height and thickness of the **heel**. The two-inch heel is a very good height for business shoes. The shoes and pantyhose must match the hemline. Stockings or pantyhose must not be darker than the shoes worn with them.

Whenever possible, stay with natural fabrics that will allow your body to **breathe**. Comfortable clothes are much more relaxing and lead to a better interview. Some natural fabrics blended with polyester make for appropriate combinations.

Five general **guidelines** to aid you in determining whether your clothes are appropriate for the interview follow: 1) Make sure clothes fit nicely and are not too loose or too tight; you do not want to squirm and fidget with your clothing while you are interviewing; 2) Make sure that the fabric in suits and jackets is colorfast so that if you have to remove a jacket or suit, there will be no stain staring everyone in the face; 3) Women should make sure slips are not showing underneath the outer garment; 4) Make sure that jackets and suits are the right fit for you; suits and jackets that are too tight or too large will not accent your appearance; 5) Make sure that suits and dresses are clean and neatly pressed (Alexrod, 2004; Brennan, 2004; Post, 2004).

### *Business Posture*

The way you carry yourself has a lot to do with another's perception of you. What is observed about your **appearance** during the first few seconds of an encounter with another individual will create such a lasting impression that it may take you a lifetime to overcome it (especially if that impression is negative). The **ruler** at the beginning of your body and the **ruler** at the end of your body will determine the perception others have of you. The ruler at the beginning of your body, from the neck up, includes the first 12 inches. The ruler at the end of your body, your feet and legs, includes the last 12 inches.

**Walking** with confidence means that an individual's head is held up and steps are at a moderate pace. A confident walk gives the impression that you know where you are going and how you are going to get there.

Sitting properly with feet on the floor and your back against the back of the chair will indicate that you are prepared to take on the business of the day. **Sitting** in a slouched position will give the impression that you are bored with the people around you and that you would rather be somewhere else. Surely, this is not the impression you will want your interviewers to have of you. Therefore, business posture is important; it may determine whether you get the job (Brennan, 2004).

## *Introductions*

Today's students must know how to be **at ease** with strangers or in groups, know how and when to congratulate someone, know how to make introductions, and know how to conduct themselves at company social functions, receptions, and meals. Knowing and practicing proper business etiquette will contribute to individual, school, and business success.

The **first rule** for introductions is always make them, even if you cannot remember names. Gender is not an issue. The most important or highest-ranking person is named first. For example, Mr./Ms. Greater Power …Mr./Ms. Lesser Power. Both first and last names should be used in introductions. To **forget** a name is human. So simply and sincerely say, "I'm sorry; I seem to have forgotten your name." It is proper to correct someone who **mispronounces** your name by clearly saying it yourself.

Extend the right hand when being introduced. Use a firm, but not bone-crushing, handshake. Pump once or twice from the elbow and make eye contact unless your culture forbids making **eye contact**. Place your **name tag** on the right to make it easy to read. Begin a conversation, but remember to steer clear of controversial topics and personal attacks (Sabath, 1998).

## DINING AND RESTAURANT ETIQUETTE

Having a college education is not enough if you have not mastered the art of getting along with people. One of the best ways to learn to get along with people is to know how to conduct yourself properly in a **social setting**. After your interviewers have interviewed you in their corporate office, school building, or governmental agency, they may choose to complete the interview over lunch at their favorite restaurant. A story is told of a young man who had a very high GPA, 3.8 overall and a 4.0 in his major. Several companies and universities were trying to recruit this young man to their business or graduate school. The company that interviewed him at their corporate headquarters liked what they saw and heard and were ready to offer him a career with the company. But they waited to make the offer over lunch. They invited other senior members of the firm to join them for lunch with the prospective employee. The young man's dining etiquette was so bad that he blew the interview over lunch. Why? His table manners were so poor that they looked upon him as a burden and an **excessive expense** to the company.

**Food** is used at many **social occasions** to entertain and to fill a physical need. It is important that college students learn how to choose meals with proper nutrition in mind and know how to exhibit proper table manners. Why do we eat food? We eat food for various reasons: 1) *Physiological Reasons:* to sustain life; to maintain healthy bodies and minds, and to assist in disease prevention. 2) *Social Reasons:* to celebrate birthdays, weddings, anniversaries, and holidays; to introduce special guests, such as at receptions, and for many other family and business gatherings. 3) *Psychological Reasons:* eating when we are in distress and eustress.

Eating out has become very common for many individuals and families, and it can be a very pleasant experience if you are at ease in the experience.

## *Special Circumstances*

**Restaurants** want returning patrons, and so they give quality services to assure your return. Some even offer special services such as having servers read menus to blind persons or having signers available for hearing-impaired individuals.

If the menu contains several international foods, servers are trained to explain what each food is and what it contains.

The remaining pages in this chapter will help you to gain the competitive edge if you apply the information to your own situation.

How do you feel when you walk into a restaurant and see the beautifully set table, with all the fine china, the sparkling flatware, the exquisite crystal, and the fine, laundered table cloth? The water is poured in the water glasses and everything is color coordinated to create an atmosphere of beauty and richness. Would you be at ease in this situation?

## *Etiquette for Receptions*

**Receptions** are usually given for a large gathering of people. The purpose of the gatherings is usually to introduce some important person or persons, to **honor** someone for outstanding achievements, or to express appreciation for a charitable gift or large financial contribution. Receptions are **economical** because they quickly feed a large group of people in a small area and utilize few servers. Because many receptions will involve a large number of people, it will be imperative that you know the appropriate behavior to exhibit. Using good manners is a form of **courtesy**.

Many receptions include a **receiving line**, where guests are introduced to the guest of honor for the occasion. A line is formed, and guests file through to shake hands and introduce themselves, or are introduced by a host or hostess to the honored guest. Some important points to remember in the etiquette for receptions follow:
1. Leave large bags and purses at home.
2. You are going to need both **hands free** to shake hands and to get and eat your food.
3. If there is no host or hostess at the beginning of the line, **introduce** yourself to the first person in line, shake his/her hand, then go to the next person in line and do the same.
4. Give the persons in the receiving line a firm **handshake**.
5. **Congratulate**, thank, or welcome the person or persons, then move through the line quickly. Remember, this is not the time to share your life history.
6. After **shaking hands** with honored guests, proceed to the food table and get refreshments.
7. In many receptions, guests will have to **stand** and eat their food; therefore, it is important to place small amounts of food on the plate at one time.
8. Go to the **buffet line**, place the napkin and silverware underneath the plate.
9. Place a **small amount** of food on the plate. Remember, you can go back for seconds, but you do not want to make several trips to the buffet table.
10. You may have room on the **plate** to place your glass or cup. If not, you will need to **balance** your plate on top of the cup or glass.

11. After you have received your food and have begun eating, you will need to **mingle** with others at the reception.
12. Remember to **thank** your host and hostess for the reception before you leave.

## *Etiquette at a Formal Dinner*
## *Why Do We Set a Table?*

A **table** is set for comfort, convenience, and aesthetic purposes. The diagram on page 222 shows how utensils are arranged so that an individual can reach and grasp each one easily and comfortably. All the **utensils** you will need for the meal are placed at your place setting or cover. A **cover** is a table setting for one person and is also known as a place setting.

The guidelines for proper dress for dining are the same as those discussed for interviewing, in the first part of this chapter.

A **formal** dinner may have from three to as many as twelve courses, and all foods are served by food servers. There is not an **empty space** on the cover or in front of the diner in a formal meal until after the main course is served. Extra plates may be placed on the table to add aesthetic appeal and to protect the table linen. A **course** is a group of foods served at one particular time in a meal. The formal style of meal service was experienced by the aforementioned young man when being interviewed over lunch. The young man would have been more at ease had he known the rules that govern dining behavior.

A. Pause for a table grace. If no one offers a grace and you would like to, ask permission first. But if your grace is going to be silent, just bow your head and silently bless the food.
B. Remove the napkin from the table, unfold it once, and place it across your lap. (When you unfold it, it should still be in half.) Place the folded crease closet to your waist.
C. The napkin is used to wipe your mouth and hands and to protect your clothing.
D. Use the napkin to wipe crumbs from your mouth before you take a drink. This will prevent crumbs from collecting around the rim of your glass.
E. At the end of the meal, place the napkin on the table above the plate.
F. Begin eating only after everyone at your table has been both seated and served, unless the table has more than ten persons. In this case, you may begin eating when those on either side of you have been served.

### *How Do You Know Which Utensil to Use First and Subsequently?*

You will recall that one of the purposes of setting a table is convenience. This is illustrated in the way in which a table is set. Note the diagram on page 222. The forks and napkins are to the left, and the cocktail fork knife, and spoon are to the right. A sample menu for a formal dinner is shown below:

*Menu*
Ocean Shrimp Cocktail
French Onion Soup, with Whole Wheat Crackers
Tossed Green Salad
Filet Mignon with Mushroom Sauce
Glazed Baby Carrots and Broccoli Spears
Buttered Crescent Rolls
Iced Tea
Baked Alaska
Coffee

1. Which utensil would be used to eat the ocean shrimp cocktail?
2. How did you decide your answer?
3. Which utensil would be used to eat the French onion soup? Defend your answer.
4. Which utensil would be used to eat the tossed salad?

Analyze the answers you gave to the four questions. Come up with a rule that determines which utensil to use first and subsequently.

### *What is the Proper Way to Eat Soup?*

**Soup** is eaten from a cup or bowl using a spoon. The soup is dipped away from you and then brought back to the mouth. Try to figure out why the soup is dipped away

*A formal place setting may include multiple glasses, utensils, plates, and linens. Everything is placed so an individual can reach and grasp each item easily and comfortably during the meal.*

from you. Eat from the side of the spoon, and try to refrain from slurping. No matter how much you want those last bits of soup, do not drink the soup from the bowl. If the soup is too hot to eat right away, wait until it cools down (refrain from blowing on the soup at the table). You may dip a few spoonfuls in and out for a short period to speed the cooling process.

**Crackers** are not to be crumbled and sprinkled in the soup. Eat them one bite at a time after a spoonful of soup has been taken into the mouth and swallowed. When you crumble crackers in your soup, they become soggy and are unsightly to others at your table. Avoid excessive use of crackers, as this may indicate that you are more of a liability to a company than an asset (Sabath, 1998).

## *Eating a Cherry Tomato*

When a tossed salad has a cherry tomato in it, many people leave it on the salad plate because they are not able to **manage** the eating of it. Try these simple steps:
1. Hold the cherry tomato with the point of a knife, then pierce the tomato with the tines of the salad fork.
2. Hold the tomato with the tines of the fork. Cut the tomato into halves or quarters, depending on the size of the tomato.
3. Be careful not to squirt another diner with the juice of the tomato.

## *Drinking from a Glass*

You may have as many as three glasses on a table at one time. The glass at the tip of the dinner knife is the **water goblet**. Water is usually served at all meals, so it will be important for you to know where the water glass is placed. The small glass over the spoon, next to the knife, is the wine glass. The large goblet to the right of the wine glass is the beverage glass. After drinking from your water glass, return it to its place at the tip of the knife. Hold the water glass about midway, lift to the mouth, and drink. Avoid placing fingers inside the top of the glass to lift it. Do you remember what to do with the napkin in regard to drinking from the glass? (Refer to the section on *Etiquette at a Formal Dinner*.) Drink small amounts at a time, and refrain from using water or other liquids to wash your food down. Try eating a fourth of the food on your plate before you take your first drink.

*Even something as simple as a cherry tomato can seem daunting if you don't know how to eat it properly in a formal dining situation.*

## *Cutting Meat on Your Plate*

You will need to use a knife and fork to cut your **meat** properly. Hold the **fork** in the left hand if you are right-handed and in the right hand if you are left-handed. The **knife** would then be placed in the other hand. Hold the meat in place with the fork, and cut three or four bite-sized pieces of meat. Do not cut up all of the meat at one time, because your plate will appear to be a child's plate–or worse, your pet's plate. During the cutting process, the **knife** should not move between the tines of the fork.

In the **American style** of meal service, after you have finished cutting the two or three bite-sized pieces of meat, you will reverse the positions of the knife and fork. The fork would again be placed in the right hand of the right-handed person and the left hand of the left-handed person and the knife in the opposite hand. In the European style of meal service, the knife and fork are not reversed, but remain in the same hands as when cutting the meat.

In the **formal style** of meal service, even chicken with bone in it is cut with a fork and knife. You may want to practice this at home in order to gain a feeling of ease and comfort when cutting chicken that contains bones.

### *Bread and Butter*

The bread-and-butter plate is placed above the forks on the left side of the plate. When **bread** is passed to you, remove it from the bread basket with your hand and place it on your bread plate; if **tongs** are provided, use the tongs to acquire a piece of bread. Do not use a fork when taking bread from the bread basket. Bread is **broken** with the hands rather than cut, unless the bread is in a loaf or it is another type of special bread.

Although many people like to **butter** the whole slice of bread or the roll at one time, it is proper to butter the bread one bite at a time. Use the butter knife supplied on the bread-and-butter plate to spread the butter on the bread. If you do not have a knife on the bread-and-butter plate, use the regular dinner knife to place butter on your bread.

### *Seasonings and Sweeteners*

For seasonings and sweeteners, the best rule of thumb is **conserve**. Taste your food before adding any seasoning or sweetener, and then use them **sparingly**. Use only one sweetener at a time, and then taste your food to make sure you have not over-sweetened or over-seasoned. Opening two or three packets of sugar at one time may signal excessive **waste** of resources and could impact negatively on your character.

Remember, **salt and pepper shakers** should be passed together, even when someone asks for only one of them. Pass the shakers to your right and set them down near the person who requested them, or near the person next to you. Fingers may get tangled if you attempt to take the shakers out of the hands of the person who passed them to you, rather than picking them up off of the table. Usually the salt and pepper shakers are placed in the center of the table near the centerpiece, and they should be returned there after each diner has used them.

### *Conversation While Dining Out*

Have you ever been at a table enjoying your meal when someone started a **conversation** about a topic so unpleasant that you were unable to finish your meal? This has probably happened to most of us. As a well-groomed, enlightened college student and adult, you do not want to be the one to cause other guests to have to discontinue their meal or to improperly digest the meal as a result of improper table manners.

*Taste your food before adding seasoning or sweetener, and then use them sparingly.*

What would be appropriate topics for conversation at a luncheon or dinner meal in which you are being interviewed? To merely talk about the weather may suggest to the interviewer that you are not well read or have a narrow focus on life. You would certainly not want to dominate the discussion by talking about yourself. If you have done a good job of researching the company or business, you may want to highlight some of the positive aspects of the company. Mention an outstanding humanitarian effort of the company that has drawn widespread attention. Ask questions of the persons interviewing you. Show interest in their lives and backgrounds. This initiative will do two things: It will say to the interviewer that you have a genuine interest in the persons who manage the company, and it will show that you have interest in learning how the persons in the company came through the ranks to get to their current positions.

Table conversations must be **pleasant** and positively charged. Try to avoid controversial and argumentative topics. Before the interview, research interests of the company and its key personnel, particularly the Chief Executive Officer (CEO). Discuss topics that interest the company, such as the latest computer technology, events in the world of sports, the company's participation in the development of the community, the company's involvement in educational programs that have assisted students in their career development, publicity for the company, and hobbies or leisure activities of the interviewers. Be sure to make an effort to include the whole group at your table in the conversation. Allow others an opportunity to participate by asking them their opinions or suggestions (Brennan, 2004; Ferguson, 2004; Johnson, 2005).

## *Paying the Bill*

If you have been invited to the luncheon or dinner by the interviewer, the interviewer is most likely prepared to pay for your meal. When the interviewer offers to pay for your meal, do not argue. Accept the offer and simply say, "Thank you." If the invitation indicated that it is a **dutch treat**, this means that each person will pay his/her own way. Try to reach an agreement in advance about who will pay. To be on the safe side, make sure you have enough money to pay your own way. Do save the embarrassment of having a **charge card** refused by carefully checking the status of the account before you attempt to use the card.

Restaurants have different ways in which they receive your payment for the meal. With formal dining, a server usually retrieves your payment for the bill, takes it to the cashier, and brings your change back to the table. You will know whether or not to pay the server if the **check** is brought to the table on a tray or if the server indicates to you in some other way that you may pay the server. In some restaurants, you will pay the bill on your way out. Regardless of how the meal is paid for, make sure the bill has been paid before you leave the restaurant.

## *Gratuity*

There are different opinions concerning paying gratuities in restaurants. **Gratuity** (the tip) is the money given to the server for the service you received. Some people believe that you tip only if you liked the food and the service was good. I believe that tipping should be done, even with the worst service; however, the server and manager need to know when the food or service was unsatisfactory. By leaving a tip when service was poor, you do two things: first, you let the server know that you respect him/her as a person; and second, you let the server know that you understand the condition of the food was not necessarily his/her responsibility, since everyone is allowed one day of poor performance. Your tip may also cause the server to make sure that you receive very good service the next time around.

In many five-star restaurants, the tip (gratuity) is already figured into your bill. This percentage may be as high as **25%** in some hotel restaurants and as low as **15%** in other establishments. Read your bill so that you do not pay gratuity twice.

### *Common Dining Etiquette*

1. *R.S.V.P.* on an invitation means that the person who invited you needs a response to know whether or not you are coming. It is imperative that you respond in a timely manner to such invitations.
2. Arrive on time if you are a dinner guest.
3. Always wash your hands with soap and water before eating.
4. Ask to have food passed rather than reach across the table or in front of someone else.
5. If you do not drink alcoholic beverages, the interviewing luncheon is not the time or the place to start. Do not be forced to do those things that run counter to your values and beliefs, even in an interview.
6. Keep jackets and suitcoats on at the table unless your host asks you to remove them.
7. Do not apply makeup at the dinner table. Excuse yourself and apply makeup in the powder room.
8. Remove a bone or pit from your mouth with your finger or a spoon in an inconspicuous way.
9. Put personal belongings on your lap or the floor, not on the table, in a restaurant.
10. If you need something from a server, call him or her quietly when the server is near the table.
11. If you drop a fork or napkin on the floor, simply ask the server for another one. You need not elaborate on what happened to the first one.
12. If you spill something, inform the server so that the server may take care of the spill. Thank the server for taking care of the spill.
13. Practice good posture while dining.
14. Try a small portion of all foods offered.
15. When in doubt about how to eat a food, follow the lead of your host. In a restaurant, you may quietly ask your server for advice.
16. After the meal, avoid leaving the table until the host or hostess rises. If you must leave the table, ask if you may be excused.
17. At the end of the meal, thank the server for serving you. Thank the host or interviewer for inviting you and providing for your meal.
18. The two most appreciated phrases in the English language are "please," and "thank you."

## SUMMARY

Knowing what to do at the right time will make you feel much more at ease when you are in a social gathering. The way you **dress** will play a pivotal role in the way you present yourself to prospective employers. The **conservative rule** of dress includes the use of natural colors and fabrics, and regular-styled suits and dresses, with lengths appropriate for business wardrobes. Faddish clothing and hairstyles may not give you the competitive edge you need to win-out over the other person.

Walking with **confidence** will cause others to take notice of you and what you have to offer. First **impressions** last. Therefore, it is important to make sure that the first meeting you have with a person interested in employing you is a positively charged one that gives the prospective employer a good feeling about you from the beginning.

Receptions are held to introduce important people to society, to congratulate people for achievements, and to express appreciation for a financial contribution or other contributions to groups or agencies. Properly **introduce** yourself as you go through receiving lines. As you go through the food line, take small portions that may be handled easily as you mingle with guests.

By using proper **etiquette** in public places, you and those with whom you dine will feel more comfortable and at ease. Keep a positive conversation going during the meal that focuses the attention away from you, but on others at the table.

Paying gratuity means giving money to the server for the service received. Since some restaurants figure the gratuity in the bill, check to make sure that you do not pay gratuity twice.

## *Professional Ethics*

**Ethics** is a branch of moral philosophy. When applied to a particular profession or field, ethics is useful in uncovering the values that drive practice. These values are sometimes expressed in formal **codes of ethics** or in the lives of practitioners.

Professionals within a given discipline can develop their own code of ethics. **Codes** in and of themselves, however, do not have value unless they are actively used, interpreted, reviewed, and revised over time. A code cannot be expected to motivate bad people to behave well, nor can a code take the place of the individual's aspiration for good character or morally reflective practice.

Codes are important when they reflect the realities of professional life. Codes also declare to those outside the field the way a certain group of professionals thinks about its responsibilities.

College students must be introduced to professional organizations within their own discipline early in the college career, preferably during the freshman year. Students will pay membership dues, fill out an application, and begin the journey toward becoming a **professional**. With membership in professional organizations comes subscriptions to refereed journals and other journals, as well as newsletters, and opportunities to attend professional meetings at a reduced cost.

Chapters of professional organizations, including **honor societies**, abound on college campuses, offering numerous opportunities for leadership development and participation by students and faculty. On some college and university campuses, membership in the discipline major or parent organization is required. **Membership** then becomes a springboard for faculty and students to attend and participate in local, state, national, and international workshops, conferences, and annual meetings to network with other professionals and preprofessionals and to enrich and enhance academic skills.

**Work ethics** are standards of conduct for successful job performance. Ethics show morality, or a sense of right and wrong. The concepts of fairness, right and wrong, and good and bad affect your work ethics.

A strong work ethic will help you achieve personal satisfaction. **Successful** employees work not only for the company but also for personal satisfaction. You may not be complimented each day for the work that you do, even if your supervisor recognizes the quality of your work and your importance to the company. Therefore, you need to develop personal feelings of satisfaction from the work you do. In turn, personal satisfaction will make your work seem more important and more enjoyable. Performance equals ability times motivation times resources. **Performance** = (ability x motivation x resources).

A study by Joan Finegan (1994) examined how personal values influence our judgment of the morality of some workplace behaviors. Sixty-nine undergraduates were asked to rank-order separately Rohearh's instrumental and terminal values in terms of their importance as guiding principles in their lives. Subjects then read four scenarios, each of which described ethically questionable behavior of the sort that might be encountered in business. Subjects were then asked to rate whether or not the behavior of the person described in the scenario was **ethical** and whether or not they had any intentions to rectify the situation. People with different value complexes perceived the targeted behaviors differently. For example, subjects who valued honesty perceived the behavior as more immoral than subjects who did not value honesty.

While the ranking of the instrumental value "honesty" was the best **predictor** of people's judgment about the morality of the behavior, their ranking of the instrumental value "ambition" was the best predictor of their behavioral intentions.

One can analyze the importance of codes within a particular profession by investigating the methods used in their construction, and by asking how the codes are included within programs of professional preparation, in-service education, and programs of certification and licensing. When codes are actively used in these ways, members of the group prove their collective will to hold each other accountable for a particular kind of behavior. A professional **culture** that finds this type of utility in codes of ethics assures the public that the group is serious about protection against harm from unethical colleagues.

A code is especially valuable in those circumstances where action by the practitioner will unavoidably result in harm to someone. Such instances may involve **conflicting rights** of students and teachers, athletes and coaches, or subjects and researchers. Ethical dilemmas require the mediation between competing interests. Codes may also provide guidance regarding professional etiquette concerning associations with colleagues, clients, and the public (Ferguson, 2004; Johnson, 2005).

When there is no instruction from the profession, the practitioner alone determines what to do. In that case, practitioners use their reasoning, intuition, and/or practical experience with matters of right and wrong. Without instruction from colleagues, this kind of decision-making is often based upon self-interest and may be no more complicated than asking, "What does my employer or the **public law** require me to do?" (Fain & Gillespie, 1990). In searching for guidance, the **practitioner** gains no benefit from the collective experience and knowledge of colleagues. As a result, the basis for determining good practice is invented by each solitary practitioner, and the opportunity for building a unified profession becomes impossible.

Codes of ethics, if properly crafted, can reflect the moral foundation of professional life. These codes provide an **opportunity** to instruct the beginning practitioner about professional responsibility, and they serve as a reminder to those in the field that continued practice is dependent upon compliance with specific expectations held by colleagues. Providing that attention is given to enforcement, codes can be instrumental in guarding against those who believe that decency in professional behavior is all relative, all a matter of personal taste, or an arbitrary preference for professional behavior.

Teaching ethics requires that instructors have **good character**, are familiar with ethical concepts, and have an interest in moral reflection. Attention must be given to moral philosophy within professional preparation and in service education. Research agendas that collect and analyze case materials and, thereby, describe how ethical principles are applied within the specializations are needed. Great benefit would be derived if each specialized discipline were to create an ongoing conversation about ethics in their respective fields. If this were to occur, the unification of practitioners who serve diverse groups of clientele across a great number of environments would be realized. It is the ethics of these practitioners that serve as a common foundation for professional practice (Johnson, 2005).

In the **twenty-first century,** all kinds of ethical considerations confront us and compel us to action. Foremost among these are genetic engineering and the **ethics of genes**. Scientists can now detect many characteristics of an individual, including the presence of life-threatening diseases before birth. Each year we learn more about genetic characteristics, and, thus, we are better able to foresee aspects of a child's future. However, with this knowledge comes an ethical challenge that will face every American and world citizen in the coming decades (Ivens, 2004).

Eventually, we may be able to test every fetus for a variety of incurable genetic diseases. Should those tests be mandated? Should parents be informed of their future child's fate? Should the prospect of an incurable disease provide grounds for abortion? It has also been suggested (though not proven) that alcoholism and other behavioral disorders may be related, at least in part, to **genetic factors**. Suppose a person were found to carry a particular gene or combination of genes that were thought to predispose them toward alcoholism? To whom should that information be conveyed? To the individual? To his or her doctor? His or her employer? The insurance company?

Taking these issues a step further, it may soon be possible to alter an individual's **DNA** in utero, perhaps even in the first weeks of pregnancy. Many people would probably agree to genetic manipulation if it could cure their child of a fatal disease, but where do we draw the line? Would you allow such a procedure to improve genetically defective eyesight or perhaps prevent crippling arthritis in later years? Would you be willing to enhance your child's **IQ** or make him or her more athletic? What about changing height or hair color? As with many other aspects of science and technology, we must come to grips with the question of whether it is ethical to do something simply because we are able to do it (Trefil & Hazen, 1998, p. 564).

## *Ethics Scenario*

A student had not done well during her last semester. A few days before graduation, she approached the chairperson of the biology department to see what she could do in order to graduate. The chairperson showed her the final exam paper, which she denied was her own, yet it was. She had failed the final exam and became very angry with the chairperson, to the point that she cursed the chairperson, began to scream, and said she would not leave the office until her grade was changed. The chairperson in turn cursed the student and threatened to slap her face if she did not leave. The police were called and took a report of the incident. The student received an "F" in the course and did not graduate. Who was right? Who was wrong? Why?

## *Scenario 2*

A couple finds out that the baby the wife is carrying has a relatively low IQ and an incurable disease. Genetics engineers indicate that they can alter the IQ and cure the disease before the baby is born. Should the parents have this information before the baby is born? Should the doctors alter the IQ and cure the disease? Discuss.

# GLOSSARY

**Banquet:** a formal meal that includes a program.
**Business Clothes:** clothes conservative in style, color, and fabric.
**Business Posture:** correct way of sitting, standing, and walking that inspires confidence.
**Cover:** a place setting for one person at a table.
**Ethics:** a branch of moral philosophy that addresses issues of right and wrong.
**Etiquette:** the set of rules that govern social behavior.
**Five-Star Restaurant:** the highest classification of restaurants, characterized by elegant service, high-quality food, and elegant atmosphere, where dinner guests are seated by a maitre 'd.
**Formal Meal:** A meal served to diners in an elegant atmosphere with advanced table setting and at least three courses.
**Gratuity or Tip:** a monetary measure of your gratitude for meal service.
**Meal Service:** the way a meal is served. Common styles of meal service are American, English, buffet, family, and formal.
**Menu:** a list of foods and prices offered at a restaurant or cafeteria.
**Natural Fabrics:** those grown in nature from plant or animal sources, such as silk, cotton, wool, and linen.
**Place Setting:** table setting for one person.
**Professional:** one who has earned at least a bachelor's degree in a discipline and follows a specific code of ethics.

**Protocol:** etiquette as it relates to affairs of state or organizational stature.
**Reception:** a social gathering for a large number of people where food is served and people are presented and thanked for some accomplishment.
**R.S.V.P.:** stands for *Repondez s'il vous plait* (respond please, or please reply).
**Rule of 12:** be well groomed from head to toe; people rate the first 12 inches–head and neck, and the last 12 inches–legs and feet.
**Table Setting:** the appropriate placement of dinnerware, flatware, and glassware on a table in anticipation of a meal being eaten.
**Wardrobe:** the complete supply of clothes for an individual.

## MENU TERMS:

**Ala carte:** featured items on a menu are priced individually. A separate price is given for soup, salads, main dish, beverage, etc.
**A la Kiev:** containing butter, garlic, and chives.
**A la King:** served with a white cream sauce that contains mushrooms, green peppers, and pimentos.
**A la Mode:** served with ice cream.
**Almandine:** made or garnished with almonds.
**Au Gratin:** served with cheese.
**Au Jus:** served with natural juices.
**Centerpiece:** a decorative item, or object, usually placed in the center of a dining table to add aesthetic appeal, beauty and interest.
**Course:** all foods served together at the same time during a meal. Examples of courses are appetizer, salad, main dish or entree, and dessert.
**du Jour:** of the day; for instance "Soup de Jour" means soup of the day.
**En Brochette:** cooked or served in small pieces on a skewer.
**En Coquille:** served in a shell.
**En Croquette:** breaded and deep fried.
**En Papillote:** cooked in parchment paper to seal juices.
**Florentine:** prepared with spinach.
**Food Guide Pyramid:** a guide to daily food choices. It groups foods into six groups on the basis of their similarity in nutrient content. The six groups are breads, cereals, rice and pasta–6-11 servings; fruit group–2-4 servings; meat, poultry, fish, dried beans, eggs, and nuts–2-3 servings; vegetable group–3-5 servings; milk, yogurt, and cheese–2-3 servings; fats, oils, and sweets–use sparingly.
**Julienne:** cut into long, thin slices.
**Marengo:** sauteed with mushrooms, tomatoes, and olives.
**Picato:** prepared with lemon.
**Provencal:** prepared with garlic and olive.
**Table d'hote:** the entire meal has one price. Sometimes the one price includes a beverage, appetizer, and dessert.

## REFERENCES

Axelrod, A. (2004). *First book of etiquette.* Quirk Books.
Baldridge, L. (1995). *Letita Baldridge's new complete guide to executive manners.* New York: Rawson Associates.
Brennan, L. (2004). *Business etiquette for the 21st century: What to do, and what not to do.* Piathus Books.
Ferguson, (2004). *Professional ethics and etiquette.* Ferguson.

Ivens, S. (2004). *The modern girl's guide to etiquette: How to get it right in every situation.* Piathus.

Johnson, D. (2005). *Etiquette intelligence: The ultimate international business tool.* Harper Resource.

MacFarlane, M. (2004). The book of etiquette. Main Street Press.

Petrin, C., & Thomas, R. (1995). *"New office etiquette."* Training and Development. 49 (14).

Purdy, C. (2004). *Urban etiquette: Marvelous manners for the modern metropolis.* Wildcat Canyon Press.

Post, P. (2004). *Emily Post's etiquette, 7th edition.* Harper Resource.

Sabath, A. M. (1993). *Business etiquette in brief: The competitive edge for today's professional.* Holbrook, MA: Bob Adams.

Sabath, A. M. (1998). *Business etiquette: 101 ways to conduct business with charm and savvy.* Franklin Lakes, NJ: Career Press.

Stewart, M., and Faux, M. (1994). *Executive etiquette in the new workplace.* New York: St. Martins Press.

Wyse, L. (1992). *Company manners.* New York: Crown Publishers.

# ACTIVITY 1

Make a place setting diagram for the meals below. Label dinnerware, flatware, and glassware used.

> Orange Juice
> Scrambled Eggs and Sausage
> Buttered Grits
> Whole Wheat Toast
> Milk

> Hamburger and French Fries
> Tossed Salad
> Fruit Punch

# ACTIVITY 2

Cream of Broccoli Soup  
Flowered Onion -Buffalo Wings  
Fruit Cup  
Sorbet  
Roasted Rock Island Cornish Hens/Wild Rice  
Julienne Carrots and French Green Beans  
Buttered Whole Wheat Rolls  
Peach Melba Cakes  
Cranberry Iced Tea  
Coffee and Mint Leaf  

Given the table diagram and menu, indicate the following:
1. What food is eaten first? Second?
2. What utensil will be used to eat the sorbet?
3. What will be the last course served?

Research social protocol in three of the following countries and contrast findings with social protocol in United States. Use the Internet to obtain the latest information on these countries.
1. Ethiopia (Africa)
2. Russia (Europe)
3. Cuba (Central America)
4. Hong Kong (Asia)
5. India (Southern Asia)
6. Sidney (Australia)

Include information on business dress, dining out, introductions, handshakes, and job interviews.

**Fats, Oils & Sweets**
*Use Sparingly*

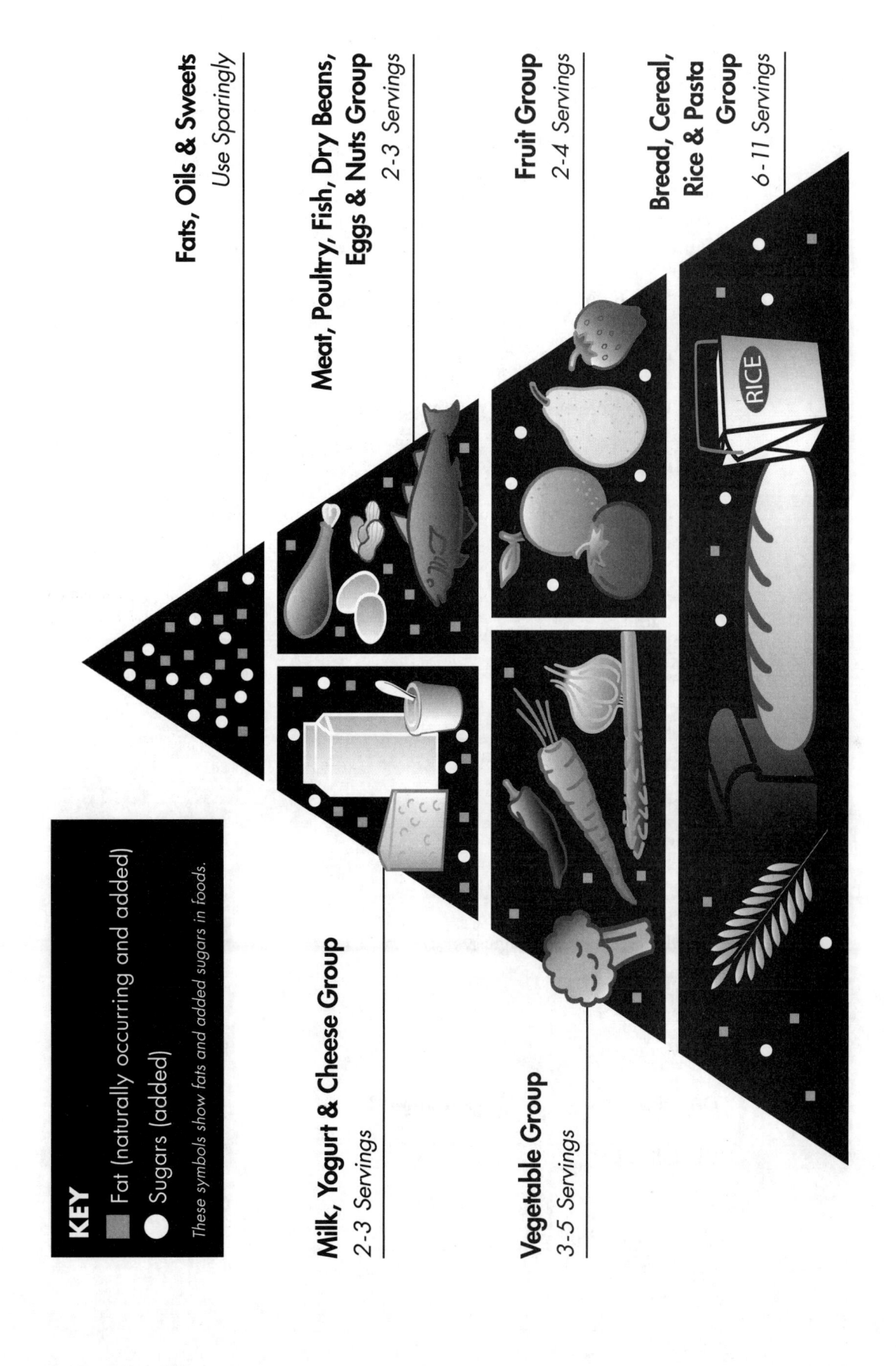

**Meat, Poultry, Fish, Dry Beans, Eggs & Nuts Group**
*2-3 Servings*

**Fruit Group**
*2-4 Servings*

**Bread, Cereal, Rice & Pasta Group**
*6-11 Servings*

**KEY**
■ Fat (naturally occurring and added)
● Sugars (added)

*These symbols show fats and added sugars in foods.*

**Milk, Yogurt & Cheese Group**
*2-3 Servings*

**Vegetable Group**
*3-5 Servings*

## ACTIVITY 3

### *Food Guide Pyramid*

Keep a record of foods you eat for three days. Compare your list of foods to the Food Pyramid. Where did most of your food fit? Were any items on the pyramid not included in your foods list?

Using the food guide pyramid as a guide to daily food choices, evaluate your food choices over a three-day period. Keep a list of the foods you eat for three days. Then count the number of servings you had from each of the six groups.

1. Did you include foods from each of the six groups?

2. In which category did you have the most servings?

3. If most of your foods were in the third and sixth groups, what should you do?

## ACTIVITY 4

Research professional organizations in the following disciplines. Choose two disciplines, and then fill out the following worksheet.

    Art
    English
    Biology
    Chemistry
    Computer Science
    Environmental Science
    Business Administration
    Accounting
    Elementary Education
    Law
    Physical Education and Recreation
    History
    Human Sciences
    Modern Foreign Languages
    Sociology
    Social Work
    Nursing
    Mathematics

**Organization I**    **Organization II**

**Discipline I**

    Founder:
    Year Founded:
    Purpose:
    Headquarters:

**Discipline II**

    Founder:
    Year Founded:
    Purpose:
    Headquarters:

# ACTIVITY 5

Secure an application for membership in a professional organization in your major. Fill it out and send in your membership dues. Make a list of the benefits of membership. Compare with a classmate's organizational benefits.

How can membership in the organization assist you in your college career? After your college career?

Describe the organization's code of ethics.

Attend one professional meeting and write a two-page report about your experience.

# CHAPTER *ten*

## Dimensions of Leadership

### INTRODUCTION

A chain is only as strong as the weakest link, and all members in the organization provide the "links" for organization. Nevertheless, a great deal of responsibility for an organization's success revolves around the leaders or officers. The **stronger** the leaders, the more likely that your organization will have a good year: one filled with goal accomplishments and recognition of members.

*A successful leader demonstrates professional conduct, dresses for success, uses acceptable manners, encourages teamwork, and efficiently performs duties.*

To ensure the **success** of the leaders, it is necessary that those who are in leadership position knows the basics of leadership theories, research, and public speaking; understand professional conduct; dress for success; understand and use acceptable manners; know how to be a team worker; and, of course, know how to carry out **specific duties** of the offices in which they serve. As an established leader or potential leader, you will find help in all of these areas in this chapter on leadership.

It is important that **leaders** always be alert to new ideas. Many opportunities for leadership development are available through workshops, seminars, and classes. As one who wishes to lead, you should take advantage of every opportunity to attend workshops and conferences that will enhance your leadership skills.

### OBJECTIVES

The objectives of this chapter are to
1. identify characteristics and definitions of effective leaders;
2. determine ways to assess effective leadership behavior;
3. articulate various differences in leadership styles and behaviors among racial and cultural groups;
4. demonstrate effective use of parliamentary procedure;
5. demonstrate ways to plan and conduct effective meetings.

> ## KEY CONCEPTS
> 
> 1. Leadership is the responsibility of the total group.
> 2. Leadership requires the ability to influence others in the achievement of goals.
> 3. The qualities of effective leadership can be learned.
> 4. There are three principal leadership styles: autocratic, democratic, and laissez-faire.
> 5. Leadership and management are different.
> 6. The effective use of parliamentary procedure can help leaders influence group goal accomplishments.
> 7. Group members can contribute to effective meetings by being prepared to take responsibility in discussions and assignments.
> 8. The best leadership style depends on how mature members of a group are at any given time.
> 9. Women leaders thrive in leadership models that inspire and communicate.
> 10. Multi-cultural organizations are more complex and especially demanding because of the potential for misunderstanding, conflict, and member dropout.

## LESSONS FROM GEESE

When you see geese heading south for the winter, flying along in a "V" formation, you might consider what science has discovered about why they fly that way.

Fact 1: By flying in the "V" formation, the whole flock adds at least 71% more flying range than is possible if each bird flew on its own. As each goose flaps its wings, it creates an "uplift" for the birds that follow.

Lesson:
People who share a common direction and sense of community can get where they are going more quickly and more easily because they are traveling on the strength and trust–i.e., the "uplift"–of the group.

Fact 2: When a goose falls out of formation, it suddenly feels the drag and resistance of flying alone. It quickly moves back into formation to take advantage of the lifting power of the bird immediately in front of it.

Lesson: If we have as much sense as geese, we will stay in formation with those who are headed in the same direction.

Fact 3: When the head goose gets tired, it rotates back in the wing, and another goose flies point.

Lesson: It is sensible to take turns doing demanding jobs, whether with people or geese flying south.

Fact 4: Geese honk from behind to encourage those up front to keep up their speed.

*Geese demonstrate some of the most important qualities of leadership: they work together, encourage each other, take turns performing difficult tasks, and stand by each other during trying times.*

What do we say when we honk from behind?

Finally, —and this is important—when a goose gets sick or is wounded by gunshot and falls out of formation, two other geese fall out with that goose and follow it down to lend help and protection. They stay with the fallen goose until it is able to fly or until it dies. Only then do they launch out on their own or with another formation to catch up with the group.

Lesson:
If we have as much sense as geese, we will stand by each other in difficult times. The next time you see a formation of geese, remember that it is a reward, a challenge, and a privilege to be a contributing member of a team.

Of such is the philosophy of a leader and of leadership. It is important that the leader have concern for the members of a group and also recognize that leadership is a shared responsibility. In addition, the goose story reminds us that there comes a time when leaders must step aside and allow others to assume leadership of the group.

**Effective leaders** not only know their strengths and weaknesses, but they also manage them. They do so through conscious objective decisions made from the perspective of a self-aware person. Further, effective leaders are those whose personal qualities inspire others to follow. An effective leader is also an effective follower.

The qualities of **leadership** can be learned and refined through awareness, feedback, and practice. Cribbin, (1982) asked managers at all levels to describe the characteristics of the most effective manger they have ever known. From presidents to supervisors, they cited similar clusters of behavior. A sample of their comments is presented below.

## THE BEST LEADERS

"He taught me to be critical of my own work, something I'm trying to do with my own people."

"She inspired confidence by having respect for and confidence in us. Often she thought that I was better than I thought I was."

"He not only accepted new ideas, he went out of his way to encourage them."

"She had a short fuse. But if your evidence was good, she'd let you try something new and give you credit."

"He was the most professional person I've worked for. He knew the business backwards and forwards."

"He insisted on high standards of performance but helped us reach them."

"She gave us as much freedom as we could handle."

"He was a good communicator. He kept us updated on things that were important to us."

"She was so well-organized that almost by osmosis you learned how to organize your work."

"He made us feel important and he convinced us that work was important." (Cribbin, 1982, pp. 15-16).

## THE WORST LEADERS

The reverse side of this exercise is interesting. A sample of the remarks made follows:

"She was demeaning. You rarely left her office without feeling worse about yourself and angry with her."

"He motivated through fear. As a result, all he got was malicious obedience, the absolute minimum that had to be done."

"She was petty. She nitpicked about things that were trivial."

"He was a politician. He used everyone for his own purposes."

"He was indecisive. He'd never make a decision if he could avoid doing so."

"He was an idea-rapist. Any good idea you gave him became his when he brought it to his boss."

"She had a wonderful division of labor. When things went well, she took all the credit. When they went wrong, you got all the blame."

"He spoke with a forked tongue. He'd tell you one story and a different one to someone else."

"She was unapproachable. She was always too busy to listen to you or give you advice." (Cribbin, 1982, pp. 16-17).

These nineteen statements give the flavor of the managers' reactions. Certain observations can be made from these managers' comments:
1. The memories are charged with feelings. Excellent leaders and terrible leaders always get an emotional reaction.
2. The **reactions** tend to cluster around two issues: the managerial skills and professionalism of the person and his or her helpfulness and supportiveness.
3. Groups do not mention unusual strengths or weaknesses. Generally, they recall simple behaviors that were motivating or alienating.
4. Under questioning, all groups agreed that the **worst managers** could have improved by gradually substituting constructive for destructive behaviors. Such change would have required no superhuman effort.
5. Under questioning, all groups agreed that the **best leaders** were aware of their impact on others, were open to feedback, knew what they had going for them, and worked hard to curb their negative tendencies. Few or none of these traits were typical of the worst leaders. Despite the unscientific nature of this evidence, the experiences of these managers offer realistic guidelines for improvement of your leadership behavior (Cribbin, 1982, p. 17).

*Bad leadership uses crticism and destructive behavior in an effort to modify coworker's productivity. Good leadership uses positive motivation and constructive behavior to inspire and direct coworkers.*

**Dimensions of Leadership**

*Leadership is primarily a function and responsibility of the total group.* Consequently, a group may function officially without a leader (often called "leaderless" groups) and perform very well indeed. A major shift in the field of social psychology in recent years affirms the view that leadership is a set of learned skills rather than a set of characteristics bestowed on one person alone.

The theory of **functional leadership** contains two basic ideas: 1) any member of the group may assume the leadership of the group by performing actions that fulfill group functional needs, and 2) every leadership function may be fulfilled by a variety of group members serving various group needs with their specific behaviors (like asking questions or making supportive statements).

Three leadership styles are autocratic, democratic, and laissez-faire. The **autocratic** leader decides all policy and gives all orders to group members. The **democratic** leader encourages group determination of policy and enables the group to interact within itself. The **laissez-faire** leader provides very minimal leadership for the group and interacts with group members in only a marginal or average manner. Most of the research upheld the democratic leadership style as the most effective. Yet, different leadership styles seem to be effective under different conditions (Turner, 1977, Stogdill, 1974).

**Leadership style and orientation** are most effective when performed in direct response to a specific situation and group need. For example, a task-oriented leader, one who has a concern that the agenda be completed or that the lesson for the day be taught, functions best when **on good terms** with the group, when the task to be done is *clearly structured*, and when the leader commands significant **power** and **authority** in the group. The task-oriented leader is also effective when the leader **directs** the group and/or assumes responsibility for making decisions. In contrast, a maintenance-oriented leader is most effective by encouraging decision-making by **broad involvement** of the group members. Clearly, situational and contextual differences in groups need to be allowed for in determining what kind of leadership orientation and style would be most helpful. An effective leader will be **flexible** enough to adjust herself/himself *to the group* and will seek a **balance** between *getting a job done*, by involving others in doing it, and **maintenance needs**, such as how people are feeling about doing the task. Group dynamics are far too complex for any one theory or style of group leadership to be effective under all conditions (Turner, 1977; Wheatly, 2001; Blanchard, Hybel, & Hodges, 2004).

## IDENTIFYING ONE'S LEADERSHIP

### *Behavior*

In order to be an **effective group leader**, it is important to assess one's own leadership behavior. It is appropriate to ask, "Am I more task or maintenance oriented? Do I have reasonable balance between needing to get the task done and the maintenance of the life of the group in my own **leadership style**? Do I feel more comfortable with one orientation compared to the other? If so, what influence does my orientation have on the groups I lead?" (Turner, 1977)

Additional questions that need to be asked are, "Am I predominantly a **democratic**, an **autocratic**, or **laissez-faire** type of leader? What does this type of leadership style do to the group(s) I lead? Am I comfortable with my style or do I want to make any changes in my style? What type of feedback and/or evaluation do I request about my style from groups I lead? How do I feel about being evaluated as a leader? Do I practice what I ask of others? Does a group's reluctance to evaluate itself or me suggest anything special to me about its dynamics?" (Turner, 1977; Blanchard, et al., 2004; Collins, 2001; & Sussman, 2004)

A person who has developed a **democratic style** of leadership is most likely the one who usually maintains an adequate balance between task and maintenance orientation. If there is an imbalance toward too much maintenance orientation, the designated leader may be leaning toward a **laissez-faire** style, whereas imbalance toward too much task orientation may indicate the **autocratic style** of leadership.

In their book, *Joining Together, Group Theory and Group Skills,* Johnson and Johnson (1991) presented the following exercise designed to enable persons to evaluate their degree of task and maintenance functions in a group. The term "dominance" was used for task, and "sociability" was used for maintenance to describe leadership behavior in their exercise.

**Instructions:** There are twenty verbs listed below that describe some of the ways in which people feel and act from time to time. Think of your behavior in groups. How do you feel and act? Check five verbs below that best describe your behavior in groups as you perceive it. Remember, members of your group may perceive you differently. Read through the verbs and choose five.

In a group, I:

| __Acquiesce | __Concur | __Lead |
| __Advise | __Criticize | __Oblige |
| __Agree | __Direct | __Relinquish |
| __Analyze | __Disapprove | __Resist |
| __Concede | __Evade | __Retreat |
| __Coordinate | __Initiate | __Withdraw |

Two underlining factors or traits are involved in the list of verbs: **dominance** (authority or control) and **sociability** (intimacy or friendliness). A lot of people tend to like to control things (high dominance) or to let others control things (low dominance). Similarly, a lot of people tend to be warm and personable (high sociability) or to be somewhat cold and impersonal (low sociability). Look in the **boxes** below and **circle** the five verbs you used to describe yourself in group activity. The box in which you have circled three or more verbs out of five represents your leadership behavior in groups.

**Dimensions of Leadership**

| High Dominance | Low Dominance |
|---|---|
| Advise | Acquiesce |
| Coordinate | Agree |
| Direct | Assist |
| Initiate | Oblige |
| High Sociability | High Sociability |
| High Dominance | Low Sociability |
| Analyze | Concede |
| Criticize | Evade |
| Disapprove | Relinquish |
| Judge | Retreat |
| Low Sociability | Low Sociability |

When you have determined your dominance-sociability pattern in groups, ask yourself if it is the kind of pattern you want. If not, why not? Are you willing to risk changing? When it comes to being an effective leader, some people may seem to have "it"; others do not. We generally know "it" when we see it. Review the list of historical and current examples of people reputed to have "it" in the public arena (regardless of whether you identify at all with their politics, methods, or goals.) Which ones of these persons were/are effective leaders?

Maya Angelou, George W. Bush, Fidel Castro, Julius L. Chambers, Shirley Chisholm, Winston Churchill, Hilary Rodham Clinton, William Jefferson Clinton, Johnetta Cole, Princess Diana, Marian Wright Edelman, Mahatma Ghandi, Saddam Hussein, Jesse Jackson, Barbara Jordan, John F. Kennedy, Martin Luther King, Jr., Sandra Day O'Connor, Eva Peron, Condelessa Rice, Roy Sano, Chief Seattle, Mother Teresa, Lech Walesa, Ophrah Winfrey, and Andrew Young have national and international reputations. What gives them this kind of recognition?

Some may believe that such leaders are **"born that way"** and have certain personality traits that made them naturals. Leaders are made, although some people may have a head start on effective leadership as a result of a combination of **heredity** and **environmental factors**. Too much emphasis has been placed on in-born personality traits. More often than not, leaders are made, not born. People who have "it" enable others to strike a balance between the human and task dimensions of working together. Leadership is an **interactive process**, and no matter what the leader does, the members will **react**. The real key to effective leadership is to be able to assess accurately what the members need from you at any point in time, and to be able to tailor your style to those needs.

The **best leadership style** depends upon how mature members are, and that level of maturity will vary from task to task. An example would be helpful to illustrate maturity of members and effective leadership. Jerod is president of the Student Government Association (SGA), which for the past twelve years has sponsored an annual homecoming concert. Students are excited about the event; committees are well established; and the chairpersons know what they are doing. Jerod assesses the maturity of the group in relation to the concert project and establish quickly that the group is highly mature. What is his choice of leadership behavior? It should be low task/ low relationship; therefore, the SGA president will want to step back, delegate, and let them get the job done. The students are well equipped to handle the job with minimal assistance and support from the president. The SGA also needs to revise its fifty-page bylaws and standing rules, which have not been revised for six years. There is a bylaws committee in place, but the chair is not excited about being responsible for this job, and three other members are new. The leadership behavior Jerod needs is high task/low relationships. The president needs to get together weekly if necessary with the chair and provide a lot of assistance. He should review the history of the organization, help develop an outline for the new bylaws, set up a timeline for the first draft to be done, and keep in close touch in case of problems along the way. He needs to be **highly directive**, specific, and focused on the tasks at hand.

Review the chart below to get an idea of the type of behavior to exhibit in various situations.

| Task-maturity | Appropriate Leadership Behavior |
| --- | --- |
| Low | High Task/Low Maintenance ("Telling") |
| Low Moderate | High Task/High Maintenance ("Selling") |
| High Moderate | High Maintenance/Low Task ("Telling") |
| High | Low Maintenance/Low Task ("Delegating") |

As member **task maturity** increases, the leader should reduce emphasis on task and increase emphasis on maintenance. When members become moderately task-mature, the leader should let them go on their own. They will be ready to give each other the support and encouragement they need to accomplish their goals.

The key to applying the right style of leadership behavior at the right time is knowing a lot about the people in the organization: their skills, attitudes, abilities, interests, likes and dislikes. If you take a quick maturity assessment before launching into a project, it could pay off in terms of member satisfaction and productivity.

## DEFINITIONS OF LEADERSHIP

The study of leadership is as old as time. Since humankind was placed upon the Earth, there have been leaders and **followers**. Leaders have influenced the actions of others and caused the group to achieve its goals, whether the goal was finding food for survival, shelter for protection, or a message from a higher authority. The study of leadership becomes important as an area of study today because of the many **emerging leaders** who come into leadership positions without any background in the definitions, theories, and research that explain the many dimensions of leadership.

**Management and Leadership** are often thought of as one and the same; however, there is an important distinction between management and leadership. Hersey and Blanchard (1982, p. 3) defined management as "working with and through individuals and groups to accomplish organizational goals." Leadership is a broader concept than management, and, therefore, management can be thought of as a special kind of leadership in which the achievement of organizational goals is paramount. Hersey and Blanchard (1982) *stated further* that the key difference between the two concepts lies in the word "organization." Leadership occurs any time one attempts to influence the behavior of an individual or group, regardless of the reason. These reasons may be one's own goals or those of others, and they may or may not be congruent with organizational goals.

Ralph Stogdill (1974) in the *Handbook of Leadership* provided several definitions of leadership based on various models and schools of thought. These included leadership as a focus of group processes, personality and its effects, the exercise of influence, an act of behavior, an instrument of goal achievement, and an effect of interaction and the initiation of structure.

Read through the definitions of leader and leadership that follow and decide which one best fits the type of leadership students are now involved in or will experience in future careers.

"**Leadership** is the activity of influencing people to cooperate toward some goal which they come to find desirable" (Stogdill, 1974, p. 10).

"**Leadership** is the process of influencing the activities of an organized group in its efforts toward goal setting and goal achievement" (Stogdill, 1974, p. 10).

"**Leadership** is entailing, envisioning, and articulating a new reality, persuading others of its benefits and inspiring them to embrace and actualize it" (Aburdene & Naisbitt, 1992 p. xii.)

"**Leadership** is the process of arranging a situation so that various members of a group, including the leader, can achieve common goals with maximum economy and a minimum of time and work. The functional relationship which is leadership exists when a leader is perceived by a group as controlling means for the satisfaction of their needs" (Stogdill, 1997, p. 13).

"**Leadership** is the ability to gain consensus and commitment to common objectives, beyond organizational requirements, which are attained with the experience of contribution and satisfaction on the part of the work group" (Cribbin, 1982, p. 13).

"**Leadership** is an influence process that enables managers to get their people to do willingly what must be done, and do well what ought to be done" (Cribbin, 1982, p. 13).

"A **leader** is one who exercises more important influence acts than any other member of the group" (Stogdill 1974, p. 10).

"**Leadership** is interpersonal influence exercised in a situation and directed, through the communication process, toward the attainment of a specified goal or goals" (Stogdill, 1974, p. 10).

## WOMEN AND LEADERSHIP

Without attaining leadership, **women** will continue to live in a world constructed and dominated by men. Women will keep responding to someone else's agenda, addressing the ills of a world they did not create.

Ultimately, it is impossible to achieve genuine liberation in a male-dominated society. That is why the old-fashioned definition of feminism–the full participation of women and the integration of their values, concerns, and opinions at every level of society–still holds.

Aburdene and Naisbitt (1992) defined leadership as **entailing**, **envisioning,** and **articulating** a new reality, persuading others of its benefits, and inspiring them to embrace and actualize it (p. xii).

In the past, the key leadership trait was to command and control; the leader emerged out of the existing power structure, which gave him the authority to command people to carry out orders or face the threat of force, expulsion, or punishment. Historically, women were largely absent from the command-control model, which is completely ineffective in a high-tech, information-based economy. That means women now possess an ironic advantage over men schooled in the old ways: women need not "unlearn" the authoritarian leadership style.

In periods of **rapid change**, the ability to envision, persuade, and inspire is critical to leadership. Women possess these traits as much as or possibly more than men. The command-and-control model of leadership is being replaced by the inspire-and-communicate model, which opens the way for women to lead (Aburdene and Naisbitt, 1992).

Women leaders strive for **excellence**, encourage participation, share power and information, enhance other people's self-worth, get others excited about their work, and **empower** others and themselves. Women are likely to thrive in organizations changing or growing rapidly. Women also succeed in companies that employ educated young professionals who demand to be treated as individuals.

## SUCCESSFUL AND EFFECTIVE LEADERSHIP

An individual's effort to change the behavior of others is **attempted leadership**. When the other members actually change, this creation of change in others is **successful leadership**. If others are reinforced or rewarded for changing their behavior, this evoked achievement is **effective leadership**. If Calvin wants Derrick to perform a task, his leadership attempt can be considered to be successful if he just gets Derrick to complete the task. However, if Calvin's style is not compatible with Derrick's expectation of his leadership, and if Derrick is angry afterwards and only did the job because Calvin exerted his power and made him feel guilty, Calvin has been successful but not effective. However, if Derrick does the job well, achieves the group's goal, and is recognized for it, Calvin's leadership is effective.

**Success** is measured by how the group or individuals actually behave when asked to do something. **Effectiveness** is measured not only in terms of task accomplishments but also by how the members feel about the process. Effectiveness is measured when leaders have the sensitivity to know what members want and need and in a conscious, careful way, are able to deliver those behaviors required to facilitate group productivity. If the leader is adjustable and consistent about employing the different styles needed for different situations, his/her behavior becomes highly predictable and a source of comfort and enjoyment for the members of the organizations.

The influence concept recognizes the fact that individuals differ in the extent to which their behavior affects activities of a group. It implies a reciprocal relationship between leader and followers, but is not necessarily characterized by domination, control, or induction of compliance on the part of the leader. Collins (2001) sums this up in his book, "Good to Great." "Good to Great leaders began the transformation by first getting the right people on the bus and the wrong people off the bus, and then figuring out with the group, where to drive them," p. 41.

The leader is a person who produces group **synality** different from that which would have existed had he/she not been present in the group. Synality means the various performances exhibited by the group in its effort to achieve a goal. This leadership may be measured in terms of its effects on group performances.

## SLAVERY AND LEADERSHIP

Nai'm Akbar (1996) reported on psychological aspects of African American leadership during slavery and the lingering impact today.

Probably one of the most **destructive** influences to grow out of slavery is the disrespect of African American leadership. The allegory is seen throughout nature that the most certain way to destroy life is to **cut off the head**. From the turkey to the cow to the human being, the most immediate way to bring death to a body is to **remove its head**. This is especially true as a social principle. One thing that was systematically done during slavery was the elimination of control of any emerging "head" or leader. Slave narratives and historical accounts are full of descriptions of atrocities brought against anyone who exemplified real leadership capability. The slave holders realized that their power and control over the slaves was dependent upon the absence of any **indigenous leadership** among the slaves.

Any slave who began to **emerge** as a **natural** head, that is, one oriented toward survival of the whole body, was identified early and was either eliminated, isolated, killed, or ridiculed. In his or her place was put a leader who had been carefully picked, trained, and tested to stand only for the masters' welfare. In other words, **unnatural heads** were attached to the slave communities. They furthered the cause of the master and frustrated the cause of the slave.

The slaves were taught to view with suspicion natural leaders who emerged from among themselves. Such heads were identified as "uppity" or "arrogant," and were branded as the kind of troublemakers who were destined to bring trouble to the entire slave community. This idea was reinforced by the public punishment of such indigenous leaders and any of their associates or sympathizers. The entire slave community was often required to carry an extra burden or be deprived of some small privilege, primarily because of such "uppity slaves" (Akbar, 1996).

## LEADERSHIP WORKING WITH CULTURAL AND OTHER DIFFERENCES

The uniqueness of individual differences is a special challenge for leaders of volunteers. Extra measures of awareness, sensitivity, and flexibility are required to involve members of different cultural backgrounds, those who are much older or younger than most members, those who may have physical disabilities, and even those who are of a "minority" gender when they are far outnumbered in your group (Bishop, 2001; Wheatly, 2001; Haines, 2004).

**Multicultural** organizations are more complex and especially demanding because of the potential for misunderstanding, conflict, and member dropout. As we choose culture as our working example of important differences among members, we trust your understanding and **flexibility** in adapting these ideas to the specific needs of your own situation.

If you have never worked with a group whose members come from a variety of backgrounds, you are missing one of the richest, most rewarding "happenings" life has to offer. At the same time, being the leader of a widely **diverse** group of people can be a bit unnerving at first. Don't let the challenge lead you to ignore or **gloss-over** the realities of the situation, however.

Whatever your role in your multicultural group, start by keeping a couple of things in mind:
- Most people of color have pretty much discarded the notion of the United States as a "melting-pot" of different races, cultures, and nationalities. They argue that this view of American society downplays the importance of their heritage and works against the retention of customs, values, and beliefs that they cherish. **Cultural integration** and equality of opportunity are worthy goals, but total assimilation into majority culture is not—at least not if the intention is to strip away the last vestiges of their heritage or to rob them of their cultural identity. Sensitive and fair-minded leaders in a multi-cultural organization prefer to accent interpersonal equality and to celebrate diversity.

*Working in a diverse group provides a rich, rewarding, and enlightening experience for all of its members.*

Dimensions of Leadership

- Those who have not had formal power tend to be suspicious of those who do. American history now clearly shows that Blacks, Asians, Native Americans, and Hispanics in this country were repeatedly used and abused by people of wealth, position, or power by virtue of race alone.

Similar feelings may exist for any group of people that comes from a different background of oppression or exploitation; use your power carefully.

## INDIVIDUAL STEPS FOR IMPROVING AWARENESS OF DIFFERENCES

- Establish a better historical perspective of the differences represented in your organization. Take the initiative by reading, asking questions, getting involved in small-group discussions, and showing a general commitment to learn and to understand.
- Develop a contemporary frame of reference about culture ...read about current events and emerging racial/cultural issues. (See Chapter 8–Diversity.)
- Be sensitive to different forms of media. Watch for stereotypes and cliches.
- Check your facts before you form a cultural opinion or make a statement.
- Be sensitive to and knowledgeable about specific, contemporary cultural differences, such as language, humor, and gestures.
- Read cultural magazines, newspapers, and books; listen to cultural radio programs.
- Take some risks. Attend an event that is programmed by and for a group other than your own.
- Seek out introductory classes, workshops, or seminars on culture and/or race relations, disabilities, equality of the sexes.
- Be open and listen–not defensively.

## ACTIVITIES FOR IMPROVING AWARENESS OF DIFFERENCES

- Set goals and objectives that reflect and embrace the cultural diversity of your membership.
- Engage in majority membership workshops on awareness of cultural differences.
- Hold discussions of tokenism: What is it? How is it used? Does it apply to your organization?
- Engage in cross-cultural exchanges (potlucks, socials, entertainment, discussions, lectures, and art exhibits ...).
- Schedule presentations by prominent local leaders from different backgrounds on culture, racism, art, politics, equal opportunity.
- Establish small support groups–"networks"–within the larger organization to help people feel welcome and secure.
- Plan programs that improve understanding of the values of people of different cultures, races, ages, physical abilities, and sexes.
- Support systems that guarantee participation for those of different backgrounds.
- Assign leadership and risk-taking roles to establish greater multicultural participation.
- Schedule meeting places and times that allow the widest possible participation.
- Establish a "buddy system" that pairs majority and minority members to discuss differences and similarities in traditions, values, and life experiences (Lawson, Donant, & Lawson, 1982 p. 23).

These suggestions only begin to scratch the surface of activities and techniques which, if sincerely used, will move your organization toward being more culturally aware and responsive. Such a commitment should not be made by the titled leaders or executive officers alone; the effort will fail miserably if the entire membership does not support it. A great deal of leader "homework" may be needed here to prepare members to act positively and to avoid awkward and potentially damaging reactions to diversity.

In order for many people of different cultures to be able to contribute their ideas, concerns, and creativity without fear, leaders must minimize procedural barriers in the organization. Some persons in ethnic groups are especially sensitive to the ways the majority culture has denied them access. This question is not one of ability, but of organizational sensitivity to language and cultural difference, access to group resources and decisions, enhanced self-confidence, and a feeling of belonging.

## *Take a close look at some of these common "roadblocks":*

While each of the roadblocks can also be used in positive ways, avoid the negative uses portrayed here:

- **Parliamentary Procedure:** For many members from other cultures, formal parliamentary procedure may be a threat. Some might even view it as oppressive. Techniques must be established for developing a greater understanding of its value and of its use to make decisions or achieve goals.
- **Bureaucratic Processes:** As is true of parliamentary procedure, long and complicated procedures may prove barriers to involvement. Unfamiliar forms and rules may represent a cumbersome way to get things done.
- **Communication Skills:** Be sensitive to language and colloquial differences among the membership. Be sure you strive for clear and precise communication, whether verbal or written. Do not try to impress anyone with your vocabulary; go for understanding, instead.
- **Assertive Skills:** When your heritage differs from that of most other members, being assertive in an organization may be very difficult.

This poem represents what may happen if we do not reconcile race and cultural relations in our leadership responsibilities:

**The Cold Within**

Six humans trapped by happenstance
    in black and bitter cold,
Each one possessed a stick of wood
    Or so the story's told.

Their dying fire in need of logs
    The first woman held hers back,
For on the faces around the fire
    She noticed one was black.

The next man looking 'cross the way
    Saw one not of his church,
And couldn't bring himself to give
    The fire his stick of birch.

The third one sat in tattered clothes
    He gave his coat a hitch,
Why should his log be put to use
    To warm the idle rich?

The rich man just sat back and thought
    Of the wealth he had in store,
And how to keep what he had earned
    From the lazy, shiftless poor.

The black man's face bespoke revenge
    As the fire passed from his sight,
For all he saw in his stick of wood
    Was a chance to spite the white.

And the last man of this forlorn group
    Did naught except for gain,
Giving only to those who gave
    Was how he played the game.

The logs held tight in Death's still hands
    Was proof of human sin
They didn't die from the cold without
    They died from the cold within.

                                                  -Author Unknown

Have a group of seven students act out this poem.

What did you learn about feelings and sensitivities toward others?

What could have been done to help this group survive?

# PARLIAMENTARY PROCEDURES

While parliamentary procedures can be a barrier to effective leadership, the effective use of parliamentary procedure can help leaders to get people to do willingly what must be done and do well what ought to be done. Below are some things leaders should know about motions:

1. A motion should be made and seconded before any discussion starts.
2. You should state the motion after it has been made and seconded, and then ask for any discussion.
3. The maker of the motion has the right to be the first to discuss it.
4. Only one main motion may be considered at a time.
5. If a motion to amend is made and seconded, the proposed amendment must be voted upon before a vote is taken on the main motion to which it applies.
6. A main motion may be changed without being formally amended by another motion. This may be done by the maker of the main motion accepting the change as a "friendly amendment."
7. When a member says "question," it means "I am ready for the question or ready to vote." When a member says, "I call for the question" or "I move the previous question," a motion is being made to stop debate and vote immediately.
8. To bring a motion to vote, say, "Are you ready for the question?" (Members are saying "yes" when they respond with "question!") "The question has been called. All those in favor say "Aye"; all those opposed say "Nay." The motion is carried (or defeated)." If some member appears not to vote, you may ask, "Does anyone abstain?" (Rap the gavel whenever a group decision has been reached.)
9. All votes take a simple majority, except those that somehow inhibit the right of members to speak; these motions require a two-thirds vote.
   - vote immediately
   - limit debate or extend the limits to debate
   - object to considering a question
   - close nominations
   - postpone to a definite time by a special order
   - suspend the rules
10. Whenever a vote requiring a two-thirds majority is taken, ask for a hand vote or a standing vote. This will save time since, invariably, someone will call "division," which demands a visual vote and you will have to call for the vote again (it's impossible to hear two-thirds anyway).
    - A "Majority Vote" is one more than half of those voting.
    - A "Two-Thirds Vote" is two-thirds of the votes cast (do not count abstentions).
    - A "Plurality" involves three or more choices and means more votes than any other candidate or alternative (a plurality does not decide the issue unless there is a special or standing rule to that effect).
11. The chairperson may vote on every issue or may choose to vote only to swing the outcome one way or the other.
12. Motions are ranked and placed in categories.
    (a) A main motion is one that brings an item of business before the group for action. It has the lowest rank, which means that any of the rest can legally be made when a main motion is on the floor.
    (b) A subsidiary motion is one to amend, postpone, limit debate, or refer the main motion. It is second-lowest in rank and only takes precedence over a main motion.

(c) An incidental motion pertains to the method of conducting business: point of order, parliamentary inquiry, division of the assembly, and withdrawal of a motion. It takes precedence over both the main motions and subsidiary motions.

(d) A privileged motion involves an immediate action of the group as a whole that it recess or adjourn. It ranks over all other motions and can be made whenever any other motion is being considered.

13. A "quorum" is the number of members eligible to vote that are required to be present in order to transact business legally. That number is generally stated in the bylaws of the organization.

## PLAN EFFECTIVE MEETINGS

1. Write out the objectives of the meeting. (Why are you having the meeting?)
2. Consider carefully who you want to attend the meeting. Invite only those who must come in order to reach your meeting's objectives. Be sure to invite the persons who will carry out the decision reached. Include the person responsible for the topic of discussion. Include an IDEA person.
3. Know what you expect each person to contribute. (What should each person bring to the meeting?)
4. For a real action meeting, meet in small groups (10 or fewer persons).
5. Don't rule out part-time attendees; some people may not need to be there for the whole meeting. Allow people to leave when their contributions are finished.
6. Plan to use an agenda and stick to it. Have others contribute agenda items. Publish the agenda and distribute it to participants prior to the meeting.
7. Choose the most appropriate time and location. Set a time limit for all meetings. Start on time and end on time.
8. Plan to summarize results and distribute copies of the follow-up report to all parties concerned.
9. If a written report or published minutes are necessary, have them distributed within twenty-four hours.

## HOW GROUP MEMBERS CAN CONTRIBUTE TO EFFECTIVE MEETINGS

1. Come prepared to take responsibility for making a good discussion group–to share ideas, questions, and information, as well as to listen.
2. Take with you all materials you will need and arrive on time.
3. Talk briefly and to the point. Stay on the topic. Avoid speeches.
4. Try to discourage, rather than encourage, wandering or unnecessary talk.
5. Listen to others in the group.
6. Encourage others to stick to the topic.
7. Be alert to the body language of others.
8. Respect the rights of others in the group to speak.
9. Take notes to help you retain key ideas.
10. If possible, help others clarify their points.
11. Be sure you understand your assignment before you leave the meeting.
12. Make a note of your assignment due date on your desk calendar.

## HOW TO CONDUCT EFFECTIVE MEETINGS

1. Start on time, no matter what.
2. Be enthusiastic; it's contagious.
3. Share the floor unless it's an information-only meeting and you're the only one giving the information.
4. Be assertive enough to wrap up each topic on time. Use body language that says you are in charge.
5. Speak with authority, yet be clear and concise in your remarks.
6. Keep the discussion on track as much as possible. When it gets off, steer it back on track.
7. Be as organized as possible.
8. Avoid the seven deadly sins meetings leaders regularly commit:
   - resenting questions,
   - monopolizing the meeting,
   - playing comic,
   - chastising someone in public,
   - permitting interruptions,
   - losing control, and
   - coming unprepared–the greatest sin.
9. Practice using the name of members of the group when you call on them.
10. Be familiar with leadership styles and use the one applicable to the situation:
    - Democratic: guides the group to decision-making.
    - Laissez Faire: allows group to do as it wills.
    - Autocratic: makes decisions for the group.
11. After you have spoken, pause until others have had a chance to talk.
12. Respect diversity in opinions. Differences can be creative.
13. Be seated so you can see the faces of every other member of the group.
14. Pace the meeting with your agenda.
15. Use visual aids if they will clarify what you're saying.
16. Search for weaknesses and strengths before the final decisions are made.
17. Be aware of your distracting mannerisms.
18. Use humor (not jokes) that comes naturally out of the exchange. Humor is a relief.
19. Praise people. Thank them. Let them know you appreciate them.
20. Close the meeting on a positive note. Make mention of the progress made and the worthy contributions submitted.

## SUMMARY

Leadership has been defined as a function of influence, interaction, achievement, power, motivation, and commitment. Leadership is a set of learned skills used to work through people to get goals accomplished. Leadership is the responsibility of the total group. Three leadership styles emerge: autocratic, democratic, and laissez faire. The democratic style of leadership has been upheld as the most effective. Leadership behavior can be assessed by using Johnson and Johnson's (1991) task and maintenance quadrant. Success in leadership is measured by how the group behaves when asked to perform a task. Effectiveness in leadership is measured when leaders have the sensitivity to know what members want and need, and in a conscious way, deliver behavior required to facilitate group productivity.

Women have the ability to envision, persuade, and inspire. These are all leadership traits needed for the twenty-first century. Women do not need to unlearn the command and control model popular in the past.

Natural leaders among slaves were systematically eliminated, isolated, or killed by the slave owner or his designee because it was feared that they would start trouble with the slaves.

Extra measures of awareness sensibility and flexibility in leadership are required to work with cultural and other differences in groups.

While parliamentary procedures can be a barrier to effective leadership, the effective use of parliamentary procedure can help a leader to get people to do willingly what must be done and to do well what ought to be done.

Effective leaders are also good followers. They plan and direct activities to accomplish goals of the group. The action includes planning and conducting effective meetings.

Good to great leaders begin the transformation by first getting the right people on the bus and the wrong people off the bus, and then they figure out with the group, where to drive them. (Collins, 2001, p. 41.)

## GLOSSARY

**Effective Leader:** one who has the sensitivity to know what members want and need and in a conscious way delivers behaviors required to facilitate group productivity.
**Leader:** one who envisions and articulates a new reality, persuading others of its benefits and inspiring them.
**Leadership:** envisioning and articulating a new reality, persuading others of its benefits, and inspiring them to embrace and actualize it (Aburdene & Naisbitt, 1992, p. xii).
**Leadership Behavior:** the leader's awareness and response to the needs, values, and interests of members of the group.
**Leadership Styles:** the manner in which a leader interacts with a group.
**Maintenance Oriented/Sociability:** concerned with how group members are feeling about performing a task.
**Management:** planning, organizing, controlling, facilitating, and motivating the use of resources to accomplish goals.
**Parliamentary Procedure:** rules that govern the transaction of business in meetings; the action and behavior of leaders and followers in a group.
**Sinality:** the various performances exhibited by the group in the effort to achieve goals.
**Successful Leader:** one who causes members to do what he/she wants done, whether the members like it or not.
**Task Oriented/Dominance:** concerned mainly with getting the job done.

# REFERENCES

Aburdene, P., & Naisbitt, J. (1992). *Megatrends for women: From reberation to leadership.* New York: Random House.

Akbar, N. (1996). *Breaking the chains of psychological slavery.* Tallahassee, Fla: Mind Production and Associates, Inc.

Banks, W. M. (1996). *Black intelluctuals: Race and responsibility in American life.* New York: W. W. Norton Company.

Bishop, C. H. (2001). *Making change happen—One person at a time: Assessing change within your organization.* New York: Glencoe.

Blanchard, K., Hybels, B., & Hodges, P. (2004). *Leadership by the book: Tools to transform your workplace.* Walter Brook Press.

Bolman, L. G., & Deal, T. E. (1996). *Leading with soul: An uncommon journey of spirit.* San Francisco: Jersey Bass Inc.

Collins, J. (2001). *Good to great.* New York: Harper Business.

Cribbin, J. L. (1981). *Leadership: Strategies for organizational effectiveness.* New York: AMACOM.

Dry, W. (1993). *Getting past no: Negotiating your way from confrontations to cooperation.* New York: Bantam Books.

Edelman, M. W. (1992). *The measure of our success.* Boston: Beacon Press.

Finzel, H. C. (2000). *The top ten mistakes leaders make.* Wheaton, IL: Victor Books.

Fraser, G. (1994). *Success runs in our race: The complete guide to effective networking in the African-American community.* New York: Avon Books.

Haines S. (2000) *A systems thinking approach to strategic planning and management.* New York: Jossey Bass.

Haines, S. (2004). *Enterprise change.* New York: Jossey-Bass.

Hersey, P., & Blanchard R. (1982). *Management of organizational behavior: Utilizing human resources.* Englewood Cliffs, NJ: Prentice Hall.

Johnson, D. W., & Johnson, F. P. (1991). *Joining together: Group theory and group skills.* Boston: Allyn and Bacon.

Johnson, E. H. (1998). *Brothers on the mend: Understanding and healing anger for African-American men and women.* New York: Pocket Books.

Lawson, L. G., Donut, F. D., & Lawson, J. D. (1982). *Lead on: The complete handbook for group leaders.* San Luis Obispo: Ca: Impact Publishers.

Northhouse, Peter G. (2004). *Leadership: Theory and Practice, 3rd Edition.* Thousand Oaks, California: Sage Publications.

Reid-Merritt, P. (1996). *Sister power: How phenomenal black women are rising to the top.* New York: John Wiley & Sons, Inc.

Stogdill, R. (1974). *Handbook of leadership.* New York: MacMillian.

Sussman, L. (2004). *Lost and found: The story of how one manager discovered the secrets of leadership, where he wasn't looking.* Hensley Publishing.

Turner, N. W. (1977). *Effective leadership in small groups.* Valley Forge: Judson Press.

Wheatly, J. (2001). *Leadership and the new sciences: Discovering order in a chaotic world.* New York: Jossey -Bass.

White, J. B. (1985). *On becoming a leader.* New York: Irrington Publisher, Inc.

White, J. (1986). *Excellence in leadership: Reaching goals with prayer, courage and determination.* Downer Grove, Il: Inter-Varsity Press.

Young, A. (1996). *An easy burden.* New York: Harper Collins Publishers.

# ACTIVITY 1

## *Traits of an Effective Leader*

Achieves
Communicates Effectively
Sets Goals
Assumes Responsibility
Honest
Energetic
Loyal to Group
Mentally Alert
Inspires Others
Cooperates with Others
Diplomatic
Self-Confident
Open-Minded
Progressive
Sense of Humor
Tolerant
Tactful
Consistent
Gives Praise and Recognition
Assertive
Available and Accessible
Capacity
Status

1. Add some other traits.

2. Place a check by each trait that describes you.

3. Are you an effective leader? Why?

Dimensions of Leadership

# ACTIVITY 2

## *Leaders Who Are Effective*

Read the characteristics of each type of leader. Can you name a leader to match each leader type? Tell why you chose the leaders.

| Executive | Motto | Characteristics Typical | Behaviors |
|---|---|---|---|
| Entrepreneur | "We do it my way. Only risk-taking achievers need apply." | Extremely competent, forceful, individualistic, egocentric, dominant, self-confident. Can be very loyal, protective, generous team player. | Unable to work well in subordinate positions, must be prime mover, offers opportunities and challenges to succeed and motivate. |
| Corporateur | "I call the shots, but we all work together on my team." | Dominant, quite, directive, consultative, sizes up people well, cordial to people but keeps them at arm's length. | Concern about the group. High task oriented, makes people feel needed, delegates and consults, very supportive. |
| Developer | "People are our most important resources." | Trustful. Intent on people reaching their potential. Excellent human relations skills. | Productivity is superior. Delegates and consults, very emotionally involved, people-oriented. |
| Craftsman | "We do important work as perfectly as we can." | Amicable, conservative, conscientious, very knowledgeable, skilled, self-reliant, high task-oriented, honest, mild minded. | Likes to innovate and build, self-demanding, likes to solve problems alone or in a small group. |
| Integrator | "We build consensus and commitment." | Supportive, egalitarian, interpersonal skills, team builder, subtle leader, prefers group decision-making. Fast-moving, mobile. | Shares the leadership. Gives great freedom and authority. Welcomes ideas, acts as synergistic catalyst. |
| Gamesman | "We win together, but I must win more than you." | Flexible, knowledgeable and skilled, risk-taking, assertive, innovative, opportunistic, but not unethical. | Wants to be respected. Enjoys competition, sharp-skilled, tough manner, eliminates the weak and non-achievers. |

# ACTIVITY 3

## *Timesaver Meeting Planner*

**Nature:** Objectives, purpose, or intended results of meeting.

**Expectations:** Who should come? What will each one contribute?

**Agenda:** What is the best way to accomplish intended results?

**Time:** What day? When to begin? When to end? Where to meet?

**Meeting Follow-up**

| WHO | WHAT | WHEN |
|---|---|---|
| Person Receiving Assignment | Nature of Assignment | Due Date of Assignment |

# ACTIVITY 4

Read the contrasting roles for traditional management and women's leadership, then write a one-page paper analyzing the two.

| **Traditional Management** | **vs Leadership/Women's Leadership** |
|---|---|
| Objective: control | Objective: change |
| Relies on order-giving | Facilitating/teaching |
| Rank | Connections |
| Knows all the answers | Asks the right questions |
| Limits and defines | Empowers |
| Issues orders | Acts as a role model |
| Imposes discipline | Values creativity |
| Hierarchy | Networking/web |
| Demands "respect" | Wants people to "speak up, act up" |
| Performance review | Mutual contract for specific results |
| Automatic annual raises | Pay for performance |
| Military archetype | Teaching archetype |
| Keeps people on their toes | Nourishing environment for growth |
| Punishment | Reward |
| Reach up/down | Reach out |
| Here's what we are going to do! | How can I serve you/bring out best in you? |
| Bottom Line | Vision |
| Closed: information = power | Openness |
| Drill sergeant | Master motivator |
| Command and control | Empowerment |
| Little time for people | Infinite time for people |
| Rigid | Flexible |
| At the top | In the center |
| Mechanistic | Wholistic |
| Impersonal/objective | Personal |

**Characteristics of Women's Leadership**

### Empower

| | |
|---|---|
| Management | Leadership |
| Punishment | Reward |
| Demands "respect" | Invites speaking out |
| Drill sergeant | Motivator |
| Limits and defines | Empowers |
| Imposes discipline | Values creativity |
| Here's what we are going to do! | How can I serve you? |
| Bottom line | Vision |

### Restructure

| | |
|---|---|
| Control | Change |
| Rank | Connection |
| Hierarchy | Network |
| Rigid | Flexible |
| Automatic annual raises | Pay for performance |
| Performance review | Mutual contract for results |
| Mechanistic | Holistic |
| Compartmental | Systemic |

### Teaching

| | |
|---|---|
| Order giving | Facilitating |
| Military archetype | Teaching archetype |

### Role Model

| | |
|---|---|
| Issues orders | Acts as role model |

### Openness

| | |
|---|---|
| Keeping people on their toes | Nourishing environment for growth |
| Reach up/down | Reach out |
| Information control | Information availability |

### Questioner

| | |
|---|---|
| Knows all the answers | Asks the right questions |

(Aburdene & Naisbitt, 1992, pp. 100-101)

**Dimensions of Leadership**

# CHAPTER *eleven*

## Dimensions of Service Learning

### INTRODUCTION

"Service-Learning is good education. It helps students take ownership of their learning, shifts teachers into the role of coach, and brings the curriculum to life. It cuts through the barriers between schools and their communities by enabling students to interact constructively with community institutions, programs and initiatives. It makes school exciting for everyone" (Jones & Anderson, 1998). Moreover, service learning builds academic, interpersonal, and civic skills. Academic skills are enhanced by applying concepts, theories, and scholarly methods to real-world issues, problems, and initiatives.

*Service-learning projects allow students to apply concepts, theories, and scholarly methods to real-world issues, problems, and initiatives.*

Interpersonal skills are developed by interacting with persons of diverse personalities, racial, ethnic, gender, age and other characteristics. And civic skills are enhanced by developing effective networks between the university and a variety of community, business, non-profit and public institutions providing goods and services to often needy populations and communities.

### OBJECTIVES

The objectives of the chapter are to
1. introduce students to academic and community service learning
2. discuss the advantages of academic and community service learning
3. identify strategies for applying classroom content to community settings.
4. help students see the relationships among learning, civic participation, and community responsibilities.

### KEY CONCEPTS

1. Service-learning is a hands-on approach to learning, with roots in the Progressive Education Movement of the 1900s.
2. Both entities in a service-learning situation must decide together what the goals for the relationship will be.

> 3. The ultimate goal of a service-learning project is to provide all parties the opportunity to gain meaningful life-long experiences.
> 4. The most important long-term impact of service-learning is on the civic development of students.

## DEFINITION OF SERVICE-LEARNING

Service-learning is an experiential learning/teaching approach that relates meaningful community service activities to the instructional goals of a class, personal awareness, and civic responsibility. From an academic perspective, service-learning is a major thrust behind academics and programs such as Tech Prep, school-to-work, transitions, work-based learning, workforce development, apprenticeships, internships, and practicums.

This active hands-on approach to learning has its roots in the Progressive Education movement of the early 1900s. The interest in service-learning decreased significantly after the first ten years, but encountered a rebirth with the passing of the National Community Service Trust Act in 1993. The renewed interest and legislation have resulted in school districts revisiting the advantages of experiential learning in community settings.

The term "service-learning" automatically implies reflection and reciprocity as major components. Reflection on one's personal experiences and values and on the community's history is critical in designing worthwhile services to be rendered. It would be a mistake to work on the premise that learning and development occur simultaneously; they do not. It is often through the reflection on one's experiences that one later realizes the lesson learned. It is the result of the experiences and reflections that the development of one's values, perspectives, and self knowledge moves from one level to another.

Reciprocity implies the need for both the individual and the community to give and take in this process. For example, while the individual gives of his or her time and energy to enhance the quality of the lives of individuals and families, the community provides an open classroom of rich legacies and experiences that promote positive self-esteem, a good self-concept, hands-on learning, interactions with people that many students would not have met, self-knowledge, and other such experiences that create the background textures of life experiences. Both entities are learners and must decide together what the goals for the particular relationship will be. Individuals who enter a service-learning activity with the belief that the other party is the "needy party" and that he or she is giving away time and energy, clearly have not internalized the mutual benefits of the relationship. (Pause and complete Activity 1 on page 264).

### *Service Learning and Pedagogy*

Theorists such as John Dewey, Jean Piaget, and Kurt Lewin have emphasized experiential learning as the most effective learning path. However, neither theorist would support the belief that the actual act, in and of itself, is the heart of the learning process. It is the reflection and engaging that takes place within the individual that allows him or her to visualize the impact of the experiences. Some participants are able to realize immediate gains, while others do not comprehend the "lessons learned" until after the activity is over or even much later.

*In the early twenty-first century, service-learning has been sponsored by state and local governments, colleges and universities, and local or regional non-profit civic and community organizations.*

Now, then, one may wonder whether one-time experiences such as assisting a person in a health care facility are more or less beneficial than extended services in the same setting. It is not the quantity of the experiences but the quality that promotes the goals of service-learning activities. A person could learn more about himself or herself, career outlooks, and the other involved individuals from participating in a one-time visit to an elder care facility than from five concentrated experiences in another setting.

## POLITICS AND SERVICE-LEARNING

There has been some discussion as to whether or not service-learning is merely a political stance taken to promote a humanistic view of political candidates. Community service and politics have a history that grew out of the establishment of the Peace Corps by President John F. Kennedy in 1961. President William "Bill" Clinton further developed the concept created by former President Kennedy into AmeriCorps: a group of national service volunteers. Was this simply a matter of political positioning? President Clinton gained control of the political arena when he declared that the nation's problems are "intensely cultural, personal and human." Coming at a time when people had lost faith in humanity and the ability of others to care, the proposal of a national service program made on March 1, 1993 (thirty-two years after President Kennedy announced the establishment of the PeaceCorp) appealed to America.

The many efforts of various groups, agencies, individuals, and politicians resulted in the passing of the National Service Bill in Congress on September 8, 1993 which was signed into law just two weeks later. A Corporation of National Service was established and funded for $155.5 million in the first year. Within one year (September 12, 1994) of the passing of the law, President Clinton swore in approximately 850 AmeriCorps members. In the early twenty-first century, service learning has been advanced through Volunteers in Service to America (VISTA) and through many initiatives sponsored jointly by state or local governments or colleges and universities and local or regional non-profit civic and community organizations.

### *Linkages BETWEEN Service and Colleges/Universities*

The concept of service and humanistic approaches did not initiate in the political arena but is linked as far back as the establishment of the YMCA and Greek organizations at colleges and universities. The thrust behind each service-learning program may be different: economic, political, sociological, cultural, or historical. And within each of these perspectives, the academic goals may be different: intellectual, professional, personal, civic, or ethical. Regardless of the focus, the ultimate goal is to provide all parties the opportunity to gain meaningful life-long experiences.

Colleges and universities have formalized the service-learning and community service efforts performed by students, faculty, and administrators. For example, North Carolina Central University (Durham, North Carolina) requires a minimum of thirty community service hours per year for each student. All of the students are required to register with the Community Service Office and must report all hours performed prior to registering for classes the following semester. Many collages and universities are pursuing similar initiatives including the university of Maryland at Baltimore County, with service learning through the Shriver Institute.

Such a position, as one could imagine, could meet with strong opposition, particularly from individuals who have never participated or even realized the value of participating in their communities. However, Community Service Offices at various universities across the country and particularly at North Carolina Central University are now reporting very positive attitudes of students regarding such requirements.

Students who have had the opportunity to perform various community services and service-learning activities have developed strong leadership skills, learned greater respect for authority, whether theirs or others, reevaluated career plans or realized new options, used their volunteer activities as hands-on experiences, learned to appreciate the personal situations of others, and gained a greater sense of personal awareness and more insight into social issues affecting the quality of lives for individuals and families. Furthermore, there is a positive correlations between student fulfilling service requirements and completing their college requirements.

## GOALS OF SERVICE LEARNING

The specific goals of service learning endeavors vary from school to school and agency to agency. There are, however, some common goals that are core to any service-learning program. The following goals developed by the Service Learning Program at North Carolina Central University, which has received national acclaim and serves as a clearing house for community service activities are to
1. enhance student learning by joining theory with experience and thought with action;
2. fill unmet needs in the community through direct service, which is meaningful and necessary;
3. enable students to help others, give of themselves, and enter into caring relationships with others.

4. assist students to see the relevance of academic subjects to the real world, while enhancing the self-esteem and self-confidence of teachers and students;
5. develop an environment of collegial participation among students, faculty, and the community;
6. give students the opportunity to do important work;
7. increase the civic and citizen skills of students;
8. expose students to social inadequacies and injustices and empower students to remedy them;
9. assist agencies in better serving their clients and in benefiting from the infusion of enthusiastic volunteers;
10. develop a richer context of student learning;
11. foster a re-affirmation of students' career choices;
12. give students greater responsibility for their learning;
13. help students know how to get things done by maximizing available resources in real-life settings;
14. significantly impact local issues and needs.

A common theme that runs through all of the goals is increasing the "Power to Care." Individuals and agencies alike tend to gain a renewed faith in humanity and realize the magic of what happens when individuals "CARE." It is through the achievement of these goals that students nationwide are experiencing personal, academic and professional success.

## STRATEGIES FOR INCORPORATING SERVICE-LEARNING INTO THE CLASSROOM

Some strategies are more effective than others in integrating service-learning into the classroom instructional plan. The instructors must first identify instructional goals that encourage and promote the implementation of "out-of-class" projects. The projects should, however, support the curriculum. Some strategies include the following:

*Service learning enable students to help others, give of themselves, and enter into caring relationships with others.*

1. Project should meet the objectives and goals of a specific course.
2. Although some applications require a little more imagination than others, most projects should start with a thorough review of the course description, purpose, goals, and objectives.
3. Times for out-of-class activities should be a part of the course schedule and final evaluation of the student's performance.
4. Continuous networking with the community will help to retain sites for such rich experiences.
5. Finally, there must be periods of reflection for the student and instructor to discuss the activities, the impact of the involvement, and the lessons learned.

The National Youth Leadership Council (NYLC) has developed a matrix composed of three clusters, which helps teachers examine the quality of their service-learning activities. The Criteria of Quality Service Learning are based on criteria established by experienced service-learning educators across the country. The three clusters are learning, service, and critical components that support learning and service (McPherson, 2004).

The instructors must first identify instructional goals that encourage and promote service learning. The learning activities must align with clear educational goals that require the application of concepts, content, and skills from the academic disciplines, and the construction of the student's own knowledge. Student engagement should challenge them cognitively and developmentally and enhance student learning. Assessment methods should document the experience and evaluate how well students have met content and skills standards.

The second cluster is service. The service cluster engages students in service tasks that have clear goals, meet genuine needs in the school and the community, and have significant consequences for students and those they serve.

The third cluster, critical components that support learning and service, maximizes student participation in selecting, designing, implementing, and evaluating the service project. Thus, service-learning activities
- Value diversity in participants, practice, and outcomes.
- Promote communication and interaction with the community.
- Encourage partnerships and collaboration.

Student preparation for all aspects of their service work includes a clear understanding of the task, the skills, and the information required to complete the task, awareness of safety precautions, and knowledge about and sensitivity to colleagues.

A major component of service-learning is student reflection, which should be take place before, during, and after service. Reflective activities should use multiple methods to encourage critical thinking and the development of skills in leadership, diversity, and ethics. The teacher's instructional plan should also include multiple methods designed to acknowledge, celebrate, and validate student service work (McPherson, 2004).

Traditional classroom learning is quite different from learning experientially, and instructors need to help students prepare for service-learning work. Preparation includes using strategies that promote cooperation and collaboration. Some of those strategies are learning stations, small-group projects, cooperative learning, project-based learning lessons, telecommunication or networking projects, short-take activities such as, "turn to your neighbor and .....3-2-1, K-W-L, think-pair-share, and workshop format lessons.

## THE CIVIC BENEFITS OF SERVICE-LEARNING

Clearly, the most important long-term impact of service-learning is on the civic development of students. Civic development refers to the process by which students discover effective ways of contributing to the development of their communities as citizens and capabilities to assume leadership roles in the development of other citizens. The National Civic League, founded in 1894 as the National Municipal League, refers to the process as the **development of the civic infrastructure**. The civic infrastructure includes the formal and informal processes and networks through which communities make decisions and attempt to solve problems (National Civic League, 1999). According to the League, the quality of a community's civic infrastructure determines that community's economic, civic, and social health. Students involved in service-learning provide a vital resource for improving the quality of the civic infrastructure by working on the key vital signs for civic health.

The League has identified ten key vital signs or components for civic health it calls **The Civic Index.** The Civic Index consists of the following components, all clearly related to student service-learning experience:
1. Community Visioning: generating a compelling vision to motivate the community;
2. New Roles for Citizens: finding innovative ways to promote citizen creativity and genius in community problem-solving or prevention;
3. New Roles for Local Government in collaborating with citizens to pursue the community vision;
4. New Roles for Non-Profit Organizations to help citizens, particularly from low-income or challenged backgrounds, to fully participate in the civic culture;
5. New Roles for Business in helping the community through corporate social responsibility, technical assistance, and financial support;
6. Bridging Diversity so that citizens of varied backgrounds all have access to and a role in the cultivation and development of the civic infrastructure;
7. Reaching Consensus in the way the community wants to address challenges or prevent problems;
8. Sharing information with the entire community through civic engagement and widespread use of information technology;
9. Crossing Jurisdictional Lines so that local governments and their citizens work with other local jurisdictions on issues, challenges, and opportunities that are regional or metropolitan in scope, scale, or implication;
10. On-Going Learning through the development of processes for archiving or keeping records of community activity and collectively working on ways to learn from the civic experience of the community or other communities.

The intimate connection between the service-learning experience of students and their development of citizenship and civic skills is a key objective of service-learning programs. The critical-thinking skills, ethics, leadership, global learning, and diversity skills in other chapters are firmly linked to service-learning goals and objectives.

# REFERENCES

Henderson, Lenneal J. (2003). "The Civic Index: Learning Across Cities in a Democracy." *Administrative Theory and Praxis.* September.

Jones, B.W. & Anderson, R.S. (1998). *Service learning at NCCU.*

**Kouzes, J.M. & Posner, B.Z. (2007). The leadership challenge. 4th ed.). New York: Jossey-Bass.**

**Marks, H. M. & Jones, S. R. (2004). Community service in the transition: Shifts and continuities in participation from high school to college. Journal of Higher Education, 75(3).**

**Cress, C.M., Collier, P.J., & Reitenaver, V. L. (2005). Learning through serving a student guidebook for service-learning across the disciplines. New Jersey: Stylus.**

**Watkins, M. & Brown, L. (2005). Service learning: From classroom to community to career. Nevada: Jist.**

<u>National/Resource Organizations</u>
**Campus Outreach Opportunity League (COOL)**
1101 15th Street, NW, Suite 203
Washington, DC 20005
Phone: 202-296-7010
Fax: 202-296-7854

COOL is a national nonprofit organization that helps college students start, strengthen, and expand their campus-based community service programs. COOL strives to provide national service movement with a network of student leaders.

**Cooperation for National Service**
1100 Vermont Avenue
Washington, DC 20525

# ACTIVITY 1

**Directions:** Take a moment to think about the definition of service-learning presented in this chapter. Is this what you thought it was all about? Write a brief statement describing your view of what service-learning is.

_____

_____

_____

_____

_____

We will re-examine this point of view later in our discussion.

# ACTIVITY 2

**Directions:** Visit the website for the NCCD Clearinghouse and review the information provided. Make a list of the ten major facts or points presented in the information.

1. _____

2. _____

3. _____

4. _____

5. _____

6. _____

7. _____

8. _____

9. _____

10. _____

# ACTIVITY 3

**Daily Journal**                                                Name _____

**Directions:** This is a five-day daily journal to record your community service/service-learning experiences. Use the sections below as a guide. However, additional pages may be used as needed. This journal should be returned to your teacher to document satisfactory completion of the service component of the course.

**Name of Project:**

**Site:** _____

**Day 2**
Describe the activities performed today (including the number of hours committed):

_____

_____

_____

_____

_____

_____

Reflect on the activities. How did you feel performing these activities? Were there any challenges, concerns, or issues that evolved as a result of this activity? If so, how were they handled?

_____

_____

Describe any lessons learned. What would you do differently? What impact do you think you had on that situation, setting, or person(s)? What skills did you learn or sharpen?

_____

_____

Do you feel especially proud of something today?

_____

_____

# ACTIVITY 3 CONT'D.

## Daily Journal                                          Name _____

**Directions:** This is a five-day daily journal to record your community service/service-learning experiences. Use the sections below as a guide. However, additional pages may be used as needed. This journal should be returned to your teacher to document satisfactory completion of the service component of the course.

**Name of Project:**

**Site:** _____

**Day 3**
Describe the activities performed today (including the number of hours committed):

_____

_____

_____

_____

_____

Reflect on the activities. How did you feel performing these activities? Were there any challenges, concerns, or issues that evolved as a result of this activity? If so, how were they handled?

_____

_____

Describe any lessons learned. What would you do differently? What impact do you think you had on that situation, setting, or person(s)? What skills did you learn or sharpen?

_____

_____

Do you feel especially proud of something today?

_____

_____

Dimensions of Service Learning

# ACTIVITY 3 CONT'D.

**Daily Journal**  Name _____

**Directions:** This is a five-day daily journal to record your community service/service-learning experiences. Use the sections below as a guide. However, additional pages may be used as needed. This journal should be returned to your teacher to document satisfactory completion of the service component of the course.

**Name of Project:**

**Site:** _____

**Day 4**
Describe the activities performed today (including the number of hours committed):

_____
_____
_____
_____
_____
_____

Reflect on the activities. How did you feel performing these activities? Were there any challenges, concerns, or issues that evolved as a result of this activity? If so, how were they handled?

_____
_____

Describe any lessons learned. What would you do differently? What impact do you think you had on that situation, setting, or person(s)? What skills did you learn or sharpen?

_____
_____

Do you feel especially proud of something today?

_____
_____

## ACTIVITY 3 CONT'D.

### Daily Journal               Name _____

**Directions:** This is a five-day daily journal to record your community service/service-learning experiences. Use the sections below as a guide. However, additional pages may be used as needed. This journal should be returned to your teacher to document satisfactory completion of the service component of the course.

**Name of Project:**

**Site:** _____

**Day 5**
Describe the activities performed today (including the number of hours committed):

_____

_____

_____

_____

_____

Reflect on the activities. How did you feel performing these activities? Were there any challenges, concerns, or issues that evolved as a result of this activity? If so, how were they handled?

_____

_____

Describe any lessons learned. What would you do differently? What impact do you think you had on that situation, setting, or person(s)? What skills did you learn or sharpen?

_____

_____

Do you feel especially proud of something today?

_____

_____

*Dimensions of Service Learning*

# CHAPTER *twelve*

## Dimensions of Career Development

### INTRODUCTION

Do you remember being asked, "What do you want to be when you grow up?" and replying with confidence–lawyer, a teacher, a doctor, or a nurse? Your answer probably mirrored your parent's chosen profession or that of someone you admired. As you grew older, the question became more difficult to answer. Somewhere between the middle grades and high school, you may have discovered that you really didn't know what you wanted to be.

*About one-half of all college freshmen and a significant number of upperclassmen and returning students have not chosen a major or career.*

### OBJECTIVES

The objectives of this chapter on Career Planning and Development include
1. expanding student consciousness of the need for early, careful, and systematic career planning;
2. identifying the key steps in the career-planning process;
3. encouraging students to think about changes in workplace, particularly those produced by information technology, as they think about and plan careers;
4. urging students to identify and pursue the skills, characteristics, and strategies that contribute to successful career planning;
5. encouraging students to link career planning to their personal, academic, and professional growth strategies; and
6. encouraging students to identify and exchange with distinguished individuals in their careers through the cultivation of a mentor or friendship relationship.

### KEY CONCEPTS

This chapter is designed to help you
1. decide on the kind of career you want to pursue.
2. examine your personal attributes in making career choices.
3. utilize professional tools in planning your career.
4. locate and communicate with a person currently in a role or job similar to your career aspirations and, where possible, recruit them as a mentor.

**Dimensions of Career Development**

As a college student, you still may not know what you want your profession to be. I know that this reality may be frightening, but before you get excited, let me assure you that it is not time to panic. About one-half of all college freshmen and a significant number of upperclassmen and returning students have not made a definite decision or selected a career (Michelozzi, Surrell, & Cobez, 2003).

Career planning is a relatively new phenomenon. Historically, one's career path was limited and to a large extent determined by gender. The career choices for women were limited to preparing to become housewives, teachers, or nurses, while men prepared to enter the world of business, government, or agriculture. Career choices were limited and static compared to the career choices that you have today. As a matter of fact, your generation is more likely to change careers as often as your parents traded in their automobiles. A global economy will offer career options that were not available just a few years ago.

The age of information is partly responsible for today's rapidly evolving workplace. The Information Age has sparked a rebirth in the way we communicate, learn, and work. Information technology is also responsible for creating many of the top jobs that exist today. These factors have put the very nature of work itself in flux. In order for you to compete in this high-tech, fast-moving workforce, you must plan your career. It doesn't matter whether you are 17 or 50, after reading this chapter and completing the exercises, you will have some idea of what you want to be when you grow up.

## DIMENSIONS OF CAREER PLANNING

Career planning is a process that will help you
- articulate who you are and what you do well.
- see where your personal characteristics fit into the work world.
- secure the job you have chosen by improving your job-hunting skills.

The career-planning process begins with self-discovery and career exploration. Throughout this text you have been challenged to analyze who you are, what is important to you, and what your expectations are. You have also been asked to clarify your values. By clarifying your values, you were identifying your wants and interests. Your career choices should be based on those interests.

## DIMENSIONS OF CAREER EXPLORATION

The next step in career planning is career exploration. Career exploration is learning about yourself and the world of work and then making choices about careers based on what you have learned. There is a direct relationship between the kind of work you are interested in doing and your values and aptitudes. Your search begins with the Dictionary of Occupational Titles (DOT). The DOT is published by the U.S. Department of Labor and contains over 20,000 occupational listings and descriptions. An easier-to-use guide is the DOT supplement entitled the Guide for Occupational Exploration. Jobs in the GOE are classified into 66 job groups. Both of these publications can be found in most libraries, the university career center, the university counseling office, and on line.

# HOW TO USE THE GUIDE FOR OCCUPATIONAL EXPLORATION

The number and name of the job group appear at the beginning of the listing. Jobs or occupations are listed under each heading. The decimal code appears to the left of the job title. For example, suppose you are interested in Job Group 55, Human Services, Child and Adult Care. The code number is 10.03. Immediately following the code number and job title, you will find information that describes the workers in the group and gives examples of where you may work. Each of the job listings is subdivided into specific job titles and identified by a six-digit number. For example, under the Child and Adult Care group is

10.03.01 Data Collection
10.03.02 Patient Care
10.03.03 Care of Others

The Occupational Outlook Handbook is an excellent reference that will help you find careers and/or occupations that interest you. Providing descriptions for 85% of all jobs found in the United States, the Handbook lends itself to career exploration. For example, a specific occupation can be found in the alphabetical index located in the back of the Occupational Outlook Handbook. If you are exploring career possibilities, occupations are grouped into clusters and are located in the Table of Contents in the front of the Handbook. Whether you are exploring by clusters or by index, you will find the same standard format of descriptions: nature of work, working conditions, employment training, other qualifications, advancement possibilities, job outlook, earnings, and related occupations.

## *Selecting a Major*

Making choices about your occupation based on your interests should help you in determining your major. If you are not sure about a career choice, ability tests and interest inventories can help. Ability tests and interest inventories will help you compare the strengths of your interests in activities performed in various occupational categories. Ability tests, often called aptitude tests, assess how quickly or easily you can learn and perform an unfamiliar task.

Ability tests measure aptitudes ranging from conceptualization to finger dexterity. Therefore, some aptitude measures can predict career success. There are different types of aptitudes.

- The aptitude to learn, called general learning ability, measures how quickly you can grasp and/or understand instructions and facts.
- Verbalization aptitude is the ability to process and use written or spoken words clearly.
- The aptitude to conceptualize means that you can find creative ways or quick solutions to problems.
- Numerical aptitudes are those in which you work quickly and correctly with numbers.
- Spatial perception aptitude is the ability to mentally understand in three-dimensional form how objects can be moved, folded, and arranged.
- Form perception aptitude is your ability "to recognize simi-

*Your major should be based on your interests. Ability tests and interest inventories can help you narrow the field.*

Dimensions of Career Development

larities and differences in shapes and shadings and to observe detail in drawings or objects.
- The eye-hand aptitude ability coordinates how quickly the eye matches the movement of the hand.
- The finger dexterity aptitude is characterized by how quickly you can move your fingers and pick up small objects.
- Your mechanical aptitude ability combines eye-hand coordination and finger dexterity with your capacity to understand machinery and its working parts.

Interest Inventories such as COPS are designed to help you plan your career by comparing the relative strengths of your interest in activities performed in a variety of occupations (Edits/Educational & Industrial Testing Service, 1992). For example, COPS asks you to respond to statements about various activities performed. Next, you plot the responses to reveal job clusters. High peak points correlate positively with career interests.

## PROFESSIONAL DEVELOPMENT PLAN

Now that you have chosen your major, you are ready to create your professional development plan. The purpose of the Professional Development Plan (PDP) is to help you strategically plan your future through self-analysis and tracking. The PDP is a guide to assist you in making assessments, exploring careers, gaining career experiences, and making a smooth transition from undergraduate to graduate school and/or the workplace. The Professional Development Plan should be a helpful tool in establishing networks, selecting mentors, and identifying potential employers. You may wish to pursue an internship or a volunteer experience in, or related to, your professional development plan so that you may gain experience and knowledge in the professional roles you seek. This can be done through service-learning, civic participation, developing a relationship with a professional or career mentor, and a study abroad experience.

## DIMENSIONS OF JOB-HUNTING

Preparing for the job hunt starts now with your choice of classes, praticums, internships, and/or cooperative education (co-ops), because one of the most effective ways to land a job is to become acquainted with the person who has the power to hire you (Bolles, 2007). A great way to get your feet in the door, learn more about your chosen field, and gain experience is to do practicums and/or internships. Practicums and internship rewards come after graduation. They make you more marketable and increase your ability to become employed full-time.

If you need money while in college, the co-op program may be the revenue source you are looking for, while gaining experience in your professional field. Students who co-op will generally work one semester and attend school the next semester. The cycle of the co-op will be determined by the employer and you. In addition, most students receive academic credit hours for full-time or continuous part-time experiences.

The five most effective ways to find the job you seek are to
1. use the creative job-hunting approach: match your best skills and cognitive abilities with potential employers. Employ the Internet to assist you in exploring your career options.

2. apply directly to an employer, office, or company in person.
3. ask friends for job leads.
4. ask relatives for job leads.
5. use the placement office at the university or college you attend (Bolles, 2007).

The tools necessary for the job hunt are the resume, cover letter, networking and negotiation skills, and interview preparation. A resume is a brief history of a person's education, work experience, and other qualifications for employment (Michelozzi, et.al. 2003). The resume is an effective way to express your qualifications on paper. By writing down your skills, you may discover things about yourself and learn how to express your qualifications. A resume can serve as your calling card. It is a quick and easy way for an employer to learn about you. The employer may use your resume as a starting point for conducting the job interview and for refreshing his or her memory of you after your interview. Preparing an effective resume requires planning. The resume should be prepared to draw a potential employer's attention to your qualifications. A person who screens resumes spends thirty seconds or less on each one (Bolles, 2007; Ellis, Toft, Stupka, &, Lankowitz, 2003). Since the aim of the resume is to get an interview, make it happen.

## RESUME-WRITING TIPS

1. Make sure that your resume is geared to the language and needs of the employer.
2. Your resume must be neat, well organized, and free of grammatical and spelling errors.
3. Make your resume easy to skim.
4. Prepare a cover letter to accompany the resume. Your cover letter should answer the question, "What can I say that would motivate this employer to meet me personally?" Mention a goal of the company and describe how hiring you will contribute directly to meeting that goal. Knowing about the company is a motivator for many employers.
5. Keep track of the job you are pursuing. Follow-up your resume with news clippings, workshop announcements, journal articles, thank-you notes, and follow-up letters (Bolles, 2007). Make sure to attach a note. The note may say, "I thought you may be interested in this" or "Please file this along with my resume."

## THE RESUME CHECKLIST

### *Do's:*

- Include an objective statement. This gives your resume focus.
- Use career-related words to feature key facts.
- Use action verbs to describe your skills and accomplishments.
- Keep descriptions of experiences short.
- Include community service experiences.
- Use major headings and bullets and organize your accomplishments under them.
- Use a format that is easy to read by placing headings in the center or in the left margin.
- Keep resumes to one page, unless you are very experienced in the field.
- Get permission for references prior to using them; place references on a separate page.
- Ask others–preferably your mentor–to critique your resume.

## Don'ts:

- Don't fill up the page with text or a variation of font styles.
- Don't use expressions that imply duties or responsibilities.
- Don't use a reproducible design based on a resume template.
- Don't use the first person "I" and other personal pronouns.
- Don't list references on the resume.
- Don't list full addresses and telephone numbers of current or former employers.

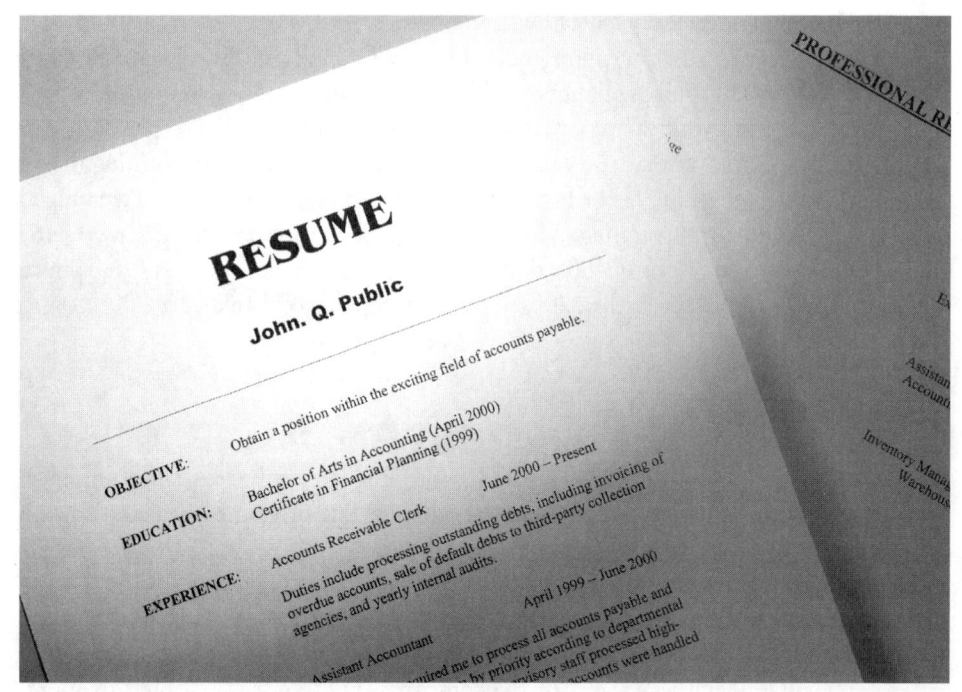

*A resume is a brief history of a person's education, work experience, and other qualifications for employment.*

## Type of Resumes

There is no one-and-only way to write a resume, but there are some basic guidelines to follow. Resumes, until recently, usually followed three formats: chronological, functional, and a combination of the chronological and functional resumes. The chronological resume is used when your work experiences are in related areas and are fairly continuous. In this case, your work experiences are listed in reverse order, starting with the present or most recent. A functional resume is used when three or four skills areas are emphasized and when work experiences have not been related and/or continuous. The combination resume usually begins as a functional resume and ends in chronological order. Mobile professionals who have been in the workforce for twelve or more years generally choose the combination format. The fourth and newest resume type is the electronic resume, which is being used by almost all midsized and large companies.

The electronic (automated) resume, or e-resume, allows a company to process and keep track of prospective employees by using databases to match applicants with jobs. Electronic cover letters and resumes are delivered via e-mail, submitted to Internet job boards, or reside on their own web page. Therefore, the technology-compatible cover letter and/or resume guidelines are different than those for traditional resumes. The electronic resume dos' are listed below:

- Use uppercase letters for emphasis in headings.
- Send the resume in a text-based format, such as ASCII.
- Keep it simple (no graphics, vertical or horizontal lines, shading, folds, or staples).
- Use capital letters and/or boldface if you wish.
- Use popular true fonts, nondecorative typefaces.
- Use white or light-colored $8\frac{1}{2}$ X 11 inch-sized paper.
- Type your name at the top of each page. Your name should be the first readable item.
- Use nouns, not verbs as key words. Employers use keywords to search for the right candidate.
- Stress results and accomplishments rather than duties and responsibilities.
- Use key characters to make your e-resume more appealing. For example, you can use equal signs = = =, plus signs +++ and tildes ~~~ to make rule lines. You can use asterisks (* * *), hyphens (- - -), lowercase letters o's (o o o), and carats (> > >) to make bullets (Bruce, 2007; Gunner, 2007;

Let's follow the process of an electronic resume. When the resume reaches the personnel department or career service center, it is assigned a code that is linked to job openings. The resume is then stored directly into a scannable database.

Next, the computer uses artificial intelligence to read recognizable text and pull out key words from each section. The computer then assigns job categories to the record and builds a skill inventory. It is now possible to use key words or specific criteria to search the database for candidate skills matching job openings. Once a match is made, the resume, along with the cover letter, is then forwarded electronically to the person doing the hiring (Bruce, 2007).

## GLOBAL RESUMES

Your job search will not be limited to the shores of America; you need at least one resume that meets the criteria of international markets. We learned in Chapter 8 (Dimensions of Culture) that different cultures have different rules, customs, values, priorities, etc. These differences are also seen in job markets. To compete in the global job market, you need to know the criteria and present your information in a culturally sensitive manner. What is acceptable in America may not be acceptable in the global job market. As a matter of fact, very few U.S. rules of resume writing apply to overseas employment. For example, the global resume is the Curriculum Vita (CV), which is very detailed.

## NETWORKING

"Networking," the term of the 90s, replaced similar terms such as "the buddy system," "the old boys' network," and "the new girls' network." Regardless of the terminology used, the fact remains that employers have always passed jobs along to people they know (Michelozzi, et.al, 2003).

"Networking is developing and maintaining relationships with others" (Ellis, et al., 1997, p. 106). It is a broad list of contacts you've met through various social, professional, and business functions that you want to assist you in looking for a job. People in your network may be able to give you job leads, offer you advice and information about a particular company or industry, and introduce you to others. The most common avenues of networking are alumni and alumnae databases, career fairs, professional organizations, and employer-sponsored events.

An effective networking job search strategy is the career fair. The most common types of career fairs are governmental fairs, health and science fairs, education fairs, and graduate and professional fairs. But all career fairs have a common theme: a chance for a company and job seeker to meet and screen a large volume of potential job candidates.

Belonging to professional organizations and associations are other avenues of networking. For every profession, there is an organization and/or association, and being a member is part of being a professional. Join your organization now and become actively involved. The benefits are tremendous. Professional organizations are designed to contribute to continuing your education. They provide up-to-date information, hold conferences, sponsor seminars, and disseminate publications in your area of study.

*Networking means developing and maintaining relationships with others who may be able to assist you in finding a job.*

Create and sustain your network:
1. Make a list of people you already know who can help you with career planning and/or job hunting.
2. Form a job-hunting team. Members of the team can draft and revise resumes, role-play interviews, and alert you about job openings.
3. Make contacts. Look for things you have in common. Memorize a short statement about your career goal. For example, "I am looking for an internship in product development. Do you know of a company that takes interns?"
4. View networking as healthy competition. Very seldom are there other people in your network actually competing for the same jobs. Ask for help, give help, and support others; any competitor could turn into a friend.

## THE INTERVIEW

Once you have delivered and/or mailed your resume and cover letter, it is time to prepare for the job interview. An interview is a "powerful conversation between an employer or delegated interviewer and a perspective employee" (Michelozzi, 1999, p. 229). Get the most out of your interview. Prior to the interview, do the following:
- Research your potential employer.
- Anticipate questions.
- Jot down essential information.
- Think positively.
- Prepare questions to ask the interviewer.
- Learn relaxation techniques.
- Conduct mock interviews with your mentor.

- Videotape and critique the mock interviews. Seek feedback from your mentor or your career service center counselor.
- Follow-up with a thank-you note.

## PREPARING FOR THE JOB INTERVIEW

The success of your interview depends on how well you prepare for it. The interviewer will form an opinion of you during the first thirty seconds after initial contact. Dress for success following the suggestions from the Social Etiquette, Professional Protocol, and Professional Ethics chapter. After choosing your outfit, practice sitting and moving in it.

The best preparation for an interview is to practice. Practice builds confidence. Practice by talking to others about their jobs. Practice by critiquing videotaped interviews. Practice good eye contact, appropriate body language, voice diction, and active listening. Prepare answers that you will give, especially about your past experiences. Interviewers often want you to elaborate about your life and work experiences.

The interviewer believes that how you handled a situation in the past tells a lot about how you will behave in the future (Job Choice, 1998). Arrange to be on time. Make sure you know where you are going and how long it takes you to reach your destination. The interview process is much different today than it was just five years ago. Employers generally use two types of interviews: the traditional job interview and the behavioral interview. The traditional job interview uses broad-based questions such as, "Why do you want to work for this company?" and "Tell me about your strengths and weaknesses." In this type of interview, the employer is assessing your ability to communicate. Employers are looking for the answer to four questions:
- Do you have the skills and abilities to perform the job?
- Do you possess the enthusiasm and work ethics of the company?
- Are you a team player?
- Will you fit into the organization?

The behavioral job interview is based on the theory that past performance is the best indicator of future behavior, and uses questions that probe specific past behaviors, such as, "Tell me about a time where you confronted an unexpected problem," "Tell me about an experience when you failed to achieve a goal," and "Give me a specific example of a time when you managed several projects at once." Companies want to know how you think, solve problems, and works with others. For example, suppose an interviewer asked you to determine how many gas stations there were in the United States. Before answering, ask yourself: Are you expected to know the answer to this question? Why did the interviewer ask you this question? Do you think the interviewer knows the answer to this question? No, you are not expected to know how many gas stations there are in the U.S. and, more than likely, the interviewer will not know the answer, either. The interviewer does, however, expect you to answer the question. The interviewer expects you to know how to approach the question to figure out the answer. The interviewer wants to see how you solve problems and handle yourself under pressure. To prepare for the behavioral interview, you need to
- recall scenarios that fit the various types of behavioral interviewing questions.
- expect the interviewer to have several follow-up questions that probe for details and explore all aspects of a given situation or experience.

- recall class projects, group situations, hobbies, and volunteer work that might lend themselves to or provide examples for these types of questions.
- frame your answers based on a four-part outline: 1) describe the situation, 2) discuss the actions you took, 3) relate the outcomes, and 4) specify what you learned from it.

Numerous types of traditional and behavioral interviews exist, and you should be prepared for any of these during your job search. The types most often used are discussed below.

The Telephone Interview: Telephone interviews are becoming more common. They save the employer time and indicate whether a face-to-face interview is warranted. Telephone interviews are typically used to make a preliminary assessment of a candidate's qualifications.

Panel Interview: In a Panel Interview, typically 3 to 6 members in different roles in the organization ask candidates questions to assess their knowledge, skills, team fit, ability to make decisions, etc.

Video-conference Interview: These interviews are becoming more common. Video conferences expand the scope of searching for qualified candidates with less cost and time involvement.

Informal Interview: This type of interview is casual and relaxed; it is intended to induce candidates to talk comfortably so that they will reveal more information than they might otherwise. Your privacy is important to remember at this point; too much information too soon could screen you out from consideration.

Performance Interview: In this interview, the interviewer asks candidates to role-play job functions to assess their knowledge and skills. (This is not the same as a Case Interview, in that it typically is only a portion of the interview and is focused on performance or knowledge rather than critical thinking.)

Case Interview: A case interview is a special type of interview commonly used by management consulting firms and is increasingly being used in many other organizations. It helps the interviewer analyze your critical-thinking skills. If you are not

*In today's workplace, it's realistic to anticipate salary negotiation; therefore, before you go into an interview, it's important to know the minimum salary you are willing to accept.*

familiar, do not have experience, or are not comfortable with case analysis, it can be one of the most difficult interviews to undergo. In a case interview, a candidate is given a problem to see how he or she would work it out on the spot. The problems that are presented come in many forms, but the interviewer wants to assess the candidate's analytical skills, ability to think under pressure, logical thought process, business knowledge and acumen, creativity, communication, and quantitative analysis skills (Boldt, 2008; Simon & Curtis, 2004).

## NEGOTIATING THE SALARY

When an employer invites you back for a second interview or to offer you the job, it is time for you to think about salary. In today's workplace, it is realistic to anticipate salary negotiation. More than likely, you are being offered a position that was once held by an experienced, more-expensive worker. "Downsizing," "layoffs," and "reorganizing the corporate structure" are terms used to describe ways companies are saving money. Even if an employer wanted to offer you the top salary right from the start, most of them cannot. Many employers are making salary their major criterion for deciding whom to hire (Bolles, 2007). Therefore, it is important for you to know the minimum salary you are willing to accept before going into the interview.

Before the job interview, determine your living expenses and estimate job-related and unforeseeable expenses. In other words, study and revise the budget you prepared in Chapter Four. Successful negotiation includes:
- waiting until the end of the interview to discuss salary. When opportunity presents itself, mention ways you may help the company save money.
- waiting for the employer to mention a salary figure first.
- knowing the minimum salary you will accept and the salary range of the job. Knowing this information will help you to determine whether the salary being offered is fixed or contains room for negotiation.

## GLOSSARY

Ability Tests: often called aptitude tests, assess how quickly or easily you can learn and perform an unfamiliar task.

Career Exploration: learning about yourself, the world of work, and making choices about careers based on what you have learned.

Career Planning: the continuous process of evaluating your current lifestyle, likes/dislikes, passions, skills, personality, dream job, and current job and career path and making corrections and improvements to better prepare for future steps in your career, as needed, or to make a career change.

Curriculum Vitae: similar to a resume, but more formal, and includes a detailed listing of items beyond the typical resume items, such as publications, presentations, professional activities, honors, and additional information. The CV tends to be used by international job seekers, and those seeking a faculty, research, clinical, or scientific position.

Interview: a "powerful conversation between an employer or delegated interviewer and a prospective employee" (Michelozzi, 1999, p. 229).

Networking: "developing and maintaining relationships with others" (Ellis, et al., 1997, p. 106).

Resume: a brief history of a person's education, work experience, and other qualifications for employment.

## REFERENCES

Boldt, A. (2008). Resumes for the rest of us: Secrets from the pros forbjob seekers with unconventional career paths. Chicago, IL.: Career Press.

Bolles, R. N. (2007). What color is your parachute ? 2008. A practical manual for job-hunter & career-changers. Berkeley, CA: Ten Speed Press.

Brickman, E., Thinnes, D., & Osmon, B. (2007). Freshman year experience: Plan for success. Dubuque, IA.: Kendall/Hunt.

Bruce, C. (February, 2007). The internet: The indispensable tool for job hunting. *Black Collegian Magazine.*

COPS. (1992). Edits/Educational & Industrial Testing Service. San Diego, CA: Educational & Industrial Testing Service.

Dean, D. (October, 2006). Career success starts with self-assessment. *Black Collegian Magazine.*

Ellis, D., Lankowitz, S., Stupka, E., & Toft, D. (1997). Career planning supplement to becoming a master student. Boston, MA: Houghton Mifflin.

Ellis, D., Toft, D., Stupka, E., & Lankowitz, S. (2003). Career planning supplement to becoming a master student. Boston, MA: Houghton Mifflin.

Gunner, M. (February, 2007). Give your resume' the electronic edge. *Black Collegian Magazine.*

Michelozzi, B. N. (1999). *Coming alive from nine to five a career search handbook,* (5th. ed.). Mountain View, CA: Mayfield.

Michelozzi, B.N., Surrell, L. & Cobez, R. (2003). Coming alive from nine to five in a 24/7 world: A career search handbook for the 21$^{st}$ century. Mountain View, CA: Mayfield.

Roth, B. (February, 2008). The college student's guide to landing a great job. *Black Collegian Magazine.*

Simons, W. & Curtis, R. (2004). The resume guide to writing unbeatable resumes. Columbus, OH: McGraw-Hill.

U.S. Department of Labor's Bureau of Labor Statistics. (2003). Dictionary of Occupational Titles. Washington, D.C.: US Government Printing Office.

U.S. Department of Labor's Bureau of Labor Statistics. (2008-2009) Occupational Outlook Handbook. Washington, D.C.: U.S. Government Printing Office.

U.S. Department of Labor and National Forum Foundation. (2003). The guide for occupational exploration. Washington, D.C.: U.S. Government Printing Office.

## WEB SITES

AT&T College Network www.att.com/college
Black Collegian Online 2004 www.bc.com
Career Mosaic www.careermosaic.com
CareerPath.com www.careerpath.com
www.HBCUCareercenter.com

**Job Searches, Job Seekers Glossary, etc.:**
www.jobweb.org/search/jobs/
The Monster Board www.monster.com
www.black-collegian.com/career/

**Work Section of Tripod:**
www.tripod.com
www.tripod.com/work/internships
www.university.toplinks.com
http://www.wetfeet.com

# ACTIVITY 1:

Guide to Occupational Exploration
Directions: Use the Guide to Occupational Exploration to do the following activities.

1. Make a list of the career groups that interest you. Include the decimal code number.

2. List all the career titles that are included in each group.

3. Answer the following questions that relate to the career you selected:

    - What kind of work would you do in the chosen career?

    - What skills and abilities do you need for this kind of work?

    - How do you know whether you would like or could learn to do this kind of work?

    - What else should you consider about these careers?

**Dimensions of Career Development**

## ACTIVITY 2:

### *Ability Testing*

Contact the University Counseling, Testing, or Career Services. Make an appointment to take an ability test, a self-discovery assessment, or an interest inventory, such as the COP Interest Inventory System. Discuss your results with a counselor. Bring your results to class. Explain below whether or not the results are consistent with your personal assessment.

# ACTIVITY 3:

## *Deciding on a Major*

After considering your career interests, ask the following questions:

1. Do you enjoy the subject?

2. Have you taken courses in this area?

3. How well did you perform?

4. What kind of jobs can this major lead to?

5. What are the requirements beyond the baccalaureate degree?

Your choice of a major should prepare you for the job market as a skilled, competent individual.

# ACTIVITY 4:

## *Occupational Outlook Handbook*

Use the Occupational Outlook Handbook to compare your highest score identified on your ability test with an occupation listed either in a career cluster or a specific occupation.

# ACTIVITY 5:

## *Professional Development Plan*

The Professional Development Plan is below. Complete Sections I through IV and Year 1 of the PDP with your instructor.

PROFESSIONAL DEVELOPMENT PLAN
Purpose/Goals of Plan:
The purpose of the Professional Development Plan (PDP) is to help you strategically plan your future through self-analysis, tracking, and implementing the plan's components to achieve your goals, dreams, and aspirations. This is a guide to assist you in making assessments, exploring careers, gaining career experiences, and making a smooth transition from undergraduate school to graduate school and/or the workplace. The Personal Development Plan should serve to be a helpful tool in establishing networks, selecting mentors, and identifying potential employers. The major components of the (PDP) include

- filling out a personal data form.
- identifying your personal goals and career objectives.
- academic planning for four years.
- developing a transition plan from college.

Implementing the Professional Development Plan (PDP):

1. Complete the Personal Data Form and Freshmen Year sections with your instructor.

2. The instructor will sort the Professional Development Plan by majors and send to the chairperson of the designated department.

3. The chairperson will assign the student to an advisor.

4. The advisor will assist the student in completing the Professional Development Plan, starting with the sophomore year.

5. The advisor will assist the student in revising and implementing components of the Professional Development Plan.

## ACTIVITY 5 CONT'D.

### *I. Personal Data Form*

Name _____ SS# _____
        (Last)      (First)      (M.)

Local Address _____ City _____

State _____ Zip _____ Phone _____

E-Mail Address _____ Fax Number _____

Permanent Address _____ City _____State __ Zip _____

In Case of Emergency Notify:
Phone ( ) _____ (Relationship) _____

Are you currently employed? ___Yes ___No  If Yes, please list employer.

Employer _____ Hours Per Week _____

Employer _____ Hours Per Week _____

Housing Arrangement: ____Off Campus ____On Campus

Approximate Travel Time (if off campus): _____

Please list all problems/concerns that you want to share and discuss with your advisors.

a.                        d.

b.                        e.

c.                        f.

List any of your special needs:

Please list any support services you currently use:

Special Talents/Hobbies:

# ACTIVITY 5 CONT'D.

## *II. Personal Goals/Objective*

1. Explain your reasons for selecting this institution:

2. List your four greatest strengths:

3. Identify areas that you would like to strengthen/improve:

4. Which inventories/assessments have you completed?

   Strong-Campbell (Vocational Interest) _____ Date

   Self-Directed Search Interest Inventories _____ Date

   Myers Briggs Personality Type _____ Date

   COPS/Keirsey Interest Inventory System _____ Date

   Other _____ Date

Career Objectives

1. Please list three career objectives:

   a.

   b.

   c.

2. Identify your Mentor/Mentor Team:

3. What is your Major? _____    Your Minor? _____

   Your Department? _____    Your School? _____

4. List professional organizations that you may join:

   a.

   b.

   c.

Dimensions of Career Development

# ACTIVITY 5 CONT'D.

## *IV. Academic Plan*

Name _____ Academic Advisor _____

Major Requirements: (Initial all that apply when you have documentation)

_____Major Credit Hours        _____Independent Study

_____GPA in Major              _____ Departmental Exams

_____Practicum                 _____Competency Exams

_____Internship                _____National Exams

_____Co-op                     _____Other

My initial indicates that I have received the following documents:

                                                                                   Date

_____University Catalog                              _____

_____Student Handbook                                _____

_____University Policies                             _____

_____Calendar of Student Events                      _____

_____Library Information                             _____

_____List of all Campus Administrators               _____

_____Copy of the Major 4-year Plan                   _____

_____Declaration of Major Form                       _____

_____Interlibrary Loan Card                          _____

_____Validated Identification Card                   _____

_____Class Schedule (Semester)                       _____

List all Honors/Awards and Dates:
            Honors/Awards                              Dates:

_____                        _____

_____                        _____

_____                        _____

Please list/describe any previous Community Service Activities:

## ACTIVITY 5 CONT'D.

### *Year 1 - Freshman Year*

I have completed the Career Inventory Assessment (Identify career choice according to assessment): Your career choice(s):

1._____   2. _____   3. _____

List jobs available on the market as related to your career choice(s):

1._____   2. _____

3._____   4. _____

Identify job, duties/responsibilities associated with career choice(s)

Career Choice 1: _____ Salary Range _____
Duties/Responsibilities: _____
Occupational Outlook: _____

Career Choice 2: _____ Salary Range _____
Duties/Responsibilities: _____
Occupational Outlook: _____

Career Choice 3: _____ Salary Range _____
Duties/Responsibilities: _____
Occupational Outlook: _____

Prospective employer(s) relative to career choice(s):
    Name of Company        Location        Phone Number
1. _____
2. _____
3. _____

List civic, community, or school organizations:

1._____   2. _____   3. _____

Total number of academic hours completed: _____

Semester grade point average: _____ Cumulative grade point average: _____

Summer Plans:
- Seek a summer job or internship to gain experience in career field.
- Focus on researching your career field.
- Acquire community services experience and hours in your career field.

Accomplishments/Results: _____

# ACTIVITY 5 CONT'D.

## *Year 2 - Sophomore Year*

Career choice: _____

Academic requirements for career choice: _____

Identify your strengths for career choice:

1. _____
2. _____

Areas of improvement needed to be successful:

1. _____
2. _____

Identify potential barriers associated with this career field:

1. _____ 2. _____
3. _____ 4. _____

List of contact persons related to career choice:

    Name of Company    Location Phone    Number

1. _____
2. _____

Have you developed a resume? Yes _____ Date _____ No _____

Have you visited the University Career Services?

    Yes _____ Date _____ No _____

Have you researched internship/work experience opportunities?

    Yes _____ Date _____ No _____

List the professional organizations you have joined:

1. _____ 2. _____

Career strategies:

- Begin thinking about graduate school.
- Research requirements for professional programs.
- Relate community service activities with career choice.
- Gain related career work experience.

Identify potential mentors in career field:

1. _____ 2. _____ 3. _____

Key questions related to career choice:

1. What do I have to offer an employer?
2. Who needs what I have to offer?
3. How do I make them want to hire me?

List civic, fraternal, community, and university organizations:

1. _____ 2. _____ 3. _____

Summer plans:

- Seek a summer job, co-op, or internship to gain experience in career field.
- Continue to explore career field.
- Continue community service experience in your career field.

# ACTIVITY 5 CONT'D.

## *Year 3 -Junior Year*

Name the members on your mentor team: _____

How many semester hours have you completed? _____

What is your cumulative GPA? _____

Has there been a career choice change? _____ Yes _____ No

If yes, what is the career choice change?

Directions: Where applicable, write your initials in the space provided for your response.

Have you visited the University Career Center?   ____Yes ____ Date ____ No
Have you filed a copy of your resume with the
   University Career Center?   ____Yes ____ Date ____ No
Have you scheduled a mock interview with the
   University Career Center?   ____Yes ____ Date ____ No
Have you a portfolio, i.e., electronic, manual?   ____Yes ____ Date ____ No
Have you conducted a graduate school search?   ____Yes ____ Date ____ No
Have you been involved in an internship
   or work experience program?   ____Yes ____ Date ____ No

Directions: Initial the professional skills you have mastered:
____Presentation   ____Leadership   ____Organizational
____Information Technology   ____Research
____Communication   ____Team Building

List the professional meetings you have attended: _____

List field experiences, internships, and or co-op experiences you've had:

Summer Plans
- Continue internship experience.
- Continue networking.
- Continue to evaluate work experience.
- Visit potential graduate/professional schools.
- Travel.

**Dimensions of Career Development**

# ACTIVITY 5 CONT'D.

## *Year 4 - Senior Year*

Section A: To be completed at the beginning of the Senior Year.

Directions: Where applicable, write your initials in the space provided for your response.

1. Academic Audit ____Yes ____ Date ____ No
2. Financial Audit ____Yes ____ Date ____ No
3. Participated in Internship/ Co-op         ____Yes ____ Date ____ No
4. Scheduled Interviews         ____Yes ____ Date ____ No

   Name of Company: _____
   Type of offer: ____Internship____Part-time job ____Other
   Results: _____Accepted ____Yes ____ No

   Name of Company: _____
   Type of offer: ____Internship____Part-time job ____Other
   Results: _____Accepted ____Yes ____ No

   Name of Company: _____
   Type of offer: ____Internship____Part-time job ____Other
   Results: _____Accepted ____Yes ____ No

5. Job Preparation with Professional/Mentor __Yes __ No

Section B: Graduate/Professional School

6. Make application to Graduate/Professional School ____Yes ____ No

   Name of Graduate/Professional School: _____
   Date of Application: _____ Results: _____

   Name of Graduate/Professional School: _____
   Date of Application: _____ Results: _____

   Name of Graduate/Professional School: _____
   Date of Application: _____ Results: _____

Section C: Graduation Checklist
7. Application for graduation ____Yes ____ Date ____ No
8. Order cap and gown ____Yes ____ Date ____ No
9. Order invitations ____Yes ____ Date ____ No
10. Take yearbook pictures ____Yes ____ Date ____ No
11. Exit interviews __ Dept. __ Career Services __ Research & Evaluation Office

Section D: Transition
10. Evaluate job offers.
11. Develop one-year, three-year, and five-year transition plans from college to workplace.

# ACTIVITY 6: RESUME

Write your resume. Critique it using the most appropriate resume-writing worksheet on the following pages; make changes. Keep your resume, update once a year and file with Career Services before applying for an internship or a co-op.

# ACTIVITY 6 CONT'D.

## *Resume-Writing Critique Worksheet for Chronological, Functional, and Combination Resumes*

Resume of _____ (Name)

**Directions:** Rate the resume on points, from 1 being low to 10 being high, in each of the categories listed. Compare your total ratings against the highest possible total score of 100. Circle the comments on how you will improve each category receiving a score of less than 6. Write additional comments in the space provided.

| ITEM | SCORE 1-3  4-6  7-9  10 | HOW TO IMPROVE |
|---|---|---|
| *Overall appearance.* Do you want to read it? Is it pleasing to the eye and easy to read? | | True font type and size, bold, no underlines, white paper, and plain text was used. |
| *Layout.* Is career objective stated and resume related to it? Does it have good margins? Does the resume look professional? | | A key word summarizes the career objective. A laser printer was used to print the resume. |
| *Length.* Is the name in the top right corner of each page? | | Lots of white space. |
| *Writing style.* Is it easy to get a picture of the qualifications? Is it free of cliches, such as "people-person," "results-oriented," "hands-on"? | | Personal qualifications build a case for finding out more about the candidate. He or she used terms such as "willing to relocate," "understanding of international marketing," "front-line experience." |
| *Descriptive Oriented.* Do sentences and paragraphs begin with nouns? | | Important information stands out. Effective words and phrases are used. |
| *Specificity.* Does resume avoid generalities and focus on specific information about projects, experiences? | | Job titles and dates of employment that would be most impressive to reader are listed. |

| ITEM | SCORE | HOW TO IMPROVE |
|------|-------|----------------|
| | 1-3   4-6   7-9   10 | |
| *Grammar.* Are there spelling and grammatical errors? | | The resume has been proofread. |
| *Format.* Is format simple? Were caps or boldface type used for delineating major headings? | | Bullets, shading graphics, acronyms, and abbreviations were avoided. |
| *Accomplishments.* Are accomplishments and problem-solving skills emphasized? Do experiences specifically match what the employer is seeking? | | Accomplishments and results are stressed, not duties and responsibilities. Honors, professional licenses, trade organizations, and certificates are examples of key words. |
| *Prioritize.* Is personal data such as name, on a line by itself? Are important dates on lines by themselves? Are important facts on the top two-thirds of the first page? | | High points have been covered. Outline format is used. Dates are given in numerical years rather than words. |
| *Extra.* Have community services, continuing education, volunteer services, and self-improvement classes been included? | | All activities are listed. Synonyms are used if key words might be described in more than one way. |
| *Bottom Line.* How well does the resume accomplish its purpose of getting interest from the employer for an interview? Is the resume scannable? | | Names of highly respected clients or people who know about your experience are included. |

Rating Point Total: _____ Out of 100 Points Maximum

How could the resume be improved?

_____

**Dimensions of Career Development**

# ACTIVITY 6 CONT'D.

## *Scannable Resumes Continues*

| ITEM | SCORE<br>1-3  4-6  7-9  10 | HOW TO IMPROVE |
|---|---|---|
| *Overall appearance.* Do you want to read it? Is it pleasing to the eye and easy to read? | | True font type and size, bold, no underlines, white paper, and plain text are used. |
| *Layout.* Is career objective stated and resume related to it? Does it have good margins? Does the resume look professional? | | A key word summarizes the career objective. A laser printer was used to print the resume. |
| *Length.* Is the name in the top right corner of each page? | | Lots of white space. |
| *Writing style.* Is it easy to get a picture of the qualifications? Is it free of cliches, such as "people-person," "results-oriented," "hands-on"? | | Personal qualifications build a case for finding out more about the candidate. He or she used terms such as "willing to relocate," "understanding of international marketing," "front-line experience." |
| *Descriptive Oriented.* Do sentences and paragraphs begin with nouns? | | Important information stands out. Effective words and phrases are used. |
| *Specificity.* Does resume avoid generalities and focus on specific information about projects, experiences? | | Job titles and dates of employment that would be most impressive to reader are listed. |

# ACTIVITY 6 CONT'D.

## *Scannable Resumes Continues*

| ITEM | SCORE<br>1-3 4-6 7-9 10 | HOW TO IMPROVE |
|---|---|---|
| *Grammar.* Are there spelling and grammatical errors? | | The resume has been proofread. |
| *Format.* Is format simple? Were caps or boldface type used for delineating major headings? | | Bullets, shading graphics, acronyms, and abbreviations were avoided. |
| *Accomplishments.* Are accomplishments and problem-solving skills emphasized? Do experiences specifically match what the employer is seeking? | | Accomplishments and results are stressed, not duties and responsibilities. Honors, professional licenses, trade organizations, and certificates are examples of key words. |
| *Prioritize.* Is personal data such as name, on a line by itself? Are important dates on lines by themselves? Are important facts on the top two-thirds of the first page? | | High points have been covered. Outline format is used. Dates are given in numerical years rather than words. |
| *Extra.* Have community services, continuing education, volunteer services, and self-improvement classes been included? | | All activities are listed. Synonyms are used if key words might be described in more than one way. |
| *Bottom Line.* How well does the resume accomplish its purpose of getting interest from the employer for an interview? Is the resume scannable? | | Names of highly respected clients or people who know about your experience are included. |

Rating Point Total: _____ Out of 100 Points Maximum

How could the resume be improved?

Dimensions of Career Development

# ACTIVITY 7:

## *Mock Interview*

Schedule a mock interview with the Career Services Office at your institution, with your mentor, or with your instructor. Evaluate your performance.

# CHAPTER *thirteen*

# Dimensions of Global Learning

## INTRODUCTION

Globalization is a reality in today's world of learning and living. Little we do, think, say, or plan is without connection to peoples, nations, institutions, cultures, trends, and forces around the world. World population, trade, economics and finance, ecological balance, global warming, ozone depletion, disease, famine, war, oppression, racial, ethnic, linguistic, and religious differences reach into our daily lives. Our academic majors, curricular and extracurricular activities involve traditions, scholarship, professional standards, and networks from past and present individuals and institutions in Europe, Asia, Africa, and islands of the Pacific, Atlantic, and Indian Oceans. We buy goods and services from foreign corporations in our downtown areas and malls. We export goods and services to many nations and peoples abroad. More and more individuals from more and more nations immigrate into our neighborhoods, rural areas, cities, and states. In the grand tradition of millions of immigrants before them, they seek to reinvent themselves and to pursue educational, employment, and cultural opportunities. Our currency, economy, employment, agriculture, and industrial capacity are all tied to those of other nations. Even the darker worlds of illegal drugs, weapons, and crime flow in and out of our nation, indeed, in and out of our neighborhoods, from overseas locations. No twenty-first century scholar or professional can be truly successful without preparing well to live, work, and grow in an international world. Consequently, in this chapter, we seek to encourage you to involve your mind, studies, career aspirations and civic and community activity in this increasingly global reality.

*Globalization has restructured our world and rewritten our cultural, economic, and academic environment.*

## OBJECTIVES

The objectives of this chapter include
1. identifying global learning as a key dimension of learning for students of any cultural background, academic major, career or professional aspiration, or civic or community orientation .
2. initiating discussion of key global trends, issues and opportunities available to students in the classroom and in constructive national and international organizations.
3. interrelating global learning with critical thinking, cultural diversity, ethical thinking, and action and career opportunities as essential to student global awareness.

4. encouraging students to think critically and independently about global trends, issues, and opportunities.
5. encouraging students to develop global networks with individuals and organizations in other parts of the world as part of their personal growth and development.

## KEY CONCEPTS

Globalization
Global learning
Trends, issues, and opportunities
Global networks

## DEFINITION OF GLOBALIZATION

**Globalization** is the process of rapid and extensive financial, intellectual, cultural and institutional exchange and interdependency between two or more nations or the peoples of two or more nations. Nations and peoples depend upon each other for education, employment, and an expanding quality of life. U.S. corporations invest and expand industrial and commercial activities in other nations; other nations invest and expand industrial and commercial activities in the U.S. Pankaj Ghemawat observes that, "Coca-Cola derived 67% of its revenues and 77% of its profits from outside of North America" (Ghemawat, Harvard Business Review, Vol. 81. No. 11, November 2003). On the darker side, American lost $70 billion in market value as a result of the 1997 Asian currency crisis. When civil war, international conflict, famine or disease run rampant in nations, many individuals and family migrate to other nations for relief and expanded social, educational, or economic opportunity. So, we know that globalization is occurring when we experience each other's social, financial, cultural and political pain, check our balance of payments and balance of trade, or observe the impact of immigration on local communities throughout the United States. Whether the imperatives of conflict following the September 11, 2001, attacks on New York and Washington, D.C., the emergence of the Euro as a new and dynamic European community currency, the perennial war in the Middle East in Israel, the Palestinians, or Iraq, the production and financial decisions of the Organization of Petroleum Exporting Countries (OPEC), the struggles over illegal distribution of drugs from various places in the world, or the need to learn several foreign languages, globalization has restructured our world and rewritten our cultural, economic, and academic environment.

## GLOBALIZATION AND LEARNING

Given these rapid and profound changes in the global contours of human relations, the learning and critical-thinking challenges and opportunities in globalization are immense and expanding. They include
- learning about the culture, history, heritage, economy, sociology, geography and politics of people and nations outside of the United States;
- learning at least one foreign language, not only as a way of promoting intercultural understanding, but also as a method of understanding the roots of the English language or whatever you identify as your native language;

**Figure 1**
**Global Thinking**

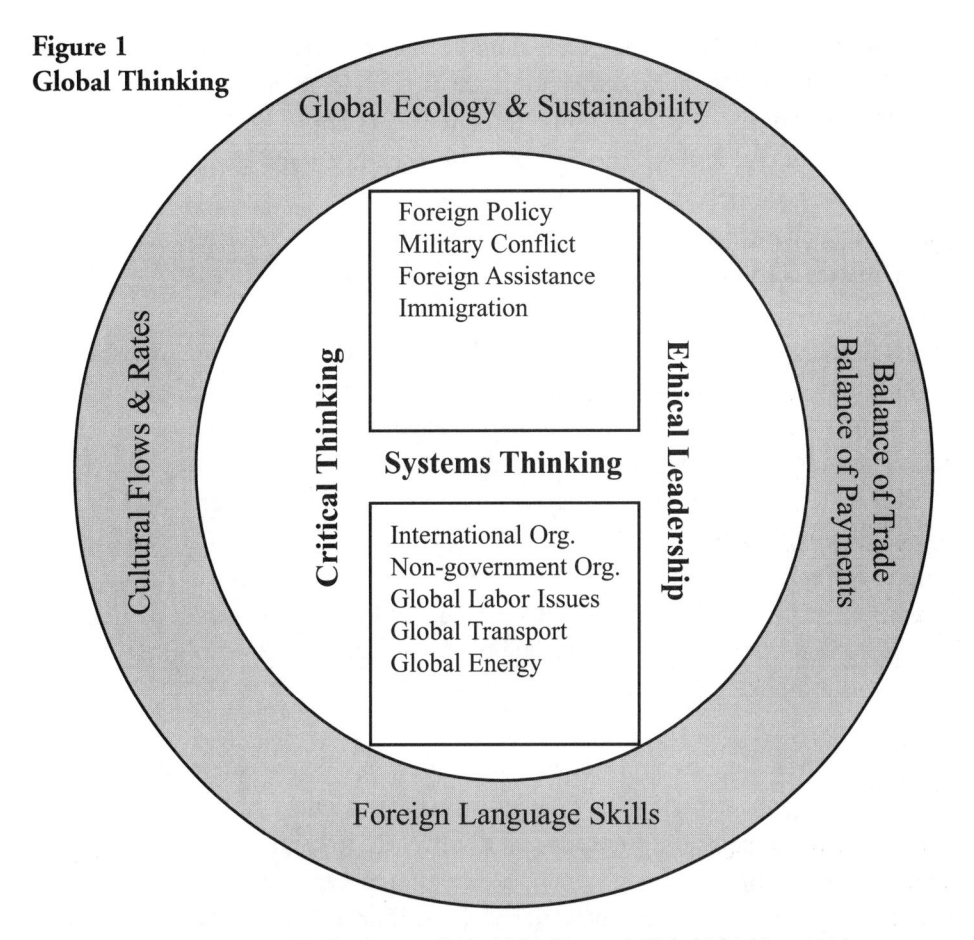

```
              Global Ecology & Sustainability

                    ┌─────────────────┐
                    │ Foreign Policy  │
                    │ Military Conflict│
   Cultural         │ Foreign Assistance│        Balance of Trade
   Flows &          │ Immigration     │        Balance of Payments
   Rates            └─────────────────┘
              Critical      Ethical
              Thinking      Leadership
                    Systems Thinking
                    ┌─────────────────┐
                    │ International Org.│
                    │ Non-government Org.│
                    │ Global Labor Issues│
                    │ Global Transport │
                    │ Global Energy    │
                    └─────────────────┘

                  Foreign Language Skills
```

Source: Lenneal J. Henderson, Critical Thinking and Global Thinking, 2004.

- learning how other cultures define and use natural, physical, social, management, engineering, and information sciences in their work, faith traditions, and cultural life;
- learning how international organizations such as the United Nations, the World Bank, the International Monetary Fund and a variety of international non-governmental organizations (NGOs) work with the diverse cultural orientations they find among nations and peoples around the world;
- learning how international trade influences economic, financial, and currency trends in the United States and other nations;
- learning how international political developments influence U.S. foreign and military policy and the policies of other nations;
- learning about the harsh realities of worldwide poverty, oppression, disease, and struggles over economic and political power among peoples and nations;
- learning about, preparing for, responding to, mitigating and recovery from natural disasters, such as earthquakes, floods, hurricanes, volcanic eruptions, desertification, and insect, bacterial, or viral disease and human-induced disasters, such as war, commercial nuclear accidents, chemical, toxic and hazardous waste contamination, air, train, or vehicular accidents, and global nutrition deficiencies and failures;
- learning about our delicate global environment and how our decisions and those of other individuals, institutions, nations, and international organizations affect our future and the futures of millions of life forms around the world;

- learning about the fascinating and complex world of nongovernmental organizations (NGOs) working throughout the world on issues of poverty, gender differences, literacy and education, sustainable development, agriculture, food quality and distribution, the development of children and youth, and disaster and emergency relief;
- learning about the gnarled roots of international crime and criminal activity as it affects societies, economies, and politics around the world.

These learning opportunities require critical thinking. They also require *systems thinking*, the ability to identify, measure, and develop strategies for complex organizations and institutions increasingly dependent on one another for money, human resources, knowledge and information, and material resources such as food, shelter, and clothing. Both critical thinking and systems thinking provide opportunities to examine how well interpersonal, inter-group, and interorganizational alliances, networks, and relationships work. Together, critical thinking and systems thinking enhance the capabilities, sensitivity, and effectiveness of a quality leader. Leadership, particularly at the global level, includes ethics, the ability to turn acts into deeds and deeds into effectiveness as both a scholar and change agent.

As Figure 1 indicates, global and systems thinking begin with the careful examination of raw data on global trends and developments. Population, economic, trade, environmental, health, education, employment, currency, transportation, and cultural trends and developments can generally be monitored through *raw statistical and descriptive data*. These data are obtained from institutions like the World Bank, the United Nations Development Program, the United States Agency for International Development, the World Trade Organization and the International Labor Organization.

Once *raw and descriptive data* are obtained, the next step is to determine the meaning, significance, and messages evident in these trends. At this point, you are moving from data to knowledge. The next step is to think critically about the alternative explanations or interpretations you can derive from your data or knowledge. Often, there are more subtle cultural or institutional messages or realities in the information and data we pursue. Indeed, varied conceptualizations are possible from the same data. As a scholar, professional or advocate, your ethical responsibilities as a leader often begin with the quality of your analysis, reflections, and observations you make about global or international data or information. These analyses, reflections, and observations can and do influence strategies for involving yourself in international activities, as well as for the way you evaluate the quality and impact of these strategies. Strategies often influence how local individuals and communities connect themselves to international issues, trends, and developments. For example, many U.S. cities and counties have sister cities or sister counties with which they collaborate on cultural, scientific, economic, or educational activities. Businesses develop joint ventures with foreign firms or nations based on their joint analysis and assessment of a business opportunity. Colleges and universities admit thousands of international students in almost every academic specialty based on their analysis of the enrollment trends and mission of their institutions.

**Figure 2. Global Thinking, Action, and Leadership**

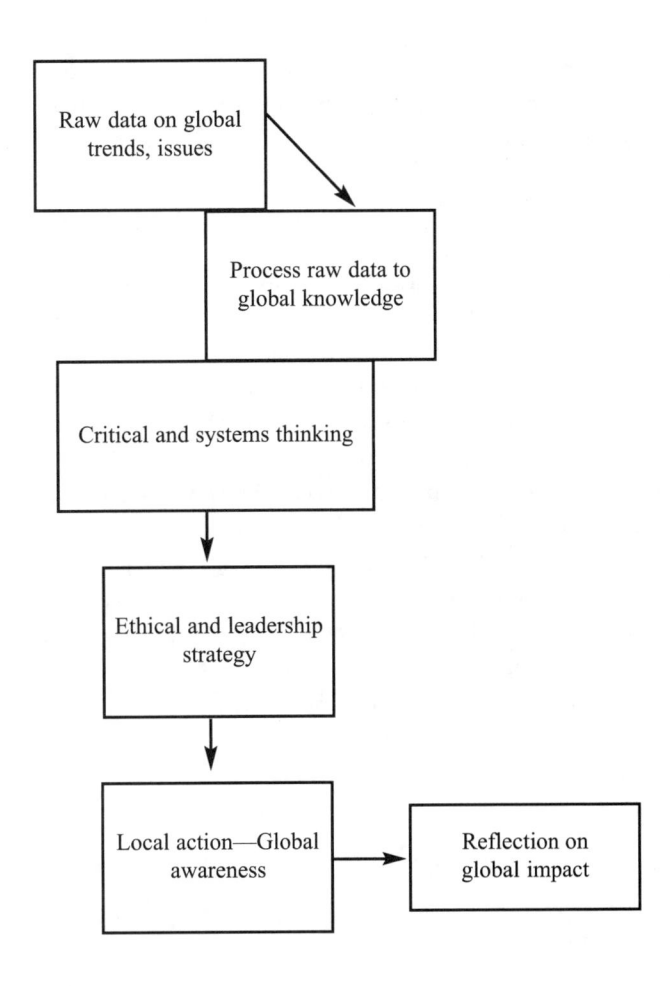

```
Raw data on global
trends, issues
       ↓
   Process raw data to
   global knowledge
       ↓
Critical and systems thinking
       ↓
   Ethical and leadership
       strategy
       ↓
Local action—Global  →  Reflection on
    awareness            global impact
```

## LEARNING AND TEACHING GOALS AND STRATEGIES

Given these trends, scholars and teachers as diverse as Robert Reich and Samuel Huntington, Hazel Henderson, and Francis Fukuyama stress the importance of infusing critical thinking, systems thinking, ethics and leadership skills into what we learn and do about globalization. They emphasize a macro perspective on world and international trends, events, and systems with a micro perspective on the ability of individuals, institutions, and communities to influence the direction of macro developments. Teachers can integrate global materials, resources, and information into existing courses and activities. Students can initiate their own global learning program to enhance their academic and professional preparation and development. Among the learning goals teachers and students may pursue include the following:

- Enhance undergraduate and graduate student learning by integrating international issues, materials, data and cases into natural, physical, social, engineering, management, and human sciences and information technology curricula and learning plans. These issues include war and peace, world inequality and poverty, world population trends, distribution of food and other basic necessities, science, technology and global issues and racial, ethnic, and gender equality. Be sure that students are encouraged to engage diverse ideological and ethical positions on these issues and to use their critical-thinking skills to become aware and active in international activities.

- Provide students with intercultural experience through global knowledge, travel, and exposure provided by such programs as the School for International Training in Brattleboro, Vermont; the Council on International Educational Exchanges; and the student Fulbright Scholar programs.
- Stimulate student interest in constructive and strategic participation of multilateral organizations like the United Nations or the World Bank or non-governmental organizations like the International Red Cross, Oxfam International, Africare, Save the Children Federation, the American Friends Service Committee, or Partners for the Americas.
- Encourage and support students to identify, appreciate, and embrace foreign students and faculty on campus in and out of the classroom.
- Support a more dynamic and diverse menu of career and professional development options including paid and volunteer work overseas, work with international and nongovernment organizations, the U.S. Foreign Service and multilateral organizations like the United Nations.
- Engender in students knowledge and appreciation of the international roots of their own cultural and family heritage in the context of global affairs, issues, and learning opportunities.
- Invite officials, experts, and international students and faculty as guest lecturers, scholars, and discussion facilitators on campus to engage students, faculty, and staff in productive discussions of global trends, issues, and innovative or best practices.

*Global and systems thinking begins with the careful examination of raw data on global trends and developments. Information on population, economic, trade, environmental, health, education, employment, currency, transportation, and cultural trends and developments can be found on the Internet, through a variety of raw data sources.*

These goals and strategies should result in the integration of global issues and dynamics into the learning environment and plans of students, faculty and the campus. They promote mutually supportive exchanges with local international agencies such as international visitor programs, faith-supported overseas programs, or local business or corporate institutions with overseas networks, products, or services. Global demographic, socioeconomic, scientific, business, ecological, and mass media materials, data, and cases are incorporated in the learning agenda. These materials encourage reflection and action on leadership, critical and systems thinking and strategic opportunities for pursuing ethical international activities and participation.

## GLOSSARY OF KEY TERMS AND AGENCIES*

**Apartheid:** the practice of rigidly separating racial and ethnic groups, which was practiced in South Africa from 1948 to 1994.

**Balance of Payments/Balance of Trade:** a record of one nation's trade dealings with the rest of the world. Balance of payments records the financial value of such trade and the balance of trade records types, levels, and volumes of commodities or services actually traded.

**Beijing Declaration:** principles, resolutions, and goals generated by the Fourth World Conference on Women in Beijing, People's Republic of China, September 1995.

**Bretton Woods Conference:** named after a small town in New Hampshire, this conference of the World War II allies established two organizations to promote world economic order: The International Monetary Fund and the World Bank (International Bank for Reconstruction and Finance).

**Central Bank:** usually a government agency responsible for regulating money supply, reserve margins, and interest rates in a nation. These activities are designed to promote economic and financial stability.

**Cold War:** a term used to describe hostile relationships between the Western bloc, led by the United States, and the Eastern bloc, led by the former Union of the Supreme Soviet Republics (U.S.S.R.) from 1945 to 1991. The Cold War included the build up of nuclear and conventional weapons, the space race, and the competition between the East and West for influence around the world.

**Colonialism:** rule of one nation by another, usually on an involuntary basis.

**Commodity Chains:** production processes carried out by "interorganizational networks clustered around one commodity or product, linking households, enterprises, and states to one another within the world economy," with greater share of control and wealth going to network nodes in core countries (G. Gereffi and M. Korzeniewicz, Editors, Commodity Chains and Global Capitalism, 1994, p. 2).

**Comparative Advantage:** a standard economic concept reflecting the advantage one country has in international trade because it can produce and transport goods for export more efficiently than other countries.

**Debt Crisis:** widespread inability in the 1980s and 1990s among some developing nations to repay loans from national and commercial lending institutions, resulting in strains on domestic development and international trade.

**Declaration:** a statement of principles calling for a worldwide environmental protection strategy and advanced by the 1992 United Nations Earth Summit conference in Rio de Janiero, Brazil.

Dimensions of Global Learning

**Foreign Direct Investment:** investment by a firm based in one country in actual productive capacity or other real assets in another country, normally through the creation of a subsidiary by a multinational corporation. A measure of the globalization of capital.

**Foreign Exchange:** the money a nation earns from its exports.

**G7:** a group of seven major economic powers, including the United States, Germany, France, the United Kingdom, Japan, Italy, and Canada, engaged in regular consultation on world and regional financial issues and stability and economic growth. Occasionally referred to as the G8 in deference to Russia.

**Globalization:** the expansion and intensification of global economic, financial, cultural, educational, diplomatic and military activities, information and organization between and among increasing numbers of nations leading to a growth in global consciousness and interactions. The Internet and other information-intensive activities are often integral to globalization.

**Human Rights:** the rights of persons to freedom of speech and conscience, equal treatment, work and health as defined in the Universal Declaration on Human Rights adopted by the United Nations in 1948 and supplemented by the 1960s Covenants on social, economic, political, and civil rights.

**IGO:** intergovernmental organization formed by restricted nation states, such as the North Atlantic Treaty Organization or a regional economic development bank.

**Indigenous Peoples:** individuals and groups identified as original residents of specified geographic areas around the world, particularly groups under threat of displacement or extinction due to local or global development and now possessing globally recognized claims to autonomy and identity fostered by supportive movements.

**International or Cultural Exchanges:** programs designed to encourage persons and institutions of different nations to interact with one another. Examples include the Council on International Educational Exchanges, the Experiment in International Living, and the Peace Corps (VISTA).

**Internet or World Wide Web:** a network of computers capable of facilitating electronic communication across the globe.

**Multiculturalism:** a doctrine asserting the value of diverse cultures coexisting within a single society or institution and, globally, a vision of cultural diversity deliberately fostered by national and international institutions.

**Multilateral Organization:** any organization involved in working with three or more nations. The United Nations, The World Bank, the Economic Community of West African States and the European Community are multilateral organizations.

**NAFTA:** North American Free Trade Agreement signed by the United States, Canada and Mexico to establish free-trade guidelines among the three countries and soon to grow to include 8 more countries including Argentina, Brazil, Chile, Columbia, Paraguay, Peru, Uruguay, and Venezuela.

**NGO:** nongovernmental organizations usually involved in education, health care, environmental protection, or services to needy population but not officially connected to a nation-state or official governmentalagency.

**North/South Relations:** the general condition of relationships between leading economic nations such as the United States, Canada, Europe, and Japan with nations of color and/or poorer nations.

**Protectionism:** an effort, usually by a nation-state or an industry, to shield domestic producers against foreign competition through tariffs, quotas, and other liberal trade policies.

**Structural Adjustment and Conditionality:** a policy advanced by the World Bank and International Monetary Fund to require nations seeking financial support to reduce governmental expenditures and deficits, lower inflation, limit imports, devalue currency, and increase economic efficiency as a condition for debt restructuring. Criticized for inducing economic decline and decreased social protection of vulnerable populations in developing nations.

**Sustainable Development:** a policy of promoting social and economic growth consistent with the protection of the environment. For example, urging a shift to renewable energy resources and local community participation in development projects.

**Transparency:** an evolving global standard for state institutions and international organizations requiring open processes for observation by any group or nation as a basis for reducing corruption and extending accountability for financial and program performance.

**The United Nations:** the major multilateral or international institution in the world. Established in 1946, the United Nations consists of constituent agencies such as the United Nations Educational, Scientific and Cultural Organization, the United Nations Development Program and the International Labor Organization. The General Assembly and the Security Council are the two most important policy-making organs of the UN, and UN peacekeeping forces are periodically deployed into areas of the world experiencing international conflict or civil war.

**Universalism:** principles considered valid for all populations, groups, and institutions across the globe, for example, universal human rights, environmental protection, or fair trade.

**The World Bank (The International Bank of Reconstruction and Finance):** established immediately after World War II, the World Bank provides financial, economic, and technical assistance to needy nations.

**The World Trade Organization (WTO):** established in 1995 by the Uruguay Round of negotiations, WTO includes 147 member nations and is responsible for administering WTO trade agreements, handling trade disputes, monitoring national trade policies, providing technical assistance for developing nations, and promoting international cooperation. Generally replaced the General Agreement on Trades and Tariffs (GATT).

*Adapted from The Globalization Website, 2004.

## REFERENCES

Anderson, Sarah, Cavanaugh, John and Lee, Thea. (2000). *Field Guide to the Global Economy.* New York: The New Press.

Appiah, Kwame Anthony, and Gates, Louis, Jr. (1997). *The Dictionary of Global Culture.* New York: Alfred A. Knopf.

Berger, Peter L., and Huntington, Samuel P. (2002). *Many Globalizations: Cultural Diversity in the Contemporary World.* New York: Oxford University Press.

Caraley, Demetrious James. (2004). *American Hegemony: Preventive War, Iraq, and Imposing Democracy.* New York: Academy of Political Science.

Charles, Daniel. (2001). *Lords of the Harvest: Biotech, Big Money, and the Future of Food.* Cambridge, England: Perseus Press.

Dam, Kenneth. (2002). *The Rules of the Global Game: A New Look at U.S. International Policy making.* Chicago: The University of Chicago Press.

Edwards, Michael, and Gaventa, John. (2001). *Global Citizen Action.* Boulder, Colorado: Lynne Rienner Publishers.

Evans, Graham, and Newnham, Jeffrey. (1998). *The Penguin Dictionary of International Relations.* New York: Penguin Books.

Fukuyama, Francis. (1992). *The End of History and the Last Man.* Hamish Hamilton, London.

Ghemawat, Pankaj. (November 2003). "The Global Corporation," Harvard Business Review, Vol. 81, N. 11.

Handelman, Howard. (2000). *The Challenge of Third World Development, 2nd Edition.* Upper Saddle River, New Jersey: Prentice Hall Publishers.

Henderson, Hazel. (1996). *Building a WinWin World: Life Beyond Global Economic Warfare.* San Francisco: Berrett-Koehlers Publishers.

Henderson, Lenneal J. (2004). "Emergency and Disaster: Pervasive Risk and Public Bureaucracy in Developing Nations." Public Organization Review: A Global Journal. 4 (1). pp. 103-119.

Huntington, Samuel P. (1973). "Transnational Organization in World Politics." World Politics. 25 (3) (August). pp. 333-368.

Huntington, Samuel P. (1997). *The Clash of Civilizations and the Remaking of the World Order.* New York: Touchstone Books.

Kenen, Peter B. (2001). *The International Economy, 4th Edition.* New York: Cambridge University Press.

Macchiarola, Frank, Editor. (1990). *International Trade: The Changing Role of the United States.* New York: The Academy of Political Science.

Meisler, Stanley. (1995). *United Nations: The First Fifty Years.* New York: Atlantic Monthly Press.

Population Reference Bureau. (2004). *World Population Data Sheet 2004.* Washington, D.C.: Population Reference Bureau.

Reich, Robert B. (1992). *The Work of Nations.* New York: Vintage Books.

Rhinesmith, Stephen H. (1993). *A Manager's Guide to Globalization: Six Keys to Success in a Changing World Homewood.* Illinois: Irwin Publishing Co.

Stiglitz, Joseph E. (2001). *Globalization and Its Discontents.* New York: W. W. Norton, Inc.

United Nations Development Program. (2004). *Human Development Report 2004.* New York: The United Nations.

The World Bank. (2004). *World Development Report 2004: Making Services Work for Poor People.* New York: Oxford University Press.

The Worldwatch Institute. (2004). *State of the World, 2004.* Washington, D.C.

## SUGGESTED JOURNALS AND PERIODICALS

*Foreign Affairs: The Harvard Journal of International Affairs*
*Global Social Policy: The International Social Science Journal*
*World Politics: The Journal of Modern African Studies*
*Current History: The Asia Development Journal*
*Middle East Journal: Latin American Studies Review*
*International Organization*
*International Studies Quarterly*
*International Labor Review*
*World Today*
*International Affairs*
*Africa Today*
*The Fletcher Forum of World Affairs*

## SUGGESTED WEBSITES

http://globaleducation.edu/ol/ Farleigh Dickson University Office of Global Learning

http://www.aacu-edu.org/issues/globallearning/resources.cfm Association of American Colleges and Universities Global Learning Center and Listserv

http://www.aacu-edu.org/issues/globallearning/studyabroad.cfm Association of American Colleges and Universities Study Abroad/International Exchange Opportunities

http://www.nafsa.org//content/PublicPolicy/NAFSAontheIssues/Nat National Association of Foreign Student Affairs/Association of International Education

http://www.worldwatch.org/ The Worldwatch Institute

http://www.sit.edu The School of International Training, Brattleboro, Vermont

http://www.iie.org/ The Institute for International Education (manages the Fulbright student and scholar international study programs)

http://www.usip.org/ The United States Institute for Peace

http://www.ciee.org/index.cfm The Council on International Educational Exchanges

http://www.afsc.org The American Friends Service Committee (Quaker organization involved in national international programs)

http://www.aed.org/ The Academy for Educational Development

http//www.psfdc.org/ The Phelps-Stokes Fund (involved in Africa and the Caribbean)

http://www.humanresources@cfr.org/ The Council on Foreign Relations Student Internship Program

http://www.globalexchange.org/ Global Exchange: human rights group dedicated to building people-to-people ties.

http://www.emory.edu/SOC/globalization/glossary.html A detailed glossary of globalization terms produced by The Globalization Website.

http://www.wto.org/ The World Trade Organization home website.

# ACTIVITY 1

## *Becoming Aware of the World*

**Collecting Raw Data on Nations and Global Trends**

1. Locate the following data on at least two nations other than your own:
   Population of the nation
   What are the major cultural or religious groups in your two nations?
   Mean or median income of the population
   Changes in population and socioeconomic status in the last five years
   The current Gross National Product (GNP) or Gross Domestic Product of these nations.
   Any key trends or changes in the last five years?
   What are the major industries or economic activities in your two nations?
   What are the key employment trends in your two nations?
   The Balance of Payment and Balance of Trade data for these nations in the past five years (imports and exports)
   What is the literacy rate and educational status of the population in the two nations you selected?
   Is literacy and education improving or not?
   What are the major health care challenges in your two nations?

2. Now that you have basic, raw or descriptive data on your two nations, write at least four paragraphs describing what observations, reflections, or insights these data suggest to you.

3. Now, putting on your critical- and systems-thinking hat, what strategic *opportunities* are your two nations pursuing to address the trends or observations you developed? What *alternative strategic approaches or opportunities* would you suggest to the policy-makers of those nations or to international, non-governmental or multilateral organizations seeking to help them?

4. Now, given what you know about global economic, political, cultural, and diplomatic conditions in the world, *how would you evaluate the strategy* you, or other international, non-governmental or multilateral organizations are using to address the challenges you identified?

# ACTIVITY 2

## *Global Academic and Professional Development Opportunities*

Go to the global or international websites in this chapter. Identify at least four international or global academic or career options for yourself.

| Academic Opportunities | Career/Professional Opportunities |
|---|---|
| Study abroad programs | Volunteer work abroad |
| Educational exchange programs | Careers in the Foreign Service |
| research opportunities in the humanities, social, natural, engineering or management sciences | Work with international businesses |
| Collaboration with a foreign student or scholar | Work in an NGO |
| Serve as an intern or fellow in a multilateral organization | Careers at the UN or World Bank |

Now develop a written global strategic plan for yourself, integrating your global academic activities with your career plan.

# ACTIVITY 3

## *The Global Neighborhood*

Now, let's bring globalization to your neighborhood, rural area, city, county, or state. Locate data on the number and national origin of immigrants in your state or locality. What are the key institutions representing persons in your community of different national origins (faith institutions, fraternal organizations, business establishments, educational institutions, cultural centers)? Make contact with these institutions. Come to know their origins, missions, and current activities. Seek at least one opportunity to collaborate with them at your college or university through a joint project or activity, a guest lecture or an information-sharing activity. Keep a record of this organization and exchange. Now, go the nation(s) from which this individual or organization is descended. Repeat the steps indicated in Activity One.

# INDEX

Absolute answer, in research, 156
Academics,
  evaluation system in, 9-10
  success in, 9
    tips for achieving, 10-11
Accreditation, 6
Adjustment,
  social, 2-4
  to living arrangements, 3-4
Administrative channels, using, 123
Admissions, 7
Anxiety, testing, 62-63
  relaxation techniques for, 63
  sources of, 62
Assets and liabilities, 96-97
Attitude, and college success, 1
Audience analysis, 118-119
Avoidance, of conflict, 124
Behavior,
  dominance, 231
  leadership, 230-233
    autocratic, 230-231
    democratic, 230-231
    laissez-faire, 230-231
  sociability, 231
Bill, paying at dinner, 211
  dutch treat, 211
Bread and butter, etiquette, 210
Budget, setting, 98-102
Business,
  dining etiquette. See Etiquette.
  dressing for, 203-204
  introductions, 205
  posture, 204-205
Calculation exams, taking, 56
Campus,
  academic evaluation system, 9-10
  administration channels, 123
  environment, 4-5
  living arrangements, 3-4
  organizational structure of, 5-6
  resources offered by, 7-8
  safety and security on, 11
Career development,
  and exploration, 268
    selecting a major, 269-270
  and planning, 268

  professional development plan for, 270
  interview, 274-275
    preparing for, 275-277
    types of, 276
  job-hunting, 270-271
  negotiating a salary, 277
  networking, 273-274
  resumes,
    types of, 272-273
    writing, 271-272
Categorical variables, in research, 161
CD-ROM and DVD, 134-135
Chat rooms, Internet, 139
Checkbook, balancing, 100-101
Cherry tomato, how to eat, 209
Civic benefit, of service learning, 259
Cognitive operations, processing, 28-29
College,
  academic evaluation system, 9-10
    success at, 9
    tips for achieving, 10-11
  accreditation of, 6
  administration, communication with, 123
  admissions, 7
  as a system, 5-11
  degrees offered by, 6-7
    selecting a major, 269-270
  environment, 4-5
  learning communities of, 8
  living arrangements, 3-4
  organizational structure of, 5-6
  resources offered by, 7-8
  safety and security at, 11
Communication, 111-131
  active listening in, 117-118
  conflict/confrontation in, 123-125
    strategies for, 124
    coping with difficult people in, 125
    defined, 124
    resolution of, 124
  diversity in, 116-117
  ethics in, 118
  key principles of, 118-123
    audience analysis, 118-118
    axioms, 120-123

    perceptual awareness in, 119-120
  process of, 113
  receiving messages in, 115-116
  sending messages in, 113-114
  through administrative channels, 123
Computer technology, 133-154
  buying considerations, 142
  CD-ROM and DVD, 134-135
  creating an electronic portfolio, 137-138
  parts of a computer, 124-135
    CPU, 134
    modem/fax board, 135
    printer, 136
    RAM, 134
    scanner, 136
    software, 136-137
    storage media, 134
  using,
    e-mail, 138
    in presentations, 136-137
    news groups, chat rooms, mailing lists, 139
    the Internet, 138
      creating a Web page, 140
      distance learning on, 140
      ethics for, 141
      research on, 139-140
Computerized exams, taking, 59
Concept map, 28
Conflict and confrontation, 123-125
  coping with difficult people in, 125
  definition of, 125
  resolution of, 125
  strategies for, 124
Continuous variables, 161
Conversation, rules of etiquette for, 210-211
Cooperative learning, 29-30
CPU, 134
Credibility, of message sender, 114
Credit,
  card, using for business dinner, 211
  managing, 102-103
  rating, 102
Critical thinking, 23-47
  cooperative learning in, 29-30

decision-making in, 32-33
deductive, 24-26
dimensions of, 23
hierarchies in building skills of, 24
mind mapping/graphic organizers, 26-28
moral reasoning in, 34-35
multiple intelligences in, 30-31
problem-solving in, 32
processing cognitive operations, 28-29
questioning in, 36-37
reflecting in, 37
Culture,
    components of, 185-187
    differences of,
        improving awareness of, 238-239
            working with, as a leader, 237-238
    diversity among individuals, groups, and, 187-188
    literacy of, 190-192
    of higher education and the workplace, 193-194
    variables of, 192-193
Data, collecting and analyzing, 164
    percentages/frequency distributions, 167-168
    pilot testing, 166
    sampling, 164-166
    using scales for, 166-167
Decision-making, 32-33
Deductive thinking, 24-26
Defusion, of conflict, 124
Degrees, offered at school, 6-7
    resources for selecting, 7
Difficult people, dealing with, 125
Dining/restaurant, etiquette, 205-212
    common rules of, 212
    conversing, 210-211
    eating
        a cherry tomato, 209
        bread and butter, 210
        cutting meat, 209-210
        drinking from a glass, 209
        soup, 208-209
        sweeteners and seasonings, 210
    for a formal dinner, 207
    for receptions, 206-207
    for special circumstances, 206
    leaving a tip, 211-212
    paying the bill, 211
    understanding a place setting, 207-208

Distance learning, on the Internet, 140
Diversity,
    among individuals, groups, and culture, 187-188
    components of culture, 185-187
    cultural,
        literacy, 190-191
        variables, 192-193
    in communication, 116-117
    in learning and teaching styles, 188-189
    stereotypes, 189-190
Dressing, for business, 203-204
Drinking. See Etiquette.
Dutch treat, 211
E-mail, using, 138
Eating. See Dining/restaurant, etiquette.
Economic resources. See Resources, managing.
Education, higher, culture of, 193-194
Electronic,
    portfolios, 137-138
    resume, 272-273
Essay exams, taking, 58
Ethics,
    etiquette, professional protocol, and, 201-223
    for using the Internet, 141
    in communication, 118
    professional, 213-216
    scenarios, 216
Ethnocentrism, 190
Etiquette,
    dining and restaurant,
        common rules of, 212
        conversing, 210-211
        eating
            bread and butter, 210
            cutting meat, 209-210
            drinking from a glass, 209
            a cherry tomato, 209
            soup, 208-209
            sweeteners/seasonings, 210
        for a formal dinner, 207
        for receptions, 206-207
        for special circumstances, 206
        leaving a tip, 211-212
        paying the bill, 211
        place settings, 207-208
    social behavior and, 202-205
        business posture, 204-205
        making introductions, 205

    successful dressing, 203-204
Exams. See Testing.
Fax board/modem, 135
Fill-in-the-blank exams, taking, 56
Finances,
    budgeting, 98-102
    credit, 102-103
    financial goals, setting in, 98
    goal-setting, 98
    management of, 95-96
    networth, assets, and liabilities, 96-97
Fraternity, 3
Frequency distributions/percentages, analyzing, 167-168
Geese, leadership lessons from, 226-227
Global resumes, 273
Globalization,
    and learning, 300-302
    definition of, 299
    goals and strategies of, 303-305
Goals, financial, setting, 98
Grading scale, 9
Graphic organizers, 26-28
Gratuity, 211-212
Hypothesis,
    formulating, 162
    types of, 162-163
        inductive and deductive, 163
Intelligences, multiple, 30-31
Internet, 138
    creating a Web page on, 140
    distance learning on, 140
    ethics for using, 141
    news groups, chat rooms, mailing lists, 139
    researching on, 139-140
Interpersonal intelligence, 30
Interviewing, 274-275
    preparing for, 275-277
    types of, 276
Intrapersonal intelligence, 30
Introductions, making, etiquette, 205
Job. See Career development.
Key-type response exams, taking, 54-55
Kinesthetic intelligence, 30
Knowledge, sources of, 158-160
Laissez-fair leadership, 230
Leaders,
    best, qualities of, 228
    worst, qualities of, 228-229
Leadership,
    definitions of, 233-234

identifying one's style of, 230-233
   autocratic, 230-231
   democratic, 230-231
   laissez-faire, 230-231
lessons from geese, 226-228
of meetings,
   conducting effective, 243
   helping members contribute, 242
   parliamentary procedures for, 241-242
   planning effective meetings, 242
quotes about leaders, 228-229
slavery and, 236
successful and effective, 235-236
women and, 235
working with cultural differences, 237-238
   improving awareness of, 238-239
Learning,
  communities, 8
  cooperative, 29-30
  critical thinking, 23-47
  distance, 140
  diversity in styles of, 188-189
  globalization and, 300-302
    goals/strategies of, 303-305
  knowledge, sources of, 158-160
  online tutorials, using, 59
  service, 253-265
   civic benefit of, 259
   definition of, 254
   goals of, 256-257
   link between colleges/universities and, 256
   pedagogy and, 254-255
   politics and, 255-256
   strategies for incorporating, 257-259
  styles, 12-13
  testing,
   and study skills, 49-81
   anxiety, 62-63
Linguistic intelligence, 30
Listening skills,
  active, 117-118
  developing, 66-67
  receiving messages, 115-116
Literacy, cultural, 190-191
Literature, reviewing, 163-164
Living arrangements, 3-4
Macroculture, 187
Mailing lists, news groups, chat rooms, 139

Major, selecting a, 269-270
Managing resources. See Resources, managing.
Manuals, and style guides, writing, 168
Matching exams, taking, 55-56
Mathematical,
  calculation exams, 56
  intelligence, 30
Meat, cutting. See Etiquette.
Meetings,
  conducting effective, 243
  helping group members contribute to, 242
  parliamentary procedures for, 241-242
  planning effective, 242
Memorization skills, 68-69
Microculture, 188
Mind mapping, 26-28
Modem/fax board, 135
Moral reasoning, 34-35
Multiculturalism, 190
Multiple intelligences, 30-31
Musical intelligence, 30
Natural intelligence, 30
Negotiating a salary, 277
Netiquette, 141
Networking, 273-274
Networth, assets, and liabilities, understanding, 96-97
News groups, chat rooms, mailing lists, 139
Note-taking skills, developing, 67-68
Occupational Outlook Handbook, using, 269
On Line Computer Library First (OCLC), for research, 140
Online tests, taking, 59
Open-book exams, taking, 58
Organizational structure, college, 5-6
Pareto's principle, 89
Parkinson's law, 90
Parliamentary procedures, 241-242
Percentages/frequency distributions, analyzing, 167-168
Philosophy, in managing resources, 85-86
Pilot testing, 166
Politics, and service learning, 255-256
Portfolio, electronic, creating, 137-138
Posture, etiquette of, 204-205
Presentations, using computers in, 136-137
Printer, 136
Problem-solving, 32
Processing cognitive operations, 28-29
Professional protocol. See Etiquette.
Purposeful change, 85
Questions, and thinking, 36-37
RAM, 134
Reading skills, developing, 69-70
Reasoning, moral, 34-35
Reflecting, 37
Research,
  characteristics of a researcher, 158
  collecting/analyzing data in, 164
   percentages and frequency distributions in, 167-168
   pilot testing, 166
   sampling, 164-166
   using scales for, 166-167
  conducting a literary review in, 164
  defining, 156
  formulating hypothesis in, 162-164
   hypotheses types, 162-163
  indentifying variables in, 161-162
  process of, 157
  reviewing the literature in, 163
  selecting the research problem in, 160-161
  sources of knowledge in, 158-160
  tools of, 163-164
  using the Internet for, 139-140
  writing styles/manuals for, 168-169
Resources, managing, 83-110
  characteristics of goals in, 86-87
  defining resources in, 87
  financial management, 95-96
   budgeting, 98-102
   credit, 102-103
   financial goals, setting, 98
   networth, assets, and liabilities, 96-97
  stress in, 91
   managing, 92-95
  tasks and responsibilities in, 87-88
   Pareto's principle, 89
  time,
   management in, 88
   orientation in, 88-91
  values and philosophy in, 85-86
Responsibilities and tasks, managing, 87-88
  Pareto's principle, 89
Restaurant. See Etiquette.

Resumes, 271-272
   types of, 272-273
   writing, 273
Roommates, adjusting to, 3-4
Safety and security, on campus, 11
Salary, negotiating, 277
Sampling data, 164-166
Scales, using to intepret data, 166-168
Scanner, 136
Schedule, as time management tool, 65
Self-actualization/self-discovery, 11-13
   learning styles, 12-13
   values clarification, 12
Service learning, 253-265
   civic benefit of, 259
   definition of, 254
   goals of, 256-257
   link between colleges/universities and, 256
   pedagogy and, 254-255
   politics and, 255-256
   strategies for incorporating, 257-259
Single-best response exams, taking, 53-54
Slavery, and leadership, 236
Social,
   adjustment, 2-4
      living arrangements, 3-4
   behavior, etiquette, 202-203
      business posture, 204-205
      making introductions, 205
      successful dressing, 203-204
Software, computer, 136-137
Spatial intelligence, 30
Stereotypes, 189-190
Storage media, computer, 134
Stress, managing, 91-95
Student,
   becoming a master, 1-21
   handbook, 1
   learning styles of, 12-13
   self-actualization/self-discovery of, 11-13
   values clarification of, 12
Study groups, 64
Study skills, 49-81
   developing, 63-70
      listening, 66-67
      memorization, 68-69
      note-taking, 67-68
      reading, 69-70

      study groups, 64
      time management, 65-66
   See also, Testing.
Style manuals, 168
Success,
   college, steps toward, 1-13
   dressing for, 203-204
   testing and study skills for, 49-81
Take-home exams, taking, 58
Talking,
   sending messages effectively, 113-114
Tasks and responsibilities, managing, 87-88
   Pareto's principle, 89
Testing, 49-81
   anatomy of,
      test-maker, 50-52
      test-taker, 59-61
   anxiety, 62-63
   developing study skills for, 63-70
      listening, 66-67
      memorization, 68-69
      note-taking, 67-68
      reading, 69-70
      study groups, 64
      time management, 65-66
   high-stakes, 61-62
   types of exam questions, 52-59
      calculations, 56
      computerized, 59
      essay, 58
      fill-in-the-blank, 56
      key-type response, 54-55
      matching, 55-56
      open-book, 58
      single-best response, 53-54
      take-home, 58
      true or false, 53
      word problems, 57
   using online tutorials to prepare for, 59
   what to do before/after the exam, 61
Thinking, critical. See Critical thinking.
Time management, skills, developing, 65-66
   time orientation in, 88-91
Tips,
   academic success, 10-11
   gratuities, 211-212
True or false exams, taking, 53
Tutorials, online, using, 59
University,

academic evaluation system, 9-10
accreditation of, 6
administration, communication with, 123
admissions to, 7
culture of, 193-194
degrees offered by, 6-7
   selecting a major, 269-270
environment, 4-5
learning communities of, 8
organizational structure of, 5-6
resources offered by, 7-8
safety and security at, 11
success at, 9
   tips for, 10-11
Values,
   clarification of, 12
   in managing resources, 85-86
Variables, identifying in research, 161-162
Web page, creating, 140
Women, and leadership, 235
Word problem exams, taking, 57
Workplace
   and higher education, culture of, 193-194
   ethics, 213-216
   etiquette,
      conversing, 210-211
      dining, 210-212
      dressing, 203-204
      introductions, 205
      posture, 204-205
World Wide Web. See Internet.
Writing, styles and manuals for, 168